COMPUTERS, CURRICULUM, AND CULTURAL CHANGE

COMPUTERS, CURRICULUM, AND CULTURAL CHANGE

An Introduction for Teachers

http://www.erlbaum.com/computer.htm

Eugene F. Provenzo, Jr.
University of Miami

Arlene Brett
University of Miami

Gary N. McCloskey, O.S.A.
St. Thomas University

 LAWRENCE ERLBAUM ASSOCIATES, PUBLISHERS
1999   Mahwah, New Jersey   London

The final camera copy for this work was prepared by the author, and therefore the publisher takes no responsibility for consistency or correctness of typographical style. However, this arrangement helps to make publication of this kind of scholarship possible.

Lawrence Erlbaum Associates, Inc., Publishers
10 Industrial Avenue
Mahwah, NJ 07430

Cover design by Kathryn Houghtaling Lacey

Library of Congress Cataloging-in-Publication Data

Provenzo, Eugene F.
   Computers, curriculum, and cultural change : an introduction for teachers / Eugene F. Provenzo, Jr., Arlene Brett, Gary N. McCloskey.
           p. cm
   Includes bibliographical references and index.
   ISBN 0-8058-2268-2 (pbk.)
   1. Computer-assisted instruction--United States--Case studies. 2. Computer-assisted instruction--Social aspects--United States--Case studies. 3. Education--United States--Curricula--Data processing--Case studies. 4. Computer managed instruction--United States--Case studies.   I. Brett, Arlene. II. McCloskey, Gary N. III. Title.
LB1028.5.P739   1998
371.33'4--dc21   98-23042
                                                           CIP

Books published by Lawrence Erlbaum Associates
are printed on acid-free paper, and their bindings are
chosen for strength and durability.

Printed in the United States of America
10 9   8   7   6   5   4   3   2   1

For
Gene's nieces and nephews Katy, Yoshiko and Jackson
and
Arlene's grandchildren Ashley, Russell, Michael, Danny, Joey, Derek, Daniel, Deanna and Marissa
and
Gary's nieces and nephews Tara, Katie, Siobhan, Ryan and John.

Using the Web Site That Accompanies This Book

An extensive web site supplements and extends the content of this book. To visit the site enter your web browser and enter the following address:

http://www.erlbaum.com/computer.htm

Credits

Book and Web Site Design	Eugene F. Provenzo, Jr.
Cover Design	Kathryn Houghtaling Lacey
Acquisitions Editor	Naomi Silverman
Production Editor	Debbie Ruel
Web Master	Robert Sidor
Technical Coordination	Art Lizza
Technology Consultant	Rob Epp (New Willow Media)

The images on pages (top to bottom) 2D, 3A, 3B, 3C, 5, 8, 14, 29, 31, 32, 36, 40B, 41, 61, 75A, 75B, 80, 81, 101C, 101D, 108, 126, 176, 186, 196A, 196B, 196C, 198, 252 A, 252B, 252C, 253, 255, 261, 262, 263A, 263B, 264A, 264B, and 268 were obtained from IMSI *Master Clips/Master Photos* © *Collection*, 1895 Francisco Blvd. East San Rafael, CA 94901-5506. Images on pages 1A, 1B, 1C, 2A, 2B, 2C, 24, 25, 26, 34, 40A, 57, 58, 101A, 101B, 104, 116, 121, 185, 200 and 256 were obtained from volumes included in the Dover *Pictorial Archive* series, Dover Publications, Inc., 31 East 2nd Street, Mineola, N.Y. 11501. Permission to use the web site banner on page 9 was provided through the courtesy of the National Council for Accreditation of Teachers. The web site banner on page 84 is used with permission from the Dade County Public Schools, Miami-Dade County, Florida. Use of the web banner on page 110 and the illustration on page 183 is with the permission of Curriculum Associates, Incorporated, North Bellerica, Massachusetts 01862. Illustrations on pages 76, 85, 102, 175, 218, 223, 224 and 229 provided by PhotoDisc. Special thanks to Lillian Lewicki for permission to use the illustrations on pages 179 and 181, and to the Bellingham Public Schools, Bellingham, Washington for the use of the illustration on page 208. Illustrations on pages 149 and 150 courtesy of Peter A. Zorn, Jr.

TABLE OF CONTENTS

PREFACE   i

CHAPTER 1—INTRODUCTION   1

How Computers Are Used Throughout the Culture   3
**The Computer as a Mediating Force in Contemporary
  Culture**   4
How Computers Are Changing Language   6
On the Non-Neutrality of the Computer   7
**How Widespread Is the Use of Technology in the
  Schools?**   7
The Promise of Technology for Teachers   8
Case Study   9
National Council for Accreditation of Teacher Education's
  Requirements for the "New Professional Teacher"   12
How Teaching Changes With the Use of Computers   13
Defining a Model of Educational Computing   13
Questions for Reflection and Discussion   16
Activities   17
**Exercise for Further Development of Your Reflective
  Practice for Teaching With Computer Technology**   17
Cyberspace   18
Sources   20

**CHAPTER 2—COMPUTERS—THE SOCIAL REVOLUTION
OF OUR TIME**   23

A Brief History of Computing   24
Augusta Ada Byron   27
Why Is the Introduction of Inexpensive Computing in Our Culture and
  Society Revelant for Educators in the Classroom?   30
The Microcomputer Revolution   30
**Parallels Between the Gutenberg and the
  Contemporary Computer Revolution**   32
Why Are the Parallels Between the Gutenberg and the Contemporary
  Computer Revolution Relevant for Educators in the Classroom?   34
The Computer as a "Singularity"   35
Why Is the Idea of the Computer Being a "Singularity" a Relevant
  Issue for Educators in the Classroom?   37
The Computer as "Augmenting" Intelligence   37
Douglas Engelbart—Computing Pioneer   38
Why Is the Augmentation of Intelligence Through Computers a Relevant
  Issue for Educators in the Classroom?   41
Questions for Reflection and Discussion   43
Activities   44

Exercise for Further Development of Your Reflective
  Practice for Teaching With Computer Technology   44
Digital Books   45
Sources   48

CHAPTER 3—THE COMPUTER AS TOOL   51

Case Study   51
Word Processors   53
Desktop Publishing   56
Keyboarding   60
Database Software   63
Spreadsheets   64
Drawing and Illustration Programs   65
Questions for Reflection and Discussion   67
Activities   68
Exercise for Further Development of Your Reflective
  Practice for Teaching With Computer Technology   68
Digital Studios   68
Sources   71

CHAPTER 4—EDUCATIONAL SOFTWARE   73

Case Study   73
Levels of Software   75
The Computer as Curricular Tool   77
Evaluating Software   81
Software Evaluation Form   83
Sources for Software   84
Computer Journals and Publications   87
Copyright Issues   91
Questions for Reflection and Discussion   93
Activities   93
Exercise for Further Development of Your Reflective
  Practice for Teaching With Computer Technology   94
Digital Evolution   94
Sources   97

CHAPTER 5—TECHNOLOGY AND THE CURRICULUM   99

Case Study   99
Content   102
National Curriculum Standards   103
Language Arts and Literacy   104
Mathematics   108
Science   116
Social Studies   121
The Arts   126

Methodology	130
Utilization	132
Assessment With Computer-Supported Curriculum	136
How Do Computers Change the Work of Teachers?	137
Questions for Reflection and Discussion	140
Activities	140
Exercise for Further Development of Your Reflective Practice for Teaching With Computer Technology	141
Digital Alteration of Documents	141
Sources	144

CHAPTER 6—TECHNOLOGY FOR INCLUSION   **147**

Case Study	147
Adaptive Input Devices	148
Adaptive Output Devices	152
Students With Disabilities	152
Adaptive Technology on Wheels	154
Selected Adaptive Technology Resources Available on the Internet	160
Technology for Inclusion	162
Questions for Reflection and Discussion	165
Activities	166
Exercise for Further Development of Your Reflective Practice for Teaching With Computer Technology	166
Wireheads	167
Sources	170

CHAPTER 7—MULTIMEDIA AND HYPERMEDIA   **173**

Case Study	173
What Is Multimedia?	176
Computers and the Movies	177
Hypertext and Hypermedia	178
Multimedia Authoring Tools	184
Mathematical Processors	185
Videodisc Technology	186
Questions for Reflection and Discussion	188
Activities	188
Exercise for Further Development of Your Reflective Practice for Teaching With Computer Technology	189
Digital Theme Parks	189
Sources	192

CHAPTER 8—NETWORKING AND TELECOMMUNICATION   **195**

Case Study	195
What Is the Internet?	198

History of the Internet   199
The World Wide Web (WWW)   **200**
Elements of a Web Page   **201**
Multicultural Education and the Internet   **202**
Protecting Students Using the Internet   **205**
Establishing an Acceptable Use Policy   **206**
The Future in Perspective   **209**
Questions for Reflection and Discussion   **210**
Activities   **210**
Exercise for Further Development of Your Reflective
  Practice for Teaching With Computer Technology   **211**
Digital Counseling   **211**
Sources   **214**

**CHAPTER 9—ETHICAL AND LEGAL ASPECTS OF
TEACHING WITH TECHNOLOGY**   **217**

Case Study   **217**
A Specific Case of Ethical and Legal Issues:
  Acceptable Use Policies for the Internet   **219**
General Ethical and Legal Issues in Teaching With
  Technology   **220**
Computer Ethics   **221**
Use of Computers as Instructional Tools   **221**
Responsible Use of Computers in the Classroom   **224**
Individual Responsible Use of Computers   **226**
Problems Arising From Computer Access   **228**
Case Study   **228**
Questions of Personal Responsibility and Safety   **230**
Case Study   **230**
Public Nature of Computer Use in the Classroom   **232**
Case Study   **232**
Copyright Protection   **233**
Privacy Rights   **234**
Privacy on the Internet   **235**
Hackers and Viruses   **236**
"The Millennium Bug"   **237**
Questions for Reflection and Discussion   **240**
Activities   **241**
Exercise for Further Development of Your Reflective
  Practice for Teaching With Computer Technology   **241**
Visual Copyright   **241**
Sources   **243**

CHAPTER 10—CONCLUSION   **245**

Questions for Reflection and Discussion   **248**
Sources   **249**

APPENDIX A—COMPUTER HARDWARE BASICS   **251**

Case Study   **251**
Machines That Count   **254**
Digital Calculating   **256**
Computer Timeline   **258**
Types of Computers   **260**
Moore's Law   **262**
Input Devices   **263**
Output Devices   **266**
The Central Processing Unit   **269**
External Storage   **271**
Questions for Reflection and Discussion   **273**
Activities   **273**
**Exercise for Further Development of Your Reflective
  Practice for Teaching With Computer Technology**   **274**
Interactive Television   **274**
Sources   **277**

GLOSSARY   **279**

INDEX   **291**

PREFACE

The purpose of this book, themes and organization, special features, acknowledgments

This book is intended to provide students with an introduction to using computers in educational settings. It is different from traditional textbooks on computers and education in that in addition to computer issues we focus on three themes which we believe have not been adequately addressed in educational computing courses: 1. the issue of how computers are redefining our culture and society and school work; 2. the idea of using the computer as a tool for increasing efficiency and productivity in curriculum; and 3. the concept of the computer not only as a tool for efficiency, but actually as a means of enhancing our intelligence.

Gutenberg: Johannes Gutenberg (c. 1400-1468) is credited with having invented moveable type and the first modern printed book.

In reference to the first of our themes—how computers are redefining our culture and society—we believe that our society has crossed a major cultural divide, one that separates us from a **Gutenberg** or **Typographic Culture** and is now forcing us to enter a **Post-Typographic Culture**. It is a culture in which people will increasingly communicate by electronic mail, in which television will not just be passively watched but interacted with, and in which schools and businesses will become even more dependent upon computers and computer-based technologies.

Typographic Culture: a culture or society based around the technology of printing.

A Post-Typographic Culture is a culture in which the computer functions as the single most important organizing point. The computer is the tool that unifies other technologies. It is the metaphor for the information age. We believe that it is critical for teachers to understand computers and their impact on

Post-Typographic Culture: an electronic non-text-oriented culture or society.

our schools and society, not just from a technical point of view, but also in terms of how the machines shape the ways in which we interpret information and how we understand the world around us.

While organized around traditional chapters intended to provide the reader with an introduction to basic skills and experience, *Computers, Curriculum and Cultural Change: An Introduction for Teachers* also provides Case Studies and Highlighted Features (Computing Timelines, Filmographies, and so on) throughout the book, as well as a text-linked glossary of key computer terms, and bibliographical sources.

Home Page: a Web screen that acts as a starting point to go to multiple sites on worldwide computing networks.

We have deliberately placed what in more traditional textbooks would have been Chapter 3 (Computer Hardware Basics) in Appendix A of this book. We have done this in the belief that more and more people are coming to courses, like the one for which this book is intended, with a basic knowledge of computers and how they work. In such a case, much of this information may be redundant. If you are largely a beginner using computers, refer to this Appendix as though it were between the second and third chapters in this book. If you are an experienced computer user, use this chapter as a reference source for facts and information you may not know or have forgotten.

World Wide Web (WWW): a browsing system that makes it possible to navigate the Internet by pointing and clicking the computer mouse. The Web connects diverse sites by the use of hyperlinks.

We have also developed a Web site to accompany this textbook that can be accessed through the Lawrence Erlbaum Associates **Home Page**. It links the reader to online sources that are being described in the book. Visit the Lawrence Erlbaum Associates Home Page to learn more about how this system works. If you are new to using the Internet and the **World Wide Web**, you may want to read Chapter 8—Networking and Telecommunication in order to become more familiar with how to link up with the **Internet**.

Internet: the successor to an experimental network built by the U.S. Department of Defense in the 1960s. Today it is a loosely configured system that connects millions of computers around the world.

Lawrence Erlbaum Associates

http://www.erlbaum.com/computer.htm

While reading this book, and using its software, you should experiment, reflect on new ideas, and discover the possibilities of educational computing. Think of yourself as being at the beginning of a new era in education and culture—one that seems to be redefining what we know and how we know it in ways that we are only beginning to understand and appreciate.

We would like to acknowledge the many people who have helped us develop this book. Asterie Baker Provenzo has provided editing, critical insights and a warm and supportive environment in which to collaborate and work. Naomi Silverman has been the consummate editor—both friend and exacting critic. Debbie Ruel, Robert Sidor and Art Lizza at Lawrence Erlbaum Associates have provided outstanding technical assistance and help. Rob Epp at Willow New Media has helped us realize many aspects of the design of this book. Alan Whitney has provided technical support as hard drives crashed and files got temporarily lost.

Eugene F. Provenzo, Jr., University of Miami
Arlene C. Brett, University of Miami
Gary N. McCloskey, O.S.A., St. Thomas University

Miami, Florida
September 1998

INTRODUCTION

How Computers Are Used Throughout the Culture, The Computer as a Mediating Force in Contemporary Culture, On the Non-Neutrality of the Computer, How Widespread Is the Use of Technology in the Schools? The Promise of Technology for Teachers, How Teaching Changes With the Use of Computers, Defining a Model of Educational Computing

Any technology tends to create a new human environment.

—Marshall McLuhan

The educational theorist C. A. Bowers (1995, p.78) maintains that although mechanical and social forms of technology surround us in our day-to-day lives, technology is one of the least understood aspects of contemporary culture. Although technologies such as television, computers, automobiles, airplanes, and telephones profoundly influence how we perceive and interact with our environment, we spend little time thinking about why this is so.

Consider the automobile, for example. How has it shaped and defined our cities, the way we shop, where we work, and where we live? How are our lives different from those of people who lived 100 years ago when the automobile had only just been invented? Would suburbs have developed in the way they have without cars? Would there be shopping malls? Would family life be different?

The fact is that technologies shape and define cultures and societies. In the Middle Ages, the introduction of stirrups from Asia made it possible for knights to ride armored horses without falling off. This meant that a new type of warfare was possible. It also changed the nature of society by necessitating the development of a feudal culture in which peasant farmers supported military lords and knights who protected them from invasion and destruction.

In the 18th century, the Industrial Revolution—through technologies like the steam engine—transformed countries such as Great Britain from a rural to an industrial economy, from a nation of farms to a nation of towns and cities. Profound changes took place in every segment of the society as a result of the introduction of new technologies.

In the United States during the second half of the 19th century, the technologies of the railroad and the telegraph profoundly affected the meaning of time and distance for the American people. With the opening of the first transcontinental railroad in 1872, the East and West Coasts were no longer 12,000 miles apart because they had been separated by an ocean voyage around the tip of South America, or by a 3,000-mile trek across a rugged and often dangerous wilderness. Important news and information no longer took weeks or months to travel from one part of the country to another, but could be communicated instantaneously via the telegraph.

Technologies such as the railroad, the telegraph, and the telephone changed how Americans in the late 19th century did business, how they communicated, and what they knew. In a similar fashion, the invention of the radio redefined our culture in the first half of this century, as did the television later on. In our own era, American society is being redefined as a result of yet another new technology—the computer.

This chapter discusses the computer and its importance for characterizing and defining not only contemporary society, but also the work of schools and teachers and the experience of children. We believe that the computer in its various forms (calculator, scanner, word processor, communications device, digital camera, and so on) is reshaping our social and economic systems, as well as our traditional approaches to teaching and learning. In doing so, it is the key to the realization of a new culture and society.

How Computers Are Used
Throughout the Culture

In less than a generation, computers have radically changed the way we live, learn, and do our work. Prior to 1950, very few people even knew what a computer was. Today they are so much a part of our lives that we hardly give them a thought. Do you own a wristwatch? Is it digital? Do you think of it as a computer? It is a computer. Do you have a camera with an electronic light meter? It probably has a small computer built into it. Does your car have a fuel injection system? If so, it almost certainly has a computer controlling it.

This book is being written using a word processor that operates on a computer. A calculator is a computer. A video game player is a computer, as is the scanning system on the cash register at your supermarket and the traffic light down the street from your home. If you have a bank account or use a credit card, then you are constantly being monitored by computers. Computers are found throughout our culture. They are the single technology that connects nearly all other technologies.

Computers represent a turning point in our culture that is as profound as the invention of the printing press proved to be to late 15th-century Europe. As argued in *Beyond the Gutenberg Galaxy: Microcomputers and the Emergence of Post-Typographic Culture* (Provenzo, 1986), we are living through the final stages of a print-based typographic culture and experiencing the creation of a post-typographic culture. Television and other forms of media are taking the place of print as our primary sources of information about the world. It is all a bit confusing, but perhaps inevitable with the advent of almost any new technology. As Marshall McLuhan (1964) argued in *Understanding Media*:

> Any technology tends to create a new human environment. Script and papyrus created the social environment we think of in connection with the empires of the ancient world. The stirrup and the wheel created unique environments of enormous scope. Technological environments are not merely passive containers of people but are active processes

that reshape people and other technologies alike. In our time, the sudden shift from the mechanical technology of the electric circuitry represents one of the major shifts of historical time. (p. iv)

We cannot ignore the "invisible" computers that are so much a part of our lives. Computers are neither "passive containers" nor, as is discussed later in this book, neutral technologies to be taken for granted.

The Computer as a Mediating Force in Contemporary Culture

Although teachers make extensive use of technology in their work (e.g., textbooks, blackboards, television, and computers), many of them have little understanding of how technology influences thinking, social relationships, or how knowledge is communicated from one generation to the next (Bowers, 1995, p. 78). How, for example, has television changed children and the ways they learn? What do they now know when they enter school that children did not know prior to the introduction of television? Do they respond differently to learning to read, or learning about mathematics, because of having been exposed to television?

The German philosopher Martin Heidegger argued that "any technology—whether the automobile, television, or the computer—*mediates human experience through its selection/amplification and reduction characteristics*" (Bowers, 1995, citing Don Ihde, p. 79). Teachers using technology must ask the following questions: How does the computer change the ecology of the classroom and the school? How does it change learning? How does it change instruction? What does the computer select and amplify? What does it reduce?

Program: software or the sequence of instructions that are executed by a computer.

If students learn through individualized computer-based drill and practice **programs**, don't they learn other skills that would be part of group instruction? What stories and ways of knowing does the computer emphasize? In video games—a type of computer learning—stories emphasizing violence, gender discrimination, and racism are prevalent. Characters act alone, not as part of a group, in most of these games. Might makes right and violence is the solution to almost any problem (Provenzo, 1991).

What happens as children increasingly deal with the real world through the screen of a computer? Computers can provide rich representations of auditory and visual information. However, these representations, by their very nature, are limited. Computers can only visually display things in two dimensions. They cannot accurately display things that are three-dimensional. They provide little tactile stimulation.

If students increasingly use computers with keyboards to write with, then what happens to learning penmanship? Do keyboarding skills become more important than learning how to write in cursive script?

Computing holds remarkable promise for education. At the same time, its limitations must be addressed. How, for example, are computer programs constructed? What assumptions are made? What values are promoted? What are the social texts underlying the computer programs being used in schools? Are we aware of the hidden curricula found in many computer programs?

A **simulation** program used in many schools, for example, is *SimEarth—The Living Planet* (Maxis). In the program/game, users are able to create their own planet by establishing animal species, modifying coastlines, designing continents, and so on. The program assumes the world can be controlled and manipulated by

Simulation (Computer): uses the power of the computer to emulate something in a real or imagined world.

master planners. This concept is also found in other titles in the same series, such as *SimCity* and *SimCity 2000*.

Maxis Corporation
http://www.maxis.com/

Sim City (Maxis Corporation)
http:/www.maxis.com/games/index.html

Sim City 2000 (Maxis Corporation)
http://www.maxis.com/games/index.html

Such an approach portrays an ecological model of the world that can be much more easily manipulated than in the real world. It puts the human being over nature rather than as a part of nature. Questions need to be raised as to whether simulation programs such as *SimEarth* and *SimCity* oversimplify the complexity of natural and urban systems. Do we create false, or at least limited, models of the world through the use of simulations? Does every simulation have a specific ideology? Is there a specific philosophy? Does being computer literate assume an understanding of the assumptions underlying a program?

How Computers Are Changing Language

New technologies create new words and new meanings for old words. Computers are changing how we use language all of the time. *Cyberspace*, which refers to the exchange of data and information inside and between computers on a worldwide basis, is a word that was invented by the science fiction writer William Gibson in his 1984 novel *Neuromancer*. A mouse is no longer just a small rodent, but an interface device for computers. *Bug* (a software problem), *handshake* (talking to and connecting with another computer), *number crunching* (doing numerical calculations) and *kluge* (a clumsy but workable solution to a computer problem) are all examples of words that are increasingly present in our vocabulary.

On the Non-Neutrality of the Computer

Bowers, in *The Cultural Dimensions of Educational Computing* (1988), questioned whether or not the use of computers in the classroom is a neutral technology. According to Bowers:

> ...the most fundamental question about the new technology has never been seriously raised by either the vocal advocates or the teachers who have attempted to articulate their reservations. The question has to do with whether the technology is neutral; that is, neutral in terms of accurately representing, at the level of the software program, the domains of the real world in which people live. (p. 24)

Bowers maintained that teachers, the educational system, and the culture in general need to critically rethink how we look at computers and the ways in which they function. Instead of simply understanding them in a technical and procedural context, we need to deal with them in a larger educational and cultural context—how they mediate and change our systems of knowledge and our ways of interpreting the world around us (p. 27).

Does this mean that computers should not be part of classroom instruction in the future? Absolutely not! Our argument is that computing within educational settings, and throughout our culture in general, should be critically understood. Computers have certain inherent values built into their design and use. We must understand this if we are to use these remarkable machines to the best educational and social advantage possible.

How Widespread Is the Use of Technology in the Schools?

In spring 1995, the Office of Technology Assessment reported that there were approximately 5.8 million computers in use in schools in the United States, or approximately one machine for every nine students. About half of the machines currently in use are based on the older 8-**bit** technology that cannot support advanced uses such

Bit: the smallest amount of data or information handled by a computer. In Binary code, it is represented as either a 1 or 0.

CD-ROM: an acronym for a "compact disc read-only memory." CD-ROMs are aluminum discs coated with plastic that are "read" by a laser and have a storage capacity of over 600 megabytes.

Network: a collection of computers and peripheral devices that are connected by a communications system.

Software: runs the computer by giving it instructions to perform certain operations.

Spreadsheet: software that allows numerical data to be entered into cells arranged as rows and columns.

Database: a file or collection of data.

as **CD-ROM** players, integrated **networks**, or increasingly complex and memory intensive **software** (Office of Technology Assessment, 1995, p. 89).

American schools have had a tendency to place computers in separate labs, rather than in classrooms (Office of Technology Assessment, 1995, p. 90). This is an important point because it means that students must go to a lab to use computers where there is less of a tendency to integrate the machines with everyday instruction. The machines are likely to become part of a separate activity, typically involving drill and instruction exercises.

High schools are more likely to have newer and more powerful machines, and in turn they are able to use more advanced software and to link themselves with online information sources (p. 90). In 1992, the average high school had 54 computers, whereas the average elementary school had approximately 25 machines. During the early 1990s, computer growth in the public schools averaged about 18% a year (pp. 92, 94). As of 1992, local area networks were in use in about 20% of all public schools in the United States—16% at the elementary level and approximately 25% in secondary schools (p. 96).

The Promise of Technology for Teachers

Computers hold remarkable promise for teachers in terms of their day-to-day work. Much of the work of teaching involves record keeping, searching for new information, and creating collections of teaching materials, as well as providing individualized instruction. Computers can help in all of these tasks.

What happens when teachers have access to powerful accounting and record keeping tools like **spreadsheets** and **databases**? How do they help them in their work?

Consider, for example, how the use of a grading and record keeping program greatly simplifies the work of a typical teacher in the following case study.

Case Study

Mr. Alvarez is a middle school social studies teacher who gives his students many short writing assignments. Each assignment is carefully graded and counts toward his students' total cumulative average. With five classes a day, an average of 30 students in each class, and two written assignments per student each week, there are a total of 300 separate grades per week that he must record and average together.

Students often turn in assignments late or need to be reminded of what they have or have not turned in. Using a grading program like *Grade Quick* (Jackson Software), a teacher like Mr. Alvarez can set up a program for his classes that not only records all of his students' grades, but automatically counts a certain percentage for late assignments. It can also generate personalized reports for students.

Grade Quick (Jackson Software)
http://www.jacksoncorp.com/gradequick//

Mr. Alvarez can connect to the Internet to talk to other teachers and find resources for his classroom. With e-mail, he can exchange curricula and ideas with teachers throughout his district, as well as with those across his state whom he has met as part of the annual statewide social studies convention.

Teachers Helping Teachers
http://www.pacificnet.net/~mandel/

For his eighth-grade American history class, Mr. Alvarez connects regularly to *Thomas*—the official government site for Congress—to find information about current legislation and government initiatives. There he finds the full text of *The Congressional Record*, tracks legislation that is going through Congress, as well as finds information about his local congressional Representatives and Senators. For a lecture on adolescent drug abuse, he can go to the home page for *Time* Magazine where he can review articles on the subject published over the last 2 or 3 years.

Thomas
http://thomas.loc.gov

Time Magazine
http://www.timeinc.com/time/

Perhaps the most valuable tool for Mr. Alvarez is his word processor. With it, he can write his lesson plans, lectures, tests, and student activity sheets. Over the years, he has developed very thorough course outlines for all of the classes he teaches. These outlines, which run seven or eight single-spaced pages, provide Mr. Alvarez and his students with a roadmap for proceeding through his courses.

Not having to retype his course outlines each semester makes it possible for him to have more time to add new materials and information. Likewise, using his word processor to set up a test bank of questions has made the construction of tests and quizzes much easier. He now keeps a running file of test questions that he adds to on a regular basis.

A word processor also helps Mr. Alvarez with correspondence to parents, and with his work on a master's degree in curriculum at a local university. Reports to his chair are easier to generate.

Using his word processor with a graphic presentation system, Mr. Alvarez has started to create very effective overheads for his classes. He recently requested $300 from his department chairperson for an electronic video connection box that will make it possible to hook his computer up to the large screen television in his classroom. With this system he can present not just sophisticated slide shows, but also animated demonstrations.

At the student level, Mr. Alvarez can have some of his brightest students go on the Internet to research a topic they are interested in, while he works with students who need additional review and instruction. When he needs time to work with his more advanced students, he can have some of his students who are having more difficulty complete a review section on the computer.

Such a model is not easy to achieve. If Mr. Alvarez teaches in more than one classroom, he has to move from room to room. Most computer equipment is not portable. The natural confusion found in most classrooms makes it hard to be sure that equipment will always work. Students play with **operating systems**. **Viruses** are introduced by outside programs—things just do not always work.

Operating System: software that controls the computer and allows it to perform basic functions.

Computers change the ecology of the classroom because they change the process of teaching and learning. They make many things much easier and introduce new levels of complexity into the instructional process. The classroom and learning environment are dramatically changed as a result of the introduction of technology. Teachers and administrators need to understand this before they decide to use technology in their classrooms.

Virus: a program that infects or corrupts other computer programs.

If computers are creating a new environment for teaching and learning, then the training of teachers must change as well. Technological literacy becomes a requirement for all teachers. This fact is leading groups like the National Council for Accreditation of Teacher Education to require that all teachers be knowledgeable about the use of computers and technology in the classroom as part of the basic requirements for accreditation.

NATIONAL COUNCIL FOR ACCREDITATION
OF TEACHER EDUCATION

National Council for Accreditation of Teacher Education
http://www.ncate.org/

What new types of understanding do teachers need to have? What new types of approaches do they need to take in the classroom? How will the traditional roles of teachers change? What types of models of professional development are needed? What new types of attitudes will teachers have to develop in order to make the most effective use of the new technologies?

National Council for Accreditation of Teacher Education's Requirements for the "New Professional Teacher"

New Understandings
Teachers need to understand the deep impact technology is having on society as a whole: how technology has changed the nature of work, of communications, and our understanding of the development of knowledge.

New Approaches
Today, teachers must recognize that information is available from sources that go well beyond textbooks and teachers—mass media, communities, etc. and help students understand and make use of the many ways in which they can gain access to information. Teachers must employ a wide range of technological tools and software as part of their own instructional repertoire.

New Roles
Teachers should help students pursue their own inquiries, making use of technologies to find, organize, and interpret information, and to become reflective and critical about information quality and sources.

New Forms of Professional Development
Teachers must participate in formal courses, some of which may be delivered in non-traditional ways, e.g., via telecommunications; they must also become part of ongoing, informal learning communities with other professionals who share their interests and concerns.

New Attitudes
Finally, teachers need an "attitude" that is fearless in the use of technology, encourages them to take risks, and inspires them to become lifelong learners.

Source: National Council for the Accreditation of Teacher Education (1997). See: http://www.ncate.org/specfoc/techrpt.html

How Teaching Changes With the Use of Computers

Using computers significantly changes the environment for teaching. Karen Sheingold and Martha Hadley (cited in Office of Technology Assessment, 1995) surveyed 608 teachers nationwide who had experience integrating computers into their teaching. Seventy-three percent of the teachers surveyed had used computers for 5 years or longer in their work. Sheingold and Hadley found that nearly 90% of the teachers sampled felt their teaching had changed as a result of introducing computers into their classrooms. Nearly three fourths reported, for example, that with the availability of computers they could expect more from their students in terms of their creating and editing their work. Over 70% reported that they spent more time with individual students, whereas 65% reported they were more comfortable with students working independently. A total of 63% stated they were better able to present more complex instruction to students; 61% felt they were better able to meet individual student needs; 52% found themselves spending less time lecturing the entire class; 43% found themselves more comfortable with small group activities; and 40% found themselves spending less time practicing or reviewing material with their whole class (pp. 52–53).

Defining a Model of Educational Computing

Before any teacher or school uses computers as part of its instructional program, careful consideration needs to be given to the issue of how the learning and teaching environment will be changed. Too often people adopt technology in their schools without thinking through its potentials and limitations—they simply use it because it is the thing to do.

All educational computing is not the same. Computers have many ways they can be used in instruction. For example, Robert Taylor (1980) argued that there are essentially three roles for the computer in education: *tutor*, *tool*, and *tutee*. As tutor, the computer functions in ways that are similar to traditional teaching or instruction. It leads the student through drills and exercises where memorization and rote learning is required. It can also take the form of simulations, problem-solving activities, as well as provide tutorials in specific areas.

Word Processor: a type of software program that makes it possible for a writer to write or compile text, edit, and revise what has been written, save what has been written, and print it.

As a tool, the computer is used by the student as a **word processor**, database manager, spreadsheet, a graphics design system, or as a link to an information resource like the Internet. As tutee, the computer is programmed by the student to perform specific operations and tasks. This can be done with a traditional programming language, or by a student-oriented program such as **Logo** (Taylor, 1980, pp. 2–4).

Logo: a programming language designed for children by the MIT professor Seymour Papert.

In using the computer in your classroom, consider which of Taylor's functions you are employing. Is your use of computers with students primarily for drill? Are you using computers mainly as tools with which to create? Are your students programming computers, or are they being programmed by them? These are very serious questions, which raise fundamental issues to be explored when developing a personal model of educational computing. As emphasized throughout this introduction, the computer is not a neutral technology. It mediates knowledge, the ways in which we interact with each other, and how we learn. It is a powerful technology that can contribute much to improving classroom instruction. But it can also be a limiting technology that ultimately distracts teachers and students from their primary purpose by imposing a set of assumed values that do not advance the purposes of instruction or individual and group development.

Is all educational computing the same? Taylor obviously argued that it is not the same. Cleborne D. Maddux (1986) basically agreed with Taylor, but took a somewhat different approach. He argued that there are essentially two types of educational computer applications. He called these *Type I* and *Type II* applications. In *Type I* applications the computer is used to do things that have always been done as part of the curriculum. Using the computer makes doing these things easier and quicker. Examples would be word processing, drill and memorization, and so on. *Type II* applications involve the use of new models of pedagogy and instruction (Maddux, 1986, p. 3).

Although *Type I* applications are extremely important, in and of themselves they will not change education. *Type I* applications of computers do not justify their expense to the schools. According to Maddux (1986), educational computing can only be justified if *Type II* applications involving new and better ways of teaching are employed (p. 3). For Maddux, a hypermedia computer program reading aloud to a dyslexic or blind child would be an example of a *Type II* application.

Maddux is raising the question of what are the best and most appropriate uses of educational computing. This is ultimately the challenge of educational computing. When and how should we use this important technology? How does its use change the ecology of the classroom and the schools? It is hoped that the answers to these questions will be clearer by the time you have completed using and reflecting on this work.

QUESTIONS FOR REFLECTION AND DISCUSSION

1. How does technology change our lives, whether it is in the form of the telephone or fax machine, television, the automobile, or computing?

2. How does computing change teaching and instruction? How does it change learning?

3. Where do computers make important contributions for improving the quality of life in our culture? Where do they cause problems? Why?

4. What is meant by the idea of computers being a form of *media*? How is this different or the same from television being a form of *media*, or newspapers and magazines as *media*?

5. Do you think that technology is neutral? If neutral, why? If not, why?

6. How widespread is the use of computers in the school with which you are familiar? Is their use sufficient, or could more be done with them?

7. How could computers help you most in your work in the classroom?

8. How do you think computers have the potential to interfere with you working effectively in the classroom?

9. How do computers potentially change traditional areas of instruction in subjects such as mathematics, language arts, social studies, and science? Are these changes good? What are their limitations, if any?

10. Outline a model of educational computing you would like to see for your own classroom and for your school. Why do you think that it would be worthwhile?

ACTIVITIES

1. Make a list of all the ways computers are at work in your personal life. How would your life be different without them?

2. Play a game of solitaire on a computer. How is the game different from playing it with a deck of cards? If you have access to a computer chess game, play against it. How is it different from playing against another person?

3. Find a cartoon about computing and share it with others in your class. What does the cartoon tell you about the nature of these machines?

EXERCISE FOR FURTHER DEVELOPMENT OF YOUR REFLECTIVE PRACTICE FOR TEACHING WITH COMPUTER TECHNOLOGY

Teachers as professionals need to be able to think critically and to enable students to develop their critical thinking. Computer technology is expanding our sense of the world. Read the following presentation on cyberspace and reflect on the following critical thinking issues related to teaching practice:

1. How are students' experiences of cyberspace making new demands on teachers for the increased teaching of critical thinking?

2. In a cyberspace world, how is the teacher's role changing from the expert giving information to teaching students to think critically about the information they are gathering with the assistance of computer technology?

3. The traditional classroom has been a place to use the door to shut the rest of the world out to ensure teacher control. How is the need to connect the classroom to cyberspace changing a teacher's control of the classroom?

Cyberspace

William Gibson, in his 1984 novel *Neuromancer,* first coined the term *cyberspace*. In *Neuromancer*, and subsequent works such as *Burning Chrome (1986)* and *Count Zero (1987)*, Gibson described a not-too-distant future in which the world is dominated by powerful multinational corporations. Urban life has collapsed. Cosmetic surgery and reconstruction are the norm. Through technology, neural implants and artificial intelligences literally take on lives of their own.

Gibson's fictional world is tied together by an electronic construct called the "matrix." This is a vast electronic network that connects all of the world's computers and information systems. Its primitive origins are found in video games and early computer experiments conducted by the military, as well as in the Internet, the computer system that today connects information users together on a global basis.

In order to navigate through the massive electronic database of the matrix, users are connected, or interfaced, through electrodes wired to their brains. The graphic representation the user sees in order to navigate through the matrix—the simulation itself—is called cyberspace.

Gibson described cyberspace as "a consensual hallucination experienced by billions of legitimate operators in every nation, by children being taught mathematical concepts.... A graphic representation of data abstracted from the banks of every computer in the human system. Unthinkable complexity. Lines of light ranged in the nonspace of the mind, clusters and constellations of datas. Like city lights, receding..." (*Neuromancer*, 1984, p. 51).

Michael Benedikt (1992), a professor of architecture and design at the University of Texas, described cyberspace as "a new universe, a parallel universe created and sustained by the world's computers and communication lines. A world in which the global traffic of knowledge, secrets, measurements, indicators, entertainments, and alter-human agency takes on form: sights, sounds, presences never seen on the surface of the earth blossoming in a vast electronic night" (p. 1).

Cyberspace exists according to Benedikt "wherever electricity runs" (p. 2). It is a realm of "pure information," a "soft hail of electrons" (p. 3). It is also a place that Benedikt argued, for the most part, does not yet exist, it is more a fantasy or desire rather than a reality.

Why then does the term *cyberspace* dominate so many current conversations involving computers and our culture? Cyberspace is a word that describes the new world that is beginning to be realized from an information point of view. It is a world describing the postmodern or post-typographic condition.

Cyberspace, at the broadest conceptual level, is the global village, the Internet, the Information Highway, and the World Wide Web. It is humanity connected by electronic information. It is also a much narrower literary construct and metaphor. At its most basic level, within novels like *Neuromancer,* it is a mnemonic device, that is, a visual construct of the world of electrons and information that flows around us, but that we cannot see or experience directly.

In this context, cyberspace is a word that is more reminiscent of a pre-Gutenberg and medieval world than of a modern or typographic culture. In Gibson's novels, artificial intelligences take on a life of their own in the matrix. Magic is rediscovered and made possible in cyberspace. It is filled with more than just data. There are ghosts and spirits in cyberspace. People are brought back from the dead (like the programmer/cyberspace cowboy Dixie McCoy in *Neuromancer).*

Cyberspace in Gibson's novel is a nontextual and closed world— what he described as "an infinite cage" (*Mona Lisa Overdrive,* 1989, p. 49). It is a world of visual images, of corporate fiefdoms, and of samurai. In many respects, it is a medieval and feudal world—a brilliant act of literary imagination.

📖 SOURCES

Benedikt, M. (Ed.). (1992). *Cyberspace: First steps.* Cambridge, MA: MIT Press.

Bowers, C. A. (1988). *The cultural dimensions of educational computing: Understanding the non-neutrality of technology.* New York: Teachers College Press.

Bowers, C. A. (1995). *Educating for an ecologically sustainable culture: Rethinking moral education, creativity, intelligence, and other modern orthodoxies.* Albany, NY: State University of New York Press.

Gibson, W. (1984). *Neuromancer.* New York: Ace.

Gibson, W. (1986). *Burning chrome.* New York: Ace.

Gibson, W. (1987). *Count Zero.* New York: Ace.

Gibson, W. (1989). *Mona Lisa overdrive.* New York: Bantam.

Maddux, C. D. (1986). Issues and concerns in special education microcomputing. *Computers in the Schools,* 3 (3–4), 3.

McLuhan, M. (1962). *The Gutenberg galaxy: The making of typographic man.* Toronto: University of Toronto Press.

McLuhan, M. (1964). *Understanding media: The extensions of man.* New York: Mentor Books. (Also see the 30th anniversary edition of this work published by MIT Press in 1994).

National Council for the Accreditation of Teacher Education. (1997). Technology and the new professional teacher: Preparing for the 21st century classroom. Washington, DC: National Council for the Accreditation of Teacher Education. See: http://www.ncate.org/specfoc/techrpt.html

Office of Technology Assessment, Congress of the United States. (1995). *Teachers & technology: Making the connectio*n (Report

No. OTA-EHR-616). Washington, DC: U. S. Government Printing Office.

President's Committee of Advisors on Science and Technology, Panel on Educational Technology. (1997). *Report to the president on the use of technology to strengthen K-12 education in the United States*. Washington, DC: U.S. Government Printing Office. See: http://ww.whitehouse.gov/WH/EOP/OSTP/NSTC/PCASTk-2ed.html

Provenzo, E. F., Jr. (1986). *Beyond the Gutenberg galaxy: Microcomputers and post-typographic culture*. New York: Teachers College Press.

Provenzo, E. F., Jr. (1991). *Video kids: Making sense of Nintendo*. Cambridge, MA: Harvard University Press.

Provenzo, E. F., Jr. (1996). *The educator's brief guide to computers in the schools*. Princeton, NJ: Eye on Education.

Provenzo, E. F., Jr. (1998). *The educator's brief guide to the inteternet and the world wide web*. Larchmont, NY: Eye on Education. See: http://www.education.miami.edu/ep/iworkshop

Provenzo, E. F., Jr. (in press). *Computing, digital culture and pedagogy: The analytical engine*. New York: Peter Lang.

Provenzo, E. F., Jr. (in press). *The Internet and the World Wide Web for Pre-Service teachers*. Boston: Allyn & Bacon.

Taylor, R. (Ed.). (1980). *The computer in the school: Tutor, tool, tutee*. New York: Teachers College Press.

United States Department of Education. (1996). *Getting America's students ready for the 21st century: Meeting the technology literacy challenge*. Washington, DC: U.S. Department of Education. See: www.ed.gov/pubs/pubdb.html

COMPUTERS—THE SOCIAL REVOLUTION OF OUR TIME

A Brief History of Computing, The Microcomputer Revolution, Parallels Between the Gutenberg and the Contemporary Computer Revolution, The Computer as a "Singularity," The Computer as "Augmenting" Intelligence

Understanding how the educational use of computers influences our pattern of thinking, and thus contributes to changes in the symbolic underpinnings of the culture, should be considered an essential aspect of computer literacy.

—C. A. Bowers

At the beginning of *The Children's Machine: Rethinking School in the Age of the Computer* (1993), Seymour Papert, mathematician and inventor of the computer language *Logo*, asked the reader to imagine a party of time travelers from an earlier century. For the sake of argument, assume that Papert's time travelers are from 1897. The group includes surgeons and schoolteachers. Papert has us imagine the surgeons visiting a hospital operating room. Almost everything they see would be new and confusing. Techniques used for sterilizing operating tools, anesthesia, and electronic monitoring devices would be totally unknown to them.

Most of what the schoolteachers from 1897 would see when visiting an elementary school would be familiar. The desks and furniture in the classroom would appear about the same. They would be able to recognize a modern textbook as being similar to the books they used. Most of the techniques and methods employed by today's teachers would probably make sense to them, and would be related to things they might have done with students in their own classrooms (Papert, 1993, pp. 1–2).

Papert made the point that unlike the world of the operating room, the world of schooling has not changed in fundamental "ways that have altered its nature" (p. 2). The one new technology in the classroom, with the exception of a television set, with which the teachers from 1897 would be unfamiliar, would be a computer. Slide projectors would correspond to magic lanterns, a tape recorder or record player would be like a victrola, and an electric typewriter would be comparable with manual typewriters of their own era. A computer, however, would be totally new, unlike any technology they had ever seen before.

Where did these machines come from? What are the origins of the contemporary computing revolution?

A Brief History of Computing

Normally we think of computers as having been introduced during the period following World War II. In fact, much of the theoretical underpinnings for contemporary computing come from the middle of the 19th century and the work of the English inventor and mathematician Charles Babbage.

Portrait of Charles Babbage (1792-1871), *Illustrated London* News, Nov. 4, 1871.

In 1822, Babbage demonstrated a very limited mechanical **binary** computer to the Royal Astronomical Society in London. Known as the *Difference Engine*, it was followed by a more advanced machine called the *Analytical Engine*. Although theoretically sound, both machines were mechanically flawed. Even the most carefully machined gears and cogs were not precise enough to undertake massive calculations. Although Babbage's machine was functional, it would need electrical switching systems before it could work on a practical basis.

Binary: information represented by 0s and 1s.

Links to Information on Charles Babbage
http://nano.xerox.com/nanotech/babbage.html

Charles Babbage
http://nano.xerox.com/nanotech/babbage.html

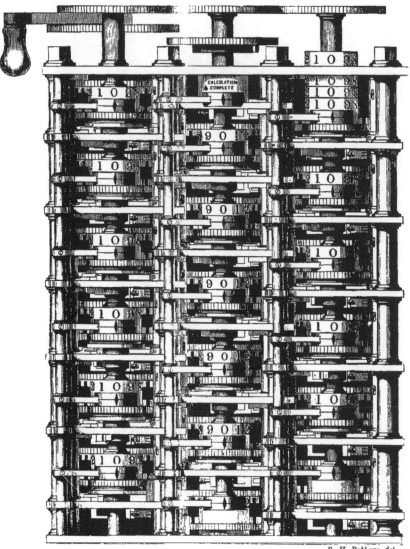

B. H. Babbage, del.

Detail of Charles Babbage's Difference Engine Number 1 illustrated in *Passages From the Life of a Philosopher* published in 1864.

Augusta Ada Byron (1815–1852)

Augusta Ada Byron (1815–1852), more widely known as Ada Countess of Lovelace, is among the most famous figures in the history of computing. The daughter of the 19th-century English poet Lord Byron, she was a gifted and largely self-taught mathematician. In 1833, when she was only 18 years old, she met the scientist and inventor Charles Babbage. Babbage, the inventor of the Difference Engine and the Analytical Engine, is widely considered to have created the first modern computer. Realizing Byron's talent, he asked her to assist him in his work. This eventually led to Byron publishing a set of notes in 1843 in Richard Taylor's *Scientific Memoirs* series, which included a set of instructions for programming the Analytical Engine and speculations about its possible applications and use in mathematical computation, artificial intelligence, and music.

Byron's work is considered a major contribution to the development of modern computing. In 1980, the U.S. Department of Defense named a computing language "Ada" in her honor. The Ada Project (TAP), a World Wide Web site on women in computing, is also named after her. To learn more about her visit:

Ada Lovelace
http://alephO.clarku.edu/~djoyce/mathhist/lovelace.html

Over 100 years passed before Babbage's ideas were used in electronic computational devices. Most experts would agree that the modern **digital computer** can trace its roots back to the 1930s and the work of Konrad Zuse, a young German engineer, who developed a simple computer using telephone switching devices that were capable of being programmed.

Konrad Zuse Biography
http://www.germany.eu.net/shop/RTD/Zuse.html

Zuse's work was interrupted by World War II. In the United States, the war encouraged the development of more advanced computing

Digital: pertaining to a single state or condition. A digital circuit controls current in a binary on or off state.

Digtial Computer: electronically stores information by representing information in two states, ON and OFF, + and -, 0 or 1.

machines. By 1946, the first general purpose computer electronic calculator was formally dedicated at the Moore School of Electrical Engineering at the University of Pennsylvania. The machine was designed to do ballistic calculations for the U.S. Army. It was known as the Electronic Numerical Integrator and Computer (ENIAC).

The ENIAC was made up of 18,000 vacuum tubes, 70,000 resistors, 10,000 capacitors, and 6,000 switches. The size of a double garage, this early computer worked only for brief periods because its vacuum tubes kept burning out. The logic chip in most watches today is a far more sophisticated calculating device than was the ENIAC.

50th Anniversary of the ENIAC
http://www.seas.upenn.edu/~museum/overview.html

Transistor: an electronic device made of semiconducting materials which amplifies or controls the flow of electrons in an electrical circuit.

Early computers were limited by the necessity of using vacuum tubes. In 1947, the **transistor** was invented by scientists at Bell Laboratories. A tiny sandwich of semiconducting materials was created so that a small amount of current entering one end of the transistor could control a larger amount of current in another transistor. The practical result was the creation of a simple switching device that could be used to control the flow of electrons. Transistors were much smaller than vacuum tubes, they generated very little heat in comparison, were very cheap to manufacture, and, unlike vacuum tubes, rarely burned out.

Microchip: a computer chip on which are etched the components of a computer's central processing unit.

Transistors made it possible to begin to make computers both smaller and more efficient. By the late 1950s, transistors were being etched onto tiny wafers of silicon. This quickly led to multiple transistors and connections being etched on single slivers of silicon. The creation of the **microchip** made it possible to put entire sections of a computer's memory, or logic system, onto a very small space.

Mister Transistor
http://ourworld.compuserve.com/homepages/Andrew_Wylie/homepage.htm

By 1971, the microprocessor had been invented. Essentially, this involved placing a complete **microprocessor**—an entire central processing unit—on a single silicon chip. Computers could now be made that would rest on the tip of your finger, which using the technology of the ENIAC, would have been the size of a football field 25 years earlier (Provenzo, 1986, p. 20).

Microprocessor: the main computing and control device on a computer. Micro-processors are used in most personal computers.

National Museum of American History—Computer History Exhibit
http://www.si.edu/resource/tours/comphist/computer.htm

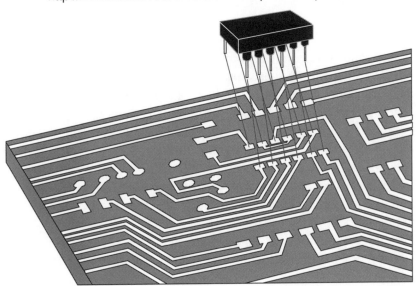

The invention of the **integrated circuit** made possible the **microcomputer**, or **personal computer**. Computers no longer had to be assembled out of millions of different parts, but could be miniaturized and mass-produced as single "integrated" units. Machines that were better and more efficient than those that would have cost millions of dollars in the 1950s and 1960s were now available to many people at an affordable price.

Integrated Circuit: a silicon chip on which transistors and other circuit elements are packed.

IEEE Annals of the History of Computing
http://www.computer.org/pubs/annals/annals.htm

Microcomputer: a computer that uses a single chip microprocessor.

The rapid evolution of computer technology is perhaps one of the most interesting aspects of the contemporary computer revolution. Machines that were only dreamed about 15 or 20 years ago are

Personal Computer: another term for microcomputer.

now available to private citizens for less than $2,000. What happens when computing power becomes so cheap and common? How does it affect the work of people, the use to which computers are put, and so on? This is a theme we will return to throughout the rest of this book.

Why is the introduction of inexpensive computing in our culture and society relevant for educators in the classroom?

The availability of inexpensive but powerful computing in our society, and in turn our schools and classrooms, means that many things are happening that were not possible even a few years ago. Migrant students going to school in one part of the country in one season are having their records follow them as their families move to another part of the country following the harvest. Rural schools with very small populations and limited resources are having students take advanced placement courses online. Teachers have productivity tools like word processors and classroom management systems to prepare lesson plans and keep records. Students are taking mass-administered intelligence and achievement tests that are being automatically scored. Individual uses of school Internet access are being tracked by school system administrators.

The Microcomputer Revolution

Today computers can be found in offices, in schools, and in many homes. They are changing not only the way we live and work, but possibly even the way we think.

Prior to 1974 there was no such thing as a personal computer. That was the year that MITS, a company in New Mexico, came up with the idea of selling a kit that made it possible to assemble a working computer. It was called an Altair 8800 and is widely considered to be the first personal computer. When purchased assembled, the Altair cost $621. If customers built it themselves, the cost was only

$395. The Altair had lots of flashing lights and switches and a very small memory. It was difficult to use. Computers that were much easier to use were developed within a short time. The most important was the Apple.

Altair Web Page
http://www.ual.mx/altair/awp.html

The Apple was designed by a young engineer named Steven Wozniak. Wozniak worked as a designer for Hewlett-Packard, a giant computer and calculator company. During his spare time, Wozniak, or "Woz" as he is more commonly known, began to design his own personal computer. Much of the technology he used in the machine already existed. A lot that went into it, however, was totally new.

Wozniak was not very interested in being a businessperson. He built his first computers mostly just for the fun of it. His friend Steven Jobs convinced him that they could start their own company to sell computers. Jobs, who was a vegetarian, came up with the name Apple for their company. It was supposed to suggest that the machine was friendly and easy to use. The first Apple computers were sold to the public in 1978. They were built by Wozniak and Jobs in the garage of Jobs' parents' home and were an immediate success. The Apple quickly evolved into the Apple II, Apple II+, Apple IIE, and in 1985, the Apple IIGS. With the introduction of the Macintosh line of computers in 1984, Apple had become one of the leading computer companies in the world. Other companies quickly followed Apple's lead into the personal computing industry. Early manufacturers included Atari, Timex, Osborne, Texas Instruments, and IBM.

The History of Apple Computer
http://www.apple-history.pair.com/

History of IBM
http://www.ibm.com/Features/ancient.html

Computer History Web Sites
http://granite.sentex.net/~ccmuseum/hist_sites.html

By 1982, nearly three million personal computers had been sold. Today, more computers are being bought each year than televisions. Besides business and educational uses, they are coming into widespread use for entertainment and communication.

Parallels Between the Gutenberg and the Contemporary Computer Revolution

There are many parallels between the invention of printing and the growth and development of microcomputing since the late 1970s. As one of this book's authors, Eugene F. Provenzo, Jr. (1986) argued in *Beyond the Gutenberg Galaxy,* "the changes that are beginning to emerge in our culture as a result of the large-scale introduction of microcomputers parallel many of the changes that took place in Europe as a consequence of the information revolution that followed the invention of printing" (p. 3).

Because of the high cost of **mainframe** computing up until the late 1970s, the machines and their programs were limited to a highly select group within the culture. Basically, only large corporations, selected academics, the government, and the military had access to computers.

Mainframe: a high-llevel computer designed for sophisticated computational tasks.

The introduction of micro, or personal, computers democratized computing. It became available to almost anyone. Computer literacy is, in turn, an increasingly important issue because such a large number of people have access to the machines (Provenzo, 1986, p. 6).

Just as the invention of printing took the writing and production of books out of the almost exclusive control of the universities and the church and put it into the hands of the individual, the personal computer has moved computing out of the largely exclusive control of groups (e.g., the government and large corporations) and into the hands of private individuals.

Many factors have contributed to this phenomenon. In recent years, computers, like early books, have become easier to read and use, cheaper to buy, and more portable. Like books during the Renaissance and Reformation, which were originally written in Latin but began to be published in vernacular languages such as English, French, and Italian, computers have become increasingly "user friendly." **Icons**—symbolic representations of complex program groups—are used to simplify the use of computers. As the cost of computers has gone down, there has been a corresponding expansion in their use. In the context of the invention of modern printing and the Gutenberg revolution, the significance of portability can be seen in the comments of Lucien Febvre and Henri-Jean Martin (1976), who argued that "thanks to printing and the multiplication of texts, the book ceased to seem a precious object to be consulted in a library: there was more and more need to be able to carry it about readily in order to refer to it or read it at any time" (p. 249). Precisely the same thing has happened with

Icon: specialized graphic image that represents an object or program that can be manipulated by the user.

computers. Computers that are more powerful than the largest mainframe machines of the 1950s are now carried as electronic calendars and pocket organizers, and laptop computers with the power of scientific workstations from the late 1980s can be carried into the classroom or on business trips.

Martin Luther (1483-1546)

Desktop Publishing: involves the use of computers to create text and graphics for the production of pamphlets, newsletters and books.

New technologies of this sort, whether the book or the personal computer, have an enormous potential to empower individuals. Martin Luther was able to supersede the censorship and control of the medieval Catholic Church because he had the power of the printing press to disseminate his ideas. To what extent is the computer, in manifestations such as the Internet and **desktop publishing**, a similarly empowering technology?

Why are the parallels between the Gutenberg and the contemporary computer revolution relevant for educators in the classroom?

The introduction of movable type made it possible to create inexpensive, highly detailed books. By the middle of the 17th century a new form of educational media called the *textbook* was created. Curriculum materials were standardized. Writers, illustrators, and publishers devoted themselves to the creation of standard texts.

The textbook created a new learning or instructional space. Likewise, the computer in our own era is creating a new type of learning space. CD-ROM discs with hypermedia programs for reading include passages where students click on a word and have a definition appear. Students also have access to files that read aloud to them. This is happening in multiple languages with illustrated animations as well as many other features.

Beyond the chalkboard, presentation systems such as Powerpoint and Astound are available through the computer. Encyclopedias are no longer print volume texts. They are now either interactive CD-ROMs or online sources on the Internet and the World Wide Web. Record keeping for the teacher has moved from the grade book to electronic grading and management programs.

The Computer as a "Singularity"

According to the science fiction writer Vernor Vinge (1989):

> When a race succeeds in making creatures that are smarter than it is, then all the rules are changed. And from the standpoint of that race, you've gone through a Singularity. That's because it's not possible before that point to talk meaningfully about the issues that are important *after* that point. (p. 116)

The computer, as it has evolved from its mainframe origins in the 1940s and 1950s, may very well be a singularity that has changed the rules of our culture and society.

Vernor Vinge on the Singularity
http://www.ugcs.caltech.edu/~phoenix/Lit/vinge-sing.html

Knowledge and our ways of knowing are redefined by the computer in much the same way that the invention of the book changed the fundamental nature and meaning of learning during the Renaissance. Memory and recitation were no longer as important with the book as they were prior to its invention. Knowledge could be precisely reproduced. With the precision provided by the printing press, thousands of copies of exactly the same book could be reproduced without the fear of variant editions being created through the errors of scribes or copyists.

Having highly accurate texts is critical to the development of modern science. The ability to produce precise scientific drawings is equally important. Imagine not having the precision of the printing press to produce these types of publications. What would maps be like if they had to be drawn rather than printed? Imagine how the world would be different if everything you used in a book format was copied by hand rather than being mass-produced.

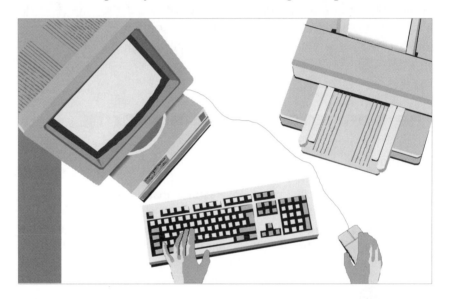

The computer, in a similar way, changes how we know and understand the world around us. We can create simulations of how things look when they move at the speed of light, we can organize huge amounts of data and retrieve them with relative ease, we can do complex mathematical computations that would take tens of thousands of hours to do by hand, and we can communicate instantaneously with people around the world.

We believe this type of shift in our ability to process information is in fact a singularity, just as the introduction of modern printing was a singularity at the end of the 15th century—a singularity of profound social and cultural significance.

Why is the idea of the computer being a "Singularity" a relevant issue for educators in the classroom?

The invention of movable type was a Singularity. As already noted, textbooks were a direct outcome of the invention of movable type. Before movable type and the textbook, neither teachers nor students regularly had books in their classrooms. Books were in libraries to be consulted by scholars. During the Middle Ages, teachers taught about what was in books. With the introduction of inexpensive printing as a Singularity, the nature of teaching changed with teachers and students having easy access to books in their classrooms. The introduction of wide access to the Internet and the World Wide Web may represent a similar Singularity affecting classroom practice. Teachers and students are no longer limited to the reference sources in their classroom or school. The Singularity of computers provides much easier access to the world's knowledge and thus is redefining recent traditions of instruction.

The Computer as "Augmenting" Intelligence

Douglas C. Engelbart (1963) wrote a prophetic essay entitled "A Conceptual Framework for the Augmentation of Man's Intellect." He outlined the basic principles of word processing, the use of icon systems for computers, as well as ideas such as the computer **mouse** and digital **scanning.**

Engelbart also postulated that the computer could "**augment**," or enhance, the intelligence of its users. He described this process as "augmenting man's intellect": "By 'augmenting man's intellect' we mean increasing the capability of a man to approach a complex problem situation, gain comprehension to suit his particular needs, and to derive solutions to problems" (Engelbart, 1963, p. 1). According to Engelbart, learning and understanding were naturally

Mouse: a pointing device that allows the user to input commands into a computer.

Scanner: a device that uses a light sensitive reader to transform text or images into a digital signal that can be used by a computer. Scanning refers to the process of using a scanner.

Augment Intelligence: to supplement, enhance or support intelligence.

facilitated by using the computer. Better solutions to problems could be produced as well. The computer would also make it possible to be more accurate (p. 1).

Engelbart talked, for example, about how using a computer as a word processor changes the entire process of composing a text:

> For instance, trial drafts can rapidly be composed from rearranged excerpts of old drafts, together with new words or passages which you insert by hand typing. Your first draft may represent a free outpouring of thoughts in any order, with the inspection of foregoing thoughts continuously stimulating new considerations and ideas to be entered. (p. 7)

Ideas can be reordered, and new ideas can be integrated more easily. More complex procedures can be introduced into the process.

Using a word processor is not just a means to more efficient typing. What Engelbart argued is that it changes the actual process of writing. Besides allowing writers to continually revise their ideas, the computer allows them to check spelling and even grammar.

Douglas Engelbart—Computing Pioneer

Douglas Engelbart is among the most important figures in the history of contemporary computing. Yet he remains a relatively obscure figure—one known largely by experts in computing. Engelbart is most famous for having invented the computer mouse, display editing, windows, cross-file editing, outline processing, hypermedia, and groupware. Working out of the Augmentation Research Center at Stanford Research Institute, which he founded in 1963, Engelbart's work has focused around the issue of using technology to augment individual and collective intelligence. His ideas were originally developed for mainframe computers and only fully came to fruition with the development of personal computers and the Internet.

Recently, with the help of Sun Microsystems and Netscape Communications, Engelbart has been working to create alliances between business, government, and civic organizations. At the heart of this alliance is the concept of *bootstrapping*, an idea drawn from engineering in which the results of an action are fed back to achieve greater results more quickly with less effort.

As director of the Bootstrap Institute, Englebart and the institute's purpose is to "Boost" the "Collective IQ." According to Engelbart, "the Collective IQ of a group is a function of how quickly and intelligently it can respond to a situation. This goes well beyond getting more information faster, to include leveraging its collective memory, perception, planning, reasoning, foresight, and experience into applicable knowledge. Such knowledge includes not only the captured knowledge products, such as documentation, plans, and source code, but also the accumulating 'web' of issues, lessons learned, rationale, commentary, dialog records, intelligence sources, and so on that iterate throughout the life-cycle of a project or situation" (Bootstrap Institute).

Bootstrap Institute
http://www.bootstrap.org

Engelbart's ideas about collective IQ are still largely untested. His remarkable insights thus far in his career would tend to suggest that these new ideas are worth very careful attention and consideration.

Boosting Collective IQ
http://beluga.dc.isx.com/bootstrap/final/vision.htm)

This is more important than it may seem. When using a **spell checker** in a word processing program the effect is that the product will have what is essentially excellent or even perfect spelling. This type of tool changes the character of our writing and what we can achieve as individuals in terms of many aspects of the written word.

Spell Checker: software that checks for spelling errors. Typically part of word processing software.

Engelbart's augmentation model has profound social and cultural implications. As Terry Winograd and Fernando Flores (1987) argued:

> All new technologies develop within the background of a tacit understanding of human nature and human work. The use of technology in turn leads to fundamental changes in what we do, and ultimately in what it is to be human. We encounter the deep questions of design when we recognize that in designing tools we are designing ways of being. (p. xi)

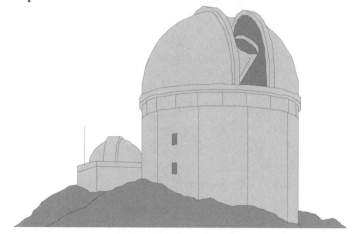

In the case of Engelbart's ideas, the computer is not just a tool for efficiency, but a tool that literally changes our ways of organizing and interpreting the world. Like the invention of the telescope and the microscope in the 17th century, which opened new ways of knowing and understanding and functionally gave us a greater and more comprehensive vision, the computer has literally expanded our capacity to understand and interpret the world. In this context, the computer represents a revolutionary intellectual and social tool—one that is as important as the inventions which made possible the scientific revolution of the late Renaissance and early modern periods.

Why is the augmentation of intelligence through computers a relevant issue for educators in the classroom?

Accurate spelling, the careful use of grammar, and precise calculation have always been important issues in education. Without them we cannot communicate well through writing, or work in mathematics or science. Arguments have recently arisen that students should use spelling and grammar checking systems to help them write, and use calculators or computers to do mathematical calculations. Some purists are horrified by this technological trend. If using a mechanical device like a computer to augment our ability to calculate, spell, or avoid a split infinitive is a bad educational practice, then is it likewise a bad practice to use a dictionary to look up a word and how to spell it? What basics do students need to learn? When should they use the computer to augment their intelligence, but not limit their abilities to think critically or solve problems? How does the use of the computer change what we need to teach and learn?

What happens when we can create a visualization model of what an object looks like at the speed of light? What happens when we can call up from our desktops virtually any of the great libraries of the world? What happens when we can manipulate words and images on the screen in ways that can only be described as a new type of electronic writing? How has the world changed?

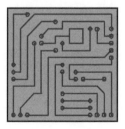

Shakespeare's *The Tempest* has a character that reflects on the "brave new world" now surrounding them. As educators, we have entered a brave new world of computing involving new ways of knowing and new types of intelligence. It is a world full of many possibilities and fraught with many potential problems. How does the computer change the nature of learning and of knowing? What new meanings can be discovered with these machines and their software? How can they contribute to our work as educators? We will address these and related questions in the chapters that follow.

QUESTIONS FOR REFLECTION AND DISCUSSION

1. What do you think classrooms will look like 10 years from now? How about 100 years from now? What role do you think computers will play in defining their character and makeup?

2. How important are computers in defining how we function and operate as a culture and society? Can you think of how contemporary culture and society would be different without computers?

3. When did computers begin to play a major role in our culture? Why is the microcomputer revolution important versus the mainframe computing revolution? Who benefited most from the microcomputer revolution? Why?

4. How do computers empower people?

5. How do computers disempower people?

6. When computers were expensive, who had access to them? For what? Why?

7. Do you think that we are indeed experiencing a Singularity in our use of computers in contemporary culture? Is the introduction of computing comparable to other Singularities in our history (*Hint*: Other Singularities include the Birth of Christ or Mohammed, the invention of movable type and modern printing, and the detonation of the first nuclear bomb)?

8. How does a screwdriver augment our strength as human beings? When people are doing certain intellectual tasks (calculating, spelling, etc.) are they using a computer to augment their intelligence?

9. What are the differences between human intelligence and the type of "intelligence" that is at work with a computer? Are they the same thing?

ACTIVITIES

1. Compile a list of computing machines beginning with the abacus. Think about how each has changed the culture in which it was used.

2. Compile a list of how computers are part of your life. Discuss with other students how your lives would be different without computers.

3. Consider the ways humans add technologies to their bodies (eyeglasses, pace makers, etc.). Is this a bad thing? Make a list of pros and cons for each of the technologies we add to our bodies and selves.

EXERCISE FOR FURTHER DEVELOPMENT OF YOUR REFLECTIVE PRACTICE FOR TEACHING WITH COMPUTER TECHNOLOGY

Teachers as professionals need to develop a strong sense of the role of the teacher in order to teach effectively in any schooling system. Computer technology is changing the context in which teachers teach. Read the following presentation on digital books and reflect on the following issues related to teaching practice:

1. With the textbook as the current fundamental resource in the classroom, how may changes in the construction of books impact the textbook?

2. How may the changes being brought about by the computer revolution change the role of the teacher from the expert giving information to the facilitator who teaches students how to gather information effectively?

3. Is reading text on a computer screen different than reading from a printed source?

Digital Books

Since the Renaissance the book has been a significant product of commerce and trade. Yet most authors make relatively little money from their books. The publisher of this book provided the authors with a small advance against royalties and will pay between 10% and 15% of the total gross receipts of the book. If one of our books is published with a university press—even though we have well-proven track records as authors—our royalty rate will be even less (perhaps as small as 5% or 7%). If the book is particularly expensive to produce, or obscure with limited potential for sales, we may receive no royalty at all.

The book you are holding probably cost $5 or $6 to bind and print. Overhead for executives and editors, warehousing costs, and profits to corporate shareholders and distributors account for much of the cost of the book. Why don't we publish our own books? We could hire technical assistance like a publisher. In fact, this book has been largely designed and laid out by its senior author. We know a printer and bookbinder in North Carolina who manufactures beautiful books of the highest quality. So, why don't we self-publish?

The issue is mostly one of distribution. We do not have a warehouse or an order system in place. We do not have the money to pay for extensive advertising and catalogues. We are more interested in writing and researching than distributing books. So, we send our books to publishers. We choose the best ones that we can find, not because they necessarily pay the best royalties or even are best at distributing what we write, but because of their reputations and the quality of the products they produce.

Nicholas Negroponte (1995) points out that when information—ideas and books—can be distributed through the flow of atoms online, then there is less of a need for the publisher. Referring to John Markoff, a communications business author for the *New York Times* whose writing he likes, Negroponte explained that he would be quite willing to pay five cents for each of Markoff's news pieces. Negroponte's logic is intriguing and the benefit for Markoff obvious.

If one fiftieth of the 1995 Internet population subscribed to this idea, and Markoff wrote 20 stories a year, he would earn $1 million, which I am prepared to guess is more than *The New York Times* pays him (Negroponte, 1995, p. 176).

As authors, we want to be read. We also like to be paid. The more money we make, the more time we have to write. We love teaching, but in the summers we like writing better. Nor do we necessarily want to teach every single semester. We would be happy to have the money to occasionally buy free time for writing from our teaching jobs.

In a digital environment, writers have the potential to break free from the tyranny of traditional publishers, their economies, and typographic distribution systems. Publishing online means eliminating the middleman between the author and the reader. Of course, there are problems for the reader because publishers act as editorial filters, weeding out bad and uninteresting authors.

But readers function as editorial filters as well when they skim through a book, a magazine, or a newspaper. They tend not to come back to authors who have disappointed them, or to subjects that have not held their interest. In the online publishing environment writers are much more subject to the free market economy than they would be through traditional publishers, because readers often buy books based on the reputation of a publishing house or of a series.

Worldwide electronic publishing systems have been proposed by a number of people, including Ted Nelson's Project Xanadu.

Nelson (1988) defined Project Xanadu as "a system designed to be the principal publishing utility of the future. It will provide for the deposit, delivery, and continual revision of linked electronic documents, servicing hundreds of millions of simultaneous users with hypertext, graphics, audio, movies, and hypermedia" (p. 225).

Nelson began Project Xanadu in 1960 as a project for a graduate course at Harvard. The Xanadu system is based on a single storage system that can be shared and organized in a variety of ways. As described by Nelson (1987) "all materials are in a shared pool of units, but every element has a unit in which it originated; new units can be built from material in previous units, in addition to new material; there can be arbitrary links between arbitrary sections of units" (pp. 5–6).

According to Nelson, the intention of Project Xanadu is not to create a database the size of the world, but instead "a repository publishing network" which could include anyone's documents and materials, and which could be combined and linked to freely.

In such a system, copyright issues are taken care of by charging a small fee, not dissimilar from what an electrical utility is paid when someone draws power for use in their own home. The creator of the document gets paid along with the utility system that provides the information.

For awhile, Nelson's efforts were supported by the computer design company Autocad. Evidently, they have recently withdrawn support for the project, which, like many of Nelson's ideas, is far-thinking but imperfectly thought-out in terms of execution. There are major problems involved with the establishment of a functional Xanadu system. Who will own such a system? What rates will be charged? Will such a system by encouraging instant publication also encourage sloppy work, creating an electronic tower of Babel in which important ideas are lost because of a largely uncontrolled mass of electronic information? What if the system is invaded by an electronic virus, or controlled and censored by a government agency? Who will guarantee the integrity of the data on the system?

Xanadu and systems like it suggest alternative modes of distributing information and ideas by researchers and writers. The invention of the printing press liberated authors such as Martin Luther from the censorship and control of the church. Something similar may be happening as authors begin to publish in the electronic and digital environments that are beginning to emerge on a global basis.

📖 SOURCES

Engelbart, D. (1963). A conceptual framework for the augmentation of man's intellect. In P. W. Howerton & D. C. Weeks (Eds.), *Vistas in information handling: vol. 1. The augmentation of man's intellect by machine* (pp. 1–29). Washington, DC: Spartan Books. Republished in (1988). *Computer supported cooperative work: A book of readings* (pp. 35–65). I. Greif (Ed.). San Mateo, CA: Morgan Kaufmann.

Engelbart, D. C. (1986, January). Workstation history and the augmented knowledge workshop. Paper presented at the ACM Conference on the History of Personal Workstations, Palo Alto, CA. Republished as The augmented knowledge workshop. In A. Goldberg (Ed.), *A history of personal workstations* (pp. 185–236). New York: ACM Press.

Engelbart, D. C., & English, W. K. (1968, December). A research center for augmenting human intellect. In AFIPS Conference Proceedings of the 1968 Fall Joint Computer Conference, San Francisco, CA. Republished in I. Greif (Ed.). (1988). *Computer supported cooperative work: A book of readings* (pp. 81–105). San Mateo, CA: Morgan Kaufmann.

Febvre, L., & Martin, H. J. (1976). *The coming of the book: The impact of printing, 1450–1800* (D. Gerard, Trans.). London: NLB.

Muffoletto, R., & Knupfer, N. N. (Eds.). (1995). *Computers in education: Social, political & historical perspectives.* Cresskill, NJ: Hampton Press.

Negroponte, N. (1995). Bits and atoms. *Wired*, January, p. 176.

Nelson, T. H. (1987). *Literary machines* (Ed. 87.1). San Antonio, TX.

Papert, S. (1993). *The children's machine: Rethinking school in the age of the computer.* New York: The Free Press.

Provenzo, E. F., Jr. (1986). *Beyond the Gutenberg galaxy: Microcomputers and post-typographic culture.* New York: Teachers College Press.

Vinge, V. (1987). *True names...and other dangers.* New York: Baen Books.

Vinge, V. (1989). Hurtling towards the singularity [interview with Michael Synergy]. *Mondo 2000,* p. 116.

Winograd, T., & Flores, F. (1987). *Understanding computers and cognition: A new foundation for design.* Reading, MA: Addison-Wesley.

THE COMPUTER AS TOOL

Word Processors, Desktop Publishing, Keyboarding, Database Software, Spreadsheets, Drawing and Illustration Programs

What computers had offered me was exactly what they should offer children! They should serve children as instruments to work with and to think with, as the means to carry out projects, the source of concepts to think new ideas. The last thing in the world I wanted or needed was a drill and practice program telling me to do this sum next or to spell that word! Why should we impose such a thing on children?

—Seymour Papert

Case Study

Mr. Zabrowski has been teaching English and journalism at a suburban high school in San Francisco for over 20 years. In addition to his courses, he supervises the monthly school newspaper.

Getting out the paper once a month used to be fun for him, but it has become more and more of a chore. The paper looked the same all of the time. Including photographs and other graphic materials is very expensive and time consuming. He would like to do more visually with the paper but does not know how.

One of his students, Luisa, has a mother who works in a graphics design shop. Luisa's mother has shown her how to use programs like Pagemaker and Adobe Photoshop and she has become very skilled in desktop publishing. From his conversations with Luisa, Mr. Zabrowski has come to realize that this can be a new way of putting out the paper. All sorts of photographs and line art can be used. Fancy type fonts can give *The Panther Gazette* a whole new look and feel. What tools are out there? Where can he learn about them and what does he need in terms of hardware and software? How can other students be taught so that it does not end with Luisa?

Mr. Zabrowski is interested in using the computer as a tool. The dictionary defines a mechanical tool like a screwdriver or hammer as "a contrivance for doing work." The computer, although primarily electronic, is a tool as well. With a program like *Adobe Photoshop,* a photograph can be manipulated. Its contrast can be raised or lowered, colors can be added, focus can be sharpened or blurred, and so on. With a word processor, words and articles can be written, spelling and grammar checked, and pages typeset. With a database, information can be compiled, sorted, and manipulated in many different ways.

Adobe Systems Incorporated
http://www.adobe.com/homepage.shtml

Robert Taylor (1980) described how students can use the computer as a tool: "They might use it as a calculator in math and various science assignments, as a map-making tool in geography, as a facile, tireless performer in music, or as a text editor and copyist in English" (p. 3).

This idea of the computer being used as a tool probably represents its single most important use currently in the schools and by the general public. This chapter examines the use of the computer as a tool for use in the classroom. On an immediate level, we talk about the computer as a productivity and efficiency tool. Although this is an important aspect of the use of computers as tools, there is the less obvious use of the machines as tools for enhancing cognition.

When using a word processor, for example, the writer not only has a tool that eliminates much of the tedium of retyping and editing, but which also acts as a framework that can help the writer organize and put together information. In writing this book, for example, the authors began with an outline that they typed into a computer and that was added to as they read and collected research materials. While working on the early chapters of the book, materials for later chapters were also found. Instead of putting these materials aside, and waiting to use them when the final chapters were written, they were placed in their appropriate places in the text.

In doing so, the writing process for this book was much less linear than it would have been if the manuscript had been written by hand or with a typewriter. By writing parts of the last chapters early on in the development of the book, materials were linked to the beginning of the book in ways that probably would not have taken place if the manuscript had not been written on a computer. Whereas this may at first seem trivial, what we are talking about is a very different way of organizing and approaching the process of writing. We believe that it is one that is much closer to how we actually think than the more traditional linear models of writing that were in place before the invention of word processing.

Word Processors

The most widespread use of computers as tools is as word processors. In the schools, word processing should not be pursued as an end in and of itself, but as a vehicle or means of meeting the objectives of the curriculum. In an elementary literacy curriculum, word processing should be integrated into the entire writing process and not stand by itself as a subject. Think for a moment about how we teach painting. The course should be about painting (i.e., creating pictorial representations with paint) and not about the paintbrushes. The purpose is not to produce "painters" but artists. In the same way, the purpose behind teaching word processing, unless it is for a secretarial course, is to create writers and not word processing technicians.

Early in the development of desktop computing there was a good deal of discussion about "dedicated word processors." These were simply computers that could only function as word processors. Such machines are still available in the form of inexpensive, but highly functional, dedicated text editing systems. Most word processing, however, is done on computers using word processing software.

Many people do not understand that computers are not necessarily word processors, but simply "Turing machines" that run word processing programs. Alan Turing, one of the important pioneers in digital computing, identified the fact in the mid-1930s that computers could operate with multiple programs that could literally be loaded or unloaded into the machine. Thus, word processors are software that is loaded into the computer's internal memory where it performs its function.

Alan Turing Home Page
http://www/wadham.ox.ac.uk/~ahodges/Turing.html

There are literally dozens of word processing programs available that are constantly being upgraded and improved. The higher the version number of word processing software, the newer it is. Thus, when you see a program like *WordPerfect* 5.1, you should know that it is older than the version 6.0. When a decimal extension is put on the version number of a word processing program or other type of software, it means that this is a minor update or revision. When the next whole number in a sequence is used, it indicates a major revision of the program.

Corel/Word Perfect
http://www.corel.com/

Word processing programs like *ClarisWorks*, *WordPerfect*, and *Microsoft Word* have evolved from having basic word processing functions into sophisticated "typesetting" and book design programs. Although sophisticated word processors such as these can be used at almost any level, they are probably more appropriate for older than for younger students.

Clip Art: commercially available art and photographs that can be bought by users interested in incorporating them into their own projects.

For younger students, particularly those at the primary level, several outstanding word processing programs are available. These programs tend to have fewer functions, but are much easier to use. In addition, they include the option of larger type, **clip art**, and graphic functions intended for children. These student-oriented programs include *Magic Media Slate* and *Creative Writer 2*.

Magic Media Slate Word Processor (Sunburst Software)
http://www.nysunburst.com/magic/magic.htm

Creative Writer 2 (Microsoft Corporation)
http://www.microsoft.com/kids/free02.htm

These programs can encourage creativity in children by making it possible for them to write and edit documents without getting encumbered with the mechanics of handwriting and spelling. This is critical. Much of what inhibits children when writing has to do with getting words down on paper clearly and neatly. A second grader typically does not have sufficient motor skills to write clearly or to be able to efficiently recopy text for editing purposes. Word processors free them from this problem, while also allowing them to integrate interesting graphic materials including drawings and photographs.

At a basic level, a word processor makes it possible for a user to enter and edit text, save and load files, and print what has been produced. Function keys, mouse commands, and arrow keys allow the user to manipulate text. Numerous capabilities are available to the user. Text can be put in *italics*, made **bold**, underlined, or made very small. Text can be written extremely large, or using a superscript or subscript. "Word Art" functions make it possible to create words and sentences that literally look like what they describe. Words like "wavy," can literally be:

Blocks of text can be moved or copied, or formatted with different justifications and spacing. Page numbers can be placed at different locations in the document. Tabs and margins can be set and so on. Few people learn all the functions and uses of the average word processor, but instead use the program at the level that fits their needs as writers.

There are many interesting functions that are now being included in most major word processing programs. On *Microsoft Word*, for example, besides a spelling and grammar checker, there is a thesaurus and even a smart **keyboard** function that can be programmed to fix standard typing errors made by the user. If you often mistype "the" as "tje," the computer will automatically correct the error. Other functions like word prediction give the user a list of possible words after typing a few letters. This can help young children who are struggling with spelling. Other functions that can be added to word processors include a read-aloud function, which reads text as it is typed.

Keyboard: device for inputting information into the computer. It works very much like a typewriter keyboard, but has a much wider range of capabilities.

Desktop Publishing

Modern printing began about the year 1450. At that time, a German jeweler, Johannes Gutenberg, realized he could cast letters to print with by pouring hot metal into molds of letters, numbers, and punctuation marks. This is what we now call movable type. When placed in a tight wooden frame, text could be composed. Inking the type, placing paper on it, and putting it under pressure made it possible to create a printed text.

The introduction of printing made possible the intellectual revolutions of the Renaissance and the Reformation. Books could be produced inexpensively, while at the same adhering to the highest editorial standards. Because printing meant that copyists and scribes were no longer needed to reproduce textual information, it eliminated introduction of errors into a text with the copying process. Along with new means of displaying graphic information, a level of accuracy unlike anything that had previously existed was now possible.

A page from Jan Vredeman de Vries's 1604 work *Perspective*. Books like this began to revolutionize the way in which the world was viewed during the late Renaissance and early Modern periods.

The implications of these changes across different fields were profound. Elizabeth Eisenstein, in *Print Culture and Enlightenment Thought* (1986) asked us to consider what happened when reference books such as maps, gazetteers, atlases, and lexicons underwent the shift from script culture to the print culture of the Reformation. She declared that, "the activities of lexicographers, map publishers and globe makers during the first centuries after printing reverberated throughout the learned world" (p. 4). The introduction of printing represented a mechanical revolution and an intellectual revolution. This is yet another example of how technology changes the way in which we understand and interpret our world.

Mechanical printing changed relatively little until the 1950s when phototypesetting was introduced that used film to reproduce type and images on metal plates. In the 1960s, mainframe computing made it possible to do the first digital typesetting. Digital typesetting was limited to large book and newspaper companies who could afford access to mainframe computers. It was an expensive and complicated process. All of this changed, however, in the middle of the 1980s with the introduction of desktop publishing.

In January 1984, the same month that Apple introduced the Macintosh computer, Paul Brainerd (a former executive with a company that made computer terminals for the printing industry) began work on the development of a typesetting and publishing system for personal computers. He referred to his concept as "desktop publishing." He called his system *Pagemaker.*

Adobe Pagemaker (Adobe Systems)
http://www.adobe.com/prodindex/pagemaker/main.html

Desktop publishing combines high-powered desktop computers with specialized software and high-quality **laser printers**. Initially, desktop publishing was different from word processing in that it allowed the user to insert complex illustrations into a document and to have text wrap around images. A variety of type fonts and headers could be used, and text and graphics could be easily revised. Pages could be viewed on the computer screen as they would appear when printed.

Laser Printer: uses the same technology as photocopiers to produce printed material. A focused laser beam and rotating mirror drum are used to create an image that is then converted on the drum into an electrostatic charge.

Steven Levy (1994) recalled how, when working as the editor of a weekly newspaper before desktop publishing, he used to shudder at the thought of laying out the paper. The paper would be taken to a design house where preliminary type specifications would be laid out. He would arrive with his staff, and:

> we would paste some of the blank "boards" on an angled table and then begin laying out our tabloid, page by page. People working the linotype machine would hand the columns of text, along with the headlines, and we'd figure out what looked good, and begin fixing things down to the boards, using hot wax to hold them down. We'd take a column of text, size it to the page and snip the excess to be jumped to another page. It was like a jigsaw puzzle with no set solution except adherence to the principles of design (as best we understood them). (p. 214)

Pictures would be resized, typos fixed, headlines rewritten, and changes made. All of this would be done with extremely expensive machinery and highly paid staff. Work would often go on into the late hours of the night, until literally the last moment possible, at which time the paper would be "sent to press."

The introduction of desktop publishing made it possible to eliminate these types of procedures and make the production of newspapers, books, brochures, and similar types of materials much simpler. Essentially, desktop publishing puts the design and layout process into the hands of the writers or creators of materials. This makes life enormously easier for those people involved in the production of printed material. At the same time, it places a considerable burden on them. Writers and editors now need to know about design.

A recent twist on desktop publishing is that advanced word processors such as *Microsoft Word* and *WordPerfect* now have the potential to do almost everything that older page layout programs like *Pagemaker* could do. The reality is that now there is very little difference between the two, and most high-level word processing programs are now typesetting and page design systems. Even printers are reaching a level unheard of in the printing industry 10 or 15 years ago. This manuscript, for example, is being printed in a camera ready format on a 1,200-dot-per-inch laser printer—one whose quality was only available on the most expensive professional printing equipment a few years ago.

Keyboarding

Critical to word processing and related types of computer programs is the problem of keyboarding. Keyboarding is traditionally thought of as a skill isolated from using the computer. In fact, it is an essential part of effective computer use. As children are using computers at younger and younger ages, they are developing habits of hunting and pecking and are becoming frustrated as a result of its inefficiency. The development of keyboarding skills early in a child's experience with a computer is extremely important. The question is, what is the best way to introduce children to keyboarding in a meaningful and enjoyable way?

Although it is not necessary to have children learn keyboarding as part of their very first computer experience, it is useful to have them establish habits of effective keyboard use as they learn to write. There are many different types of keyboarding programs currently available on the market. When choosing a keyboarding program, take into account the children's age and their developmental level. Speed is often emphasized in keyboarding programs, which is a problem for children at the early elementary level who can become extremely tense and frustrated as they are pushed by the program to work at the maximum rate. This may be a desirable thing to promote in older students who are trying to develop speed in their typing, but it is not appropriate for younger children. Why should speed be emphasized in keyboarding, when we do not necessarily emphasize it in handwriting?

Programs like *Master Type, Kid's Creative Writer 2, Mario Teaches Typing,* and *Kid Key*s, for example, provide users with basic keyboard skills. These programs, however, do not try to integrate keyboarding skills with the process of learning to read and write. An extremely interesting example of an integrated approach at the first and second grades is The Learning Company's *Read, Write & Type.*

The Learning Company
www.learningco.com

Dear Aunt Asterie and Uncle Eugene,

   I have a new kitten his name is Ming he is very fiesty ! Our neighbors found him on their porch they had a dog so they couldn't take care of him. They called us and asked if we could take care of him. My mom said "yes" we have had him for three weeks now. I think he's going to stay !
   I have two other cats who aren't getting along with him because he chases them. He acts like a dog ! He can catch a ball in his mouth.
   He talks to himself when he's walking around the house. He has a low voice which is common for this kind of cat. He is a seal-point Himalayan. Ming is very beautiful. I like his blue eyes.

Love ,
Katy

A letter to one of the authors and his wife from Katy Baker, written when she was nine, using Microsoft *Creative Writer 2.*

Read, Write & Type is a fully integrated keyboarding, reading and writing program. It teaches keyboarding by associating sounds with specific fingers. Thus the index finger of the student's left hand says "FFF." The left pinkie finger says "AAA." The advantage of a program like this is that children are learning to use phonics in a whole language context.

Read, Write & Type is a very effective tool in enhancing the writing process of children because it makes it possible for them to express their ideas without getting slowed down by the mechanics and fine motor skills necessary for handwriting. As a result, children can focus their attention on writing and creating, rather than on the mechanics of the handwriting process.

Read, Write & Type eliminates the question of when keyboarding skills should be learned by children. Instead, it integrates these skills with the reading and writing process, making them a natural part of learning to use the alphabet as a code for speech. Such an approach integrates keyboarding into the very process of developing phonemic awareness and reading and writing skills.

Classroom-based experience with *Read, Write & Type* suggests that keyboarding can become an enjoyable part of the reading and writing experience of first graders, rather than an onerous task encountered by fourth graders or even adults who learn to type by using more traditional typing tutor software.

This type of integrated instructional model is important to understand, because it illustrates the concept of the computer and its software as an integrative tool. When computers were first introduced into classrooms in the late 1970s and early 1980s, people were given courses in computer literacy (i.e., how to program the machine and use the computer) rather than how to accomplish specific goals or tasks with the machine and its programs. Programs such as *Read, Write & Typ*e embed the mechanics of the computer within the larger context of reading and writing. This is how computers and software are actually used by real people in the real world, rather than the artificial constructs created by many of our educational institutions and settings.

Database Software

A database is any collection of information. An electronic database consists of a *file*, *records,* and *fields*. A *file* is the entire collection of data in a database. It includes all the records in the database. A *record* is all the information about a particular subject. Thus, if you were creating a database of children's books, a record would be the information for each book. Thus the record for *Charlotte's Web*, by E. B. White, would include all of the information that you had entered about the book. These would be categorized and entered in different *field*s. For example, you might have a field for the author. The title field would be the book's title *Charlotte's Web*. Other fields might include publisher, date of publication, age level, and so on.

Suppose you entered several thousand books into your database of children's books. Once they were entered, you could sort them according to different criteria. Perhaps you want to find other books by E. B. White. The database would make it possible to sort them according to their date of publication, their alphabetical order, or some other similar criteria. Maybe you are interested in finding books published in a certain year, or from a particular publisher. A database lets you search for records that match one or more criteria.

Different layouts can be set up for viewing and printing information in a database. As a result, a database can be reconfigured for different needs, not only in terms of information, but graphic presentation. Databases have many potential applications in the classroom. Students can use ready-made databases that are available on CD-ROM, online, and in certain specialized types of software. They can also create their own databases with programs such as *ClarisWork*s and *Microsoft Work*s. We describe specific curricular uses of databases in Chapter 5.

Spreadsheets

Electronic spreadsheets organize, manipulate, and store information. Spreadsheets are similar to database management systems, but are numerically oriented. Spreadsheets are, in fact, electronic ledger systems. They automatically calculate columns and rows of numbers, providing the user with sums, averages, and percentages, as well as additional functions.

Spreadsheets are particularly good for use with tedious and repetitive lists of numbers that often need to be recalculated. For example, spreadsheets are the basis for teacher gradebook systems.

Each time a new grade is entered, the total is recalculated. Reports for individual students can be compiled and printed off, as well as the average for the class, or for a particular test or assignment.

Spreadsheets allow quick and easy changes to be made to an entry. With a grading program, the grade for a student taking a makeup quiz can be automatically averaged into the class's total score. Spreadsheets can also be used to analyze the effects of changing specific variables. An architect can use a spreadsheet to estimate what different costs might be using different materials. What, for example, would be the cost of building a skyscraper with floors covered in linoleum at a particular cost per square foot, versus using ceramic tile at a different price? "What if?" scenarios become relatively easy to explore.

Drawing and Illustration Programs

Drawing and illustration programs are available in many different formats for computers. Stand-alone programs like *Adobe Illustrator* and *Corel Draw* are intended for professional artists. Word processors like *Microsoft Word* and *WordPerfect* also include drawing and illustration programs. There are many drawing programs designed specifically for children such as *Kid Pix* from Broderbund, which has paint and drawing features, as well as sound effects and type setting capabilities.

Adobe Illustrator (Adobe Systems)
http://www.adobe.com/prodindex/illustrator/main.html

Corel Draw (Corel)
http://www.corel.com/products/drawformac.htm

Kid Pix (Broderbund)
https://store1-1.broderbund.com/

With the recent introduction of inexpensive color printers, the ability to do sophisticated artwork has been greatly expanded. Inkjet and laser printing has also made it possible, at very affordable prices, to print examples of complex and subtle artwork—something that was impossible a few years ago.

A note to his grandmother written by Derek Thomas, when he was four years old, using *Kid Pix.*

When combined with image manipulation software like *Adobe Photoshop*, illustration and drawing programs have the potential to open new creative possibilities for student artists. Keep in mind that many of the best drawing and image manipulation programs that are available were designed for use by professionals and they may not be suitable for younger students.

At the beginning of this chapter we introduced Mr. Zabrowski and *The Panther Gazette.* Consider how the tools now widely available on most computers can help him with his school newspaper. Desktop publishing allows his students to manipulate text and images with relative ease. Deadlines can be met more easily, and the graphic and design value of products can be greatly improved. Databases can be used to keep track of student reporters, subscribers, and suppliers. Spreadsheets can be used to keep track of expenses. Drawing programs can be used to create art that can be used in the newspaper. Image manipulation programs can be used to touch up photographs or create specialized artwork.

Chapter 5 discusses the use of the computer as a tool—more specifically a curricular tool. Word processing, databases, spreadsheets, and drawing and painting programs all have major potential for use in the classroom; this potential is particularly important in terms of teaching students to be critical thinkers and creators. As previously mentioned this aspect of the computer as tool is discussed in more detail later in this book.

QUESTIONS FOR REFLECTION AND DISCUSSION

1. Where do you think computers can make the most difference in instruction? Is their use different for different levels of instruction?

2. What is the difference between a dedicated word processor and one that runs on a "Turing" machine?

3. What are the advantages provided by using a computer to help a child learn how to write? What are some of the problems?

4. What happens when people have access to a wide range of fonts and graphic aids for desktop publishing? Do they necessarily lead to good design?

5. How do writing and the presentation of written reports and materials change as users have access to desktop publishing technology?

6. Should keyboarding be included as a basic skill for students at the elementary level?

7. Is learning to draw on a computer a good idea, or should students learn to draw first with paper and pencil? How is drawing different on a computer when compared with using more traditional tools?

8. Is having access to a computer something that is so important that it should be a right of students?

9. How powerful do programs and computers need to be for students to make effective use of them in the classroom? Is a basic program or machine as valuable as a more advanced technologies?

10. What does the use of computers do to traditional social interaction in the classroom? Does this differ according to the subject?

ACTIVITIES

1. Use a desktop publishing system or high level word processor to create a newsletter for your class.

2. Create a database on a subject that is of interest to you (the addresses for a group you belong to, an inventory of a collection, etc.).

3. Use a spreadsheet to track a stock, or calculate a set of grades for your classroom.

EXERCISE FOR FURTHER DEVELOPMENT OF YOUR REFLECTIVE PRACTICE FOR TEACHING WITH COMPUTER TECHNOLOGY

Teachers as professionals need to create effective learning environments for students to achieve success. Computer technology is broadening the spectrum of tools a teacher has for creating learning environments. Read the following presentation on digital studios and reflect on the following issues related to teaching practice:

1. How can teachers use simulations to create experiences of other realities in the classroom?

2. With students experiencing hyperreality all around them, how can teachers help students differentiate hyperreality from reality?

Digital Studios

The political reporter and commentator Cokie Roberts was severely criticized for filing a news report from what appeared to be the steps of the Capitol building in Washington, DC, when in fact she was in a television studio some distance away. She actually stood in front of a blue screen while an electronic image of the Capitol building using chroma key technology was merged behind her.

This type of technology has been used for years by weatherpeople. Its technological ancestor is the Elvis Presley film in which the singer effortlessly water skis on a sound stage while a film shot from a fast-moving speed boat is projected behind him.

This type of phenomenon is what Jean Baudrillard referred to as "hyperreality." It is a simulation in which the difference between the real (the Capitol) and what is created in the studio (Cokie Roberts in front of a blue chroma key screen) becomes eroded.

The creation of hyperreality by the media occurs all of the time. Most advertising is a type of hyperreality. Roberts was so severely criticized for what she had done not because things like this are not common, but because she is perceived as someone who has the obligation as a news reporter to objectively present reality.

Of course, there is no absolute reality or objectivity. Reporters have their point of view and every medium has an ideology, or way of looking at the world, built into its content. Does it really matter whether or not Roberts was actually standing outside of the Capitol as she gave her report?

The issue is one that is going to be an increasing problem in years to come. A research and development project by the European Union called ELSET (Electronic Set System) goes to the heart of the matter. The purpose of the project is to develop a digitally created studio set. The system is coordinated with live action shots of people in real time. If announcers move across the set, for example, a computer- generated globe of the world can move with them. Light sources are synchronized between the live set and the digitized constructs for the set. The result is that the computer-constructed reality blends in perfectly with the real time action put together by the announcers (Set-Top Studio, 1994, p. 44).

The system has the potential to revolutionize set design for television. According to Jens Bley, one of the project's managers,

"You could shoot Notre Dame de Paris, analyze the images, build up a completely new virtual cathedral from this data, and even produce a live TV show in it" (Set-Top Studio, 1994, p. 44).

Baudrillard's concern about living in a world of simulation rather than reality obviously is an issue here. Is the news the news if a reporter reconstructs a simulation of an accident or a meeting of political leaders, rather than showing a film or video of the actual events? These issues have already arisen to some extent in films like Oliver Stone's *JFK*. Simulations (i.e., Stone's cinematic recreation of Kennedy's assassination) have the potential to take the place of the reality that actually took place on November 23, 1963.

As we watch more and more electronic simulations and reconstructions of the news, to what degree do we increasingly become detached from "the real world" where the news is actually happening?

In *Simulations*, Baudrillard (1983) described how the Argentinean writer Borges created a tale where the cartographers of an Empire drew a map that is so detailed that it covers all of the things it was supposed to represent. When the Empire fell into decline, the map rotted away, merging with the soil it had once covered and obscured.

At what point does the simulation act as a map or guide to the reality we are trying to decode? At what point does it obscure that reality? When does it become reality? At what point is the news no longer really the news?

📖 SOURCES

Baudrillard, J. (1983). *Simulations* (Translated by P. Foss, P. Patton and P. Beitchman). New York: Semiotext(e).

Eisenstein, E. (1986). *Print culture and enlightenment thought.* Chapel Hill, NC: Hanes Foundation.

Levy, S. (1994). *Insanely great: The life and times of the Macintosh, the computer that changed everything.* New York: Viking.

Taylor, R. (Ed.). (1980). *The computer in the school: Tutor, tool, tutee.* New York: Teachers College Press.

Set-top studio. (1994). *Wired*, December, p. 44.

EDUCATIONAL SOFTWARE

Levels of Software, The Computer as Curricular Tool, Evaluating Software, Sources for Software, Copyright Issues

We may be a society with far fewer learning-disabled children and far more teaching-disabled environments than currently perceived. The computer changes this by making us more able to reach children with different learning and cognitive styles

—Nicholas Negroponte

Case Study

Ms. Ackerman is a fifth-grade teacher at a private elementary school. Her school has limited funds and after years of talking about getting into educational computing, a machine has finally been purchased for her classroom by the Parent–Teacher Association. She has a very limited software budget and can not afford to make any mistakes about what she buys for her class.

Ms. Ackerman has the advantage of having used a computer at home for several years—mainly as a word processor. She understands the basics of computing, but this is the first time she has been able to use a machine in conjunction with her teaching.

All of a sudden she is faced with a set of decisions about what type of software to use with her students. The question is more difficult than she thought it would be. Does she want to use the computer to enhance what she is already teaching? Is the machine best used for programmed or managed instruction to help students who need tutoring or supplemental work? Should she use it primarily as a presentation system—an electronic overhead—that she can integrate into whole class instruction? Should she use it to connect her students to the outside world through telecommunications and the Internet? Should she use it as an electronic reference source with a CD-ROM encyclopedia or atlas? Should she use it as a management tool to keep track of grades and other types of classroom and student records? Can she do more than one of these things with a single machine?

Most of Ms. Ackerman's questions focus around issues related to software. Selecting software that is appropriate for your students is a difficult and challenging task. Every educational software package has a set of curricular assumptions underlying it. How do the assumptions and strategies of a particular program fit into your personal model of teaching? In what ways does a particular model of software have the potential to change the way you teach?

One of the authors, for example, has recently begun to use an electronic presentation system with his lectures at the university. For each of his 75-minute lectures, he had put together 30 or 40 electronic slides, or "overheads." The machine that he used to present his slides on was old and took 5 or 10 seconds to move from one slide to another. He soon found that this interfered with the natural rhythm of his presentation, which was something he had carefully developed and honed through many years of teaching. Using the computer presentation system that made transitions almost instantaneous, while graphically very impressive, was seriously throwing off the timing of his lectures and his ability to interact with students in class.

The solution to this problem was to use electronic slides only to illustrate the major points of the lecture or to show an occasional quote or highlight. Thus, he made the software package meet his actual teaching needs. The following chapter looks in detail at educational software and tries to provide answers to the types of questions raised by Ms. Ackerman in this chapter's introductory case study.

Levels of Software

There are several different levels of software that operate in a computer. Every computer has information stored in its read-only memory (**ROM**). This makes it possible, when the machine is turned on, for it to respond to a basic set of commands from the operator or user. You might want to think of this as being like a wake-up call for the computer.

ROM: an acronym for read-only memory. This refers to information or data that can be read by the computer, but not modified or changed.

Once the computer is activated through its read-only memory, it calls up the operating system from a **floppy disk** or from the hard drive. The operating system is basically what runs a computer. It is the software responsible for controlling hardware resources such as memory, the **central processing unit** (CPU), disk space, and peripheral devices such as printers and scanners. The operating system manages the computer's activities and functions.

Floppy Disk: a mass storage device used mainly with microcomputers.

Operating system software is necessary to run **application software**. Application software is what most people think a computer is primarily about. Application programs perform and solve specific problems. A word processor, an educational simulation, a spreadsheet, and computer games are all examples of application software.

Central Processing Unit (CPU): the main computing and control device on a computer. It is also called a microprocessor.

The two most common operating systems presently used in computers are the Microsoft Disk Operating System (MS-DOS) and the Macintosh Operating System (System Software). When a computer is referred to as an IBM clone or IBM compatible, this means it is using MS-DOS as its operating system.

Application Software: software written for a particular purpose, such as word processing.

In the mid-1980s, Microsoft introduced a program that would emulate the visual look and feel of the Macintosh operating system.

Windows: multitasking software that creates a graphical user interface that runs MS-DOS-based machines.

This system, called *Windows*, is a **graphical user interface** (GUI), that functions on top of the MS-DOS operating system. A GUI uses icons or symbols to represent operating software, utilities, and applications software. Clicking on these icons with a computer mouse, or some other type of pointing device, activates the programs they symbolize.

A widely held misconception is that *Windows* is an operating system. In fact, the early versions of *Windows* were a multitask graphical user interface environment that ran on MS-DOS-based computers. Programs designed only for use with DOS could not take advantage of the Windows environment. When you purchase educational software, keep in mind that it will typically be designated for use specifically on Macintosh, DOS, or *Windows*.

Graphical User Interface (GUI): allows the computer user to run the machine by pointing to and activating a pictorial representation or icon shown on the screen.

This situation was further complicated by the introduction of *Windows* '95, which is a revision of the *Windows* system and is not dependent on the MS-DOS operating system. This means that what was a program that began as an add-on to MS-DOS has become a separate operating system of its own. If all of this seems a bit confusing, then the situation is only likely to become more complicated as operating systems and interfaces continue to evolve.

Application software must be compatible with the operating system of a particular computer. Most computers have a single operating system. As a result, they can only run software designed for their operating system. This leads to a serious problem in terms of cross-computer or cross-platform compatibility. In schools, for example, teachers and students are often frustrated by the fact that software from an Apple Macintosh-based computer operating system cannot be run on a MS-DOS or *Windows* operating system.

The Computer as Curricular Tool

One way of deciding about software is to consider how you are going to be using the computer. As noted previously, Taylor (1980) defined three potential roles of the computer in education. These include the computer as tool, tutor, and tutee.

Tool. The computer is used as a tool by students to extend their capabilities. For example, a word processor extends the ability to write, while a drawing program extends the ability to sketch or produce drawings. Database, spreadsheet, and graphing software are all examples of the use of the computer as a tool. Tool applications and software are the most widespread and versatile use of the computer in education.

Tutor. The computer takes on many of the traditional roles and functions of the teacher. These include drill and practice, tutorial, simulation, and problem-solving software.

Tutee. The computer is the "learner" being programmed by the student to accomplish specific tasks. In the programming language *Logo*, for example, the student writes a specific set of instructions or program to teach the computer to draw a shape such as a square or circle. Other programming languages in common use include *Basic*, *Cobol*, *Fortran*, *Pascal* and *HTML*.

Hypermedia: any combination of text, sound, and motion pictures included in an interactive format on the computer.

Using the computer as a tool, tutor, or tutee requires the use of different types of software that accomplish different tasks. Although Taylor's model is a useful means of categorizing computer use in education, not all software fits neatly into each of his three categories. **Hypermedia** software (e.g., *HyperCard*, *Toolbook*, and *HyperStudio*) can be used as a tool to organize and present information, as a tutor from which to receive instruction, and as tutee for the creation of new programs.

Another way of looking at software is from the perspective of learning theory. A behaviorist model would emphasize the use of software that reinforces correct responses in the user. This is actually very close to what happens in a video or computer game, where the user is taught to respond to stimuli in a very specific way. This translates into the idea that there is only one way to play the game and to win.

In terms of educational software, this approach is most clearly represented in drill and practice software in which the objective is for the student to get the correct answer. Davidson's *Math Blaster: Episode 1—In Search of Spot*, for example, is an excellent drill and practice program for helping students to become "automatic" in multiplication and division. Similarly, *Word Munchers* (MECC) provides practice in identifying vowel sounds in words. Each of these programs, and many others like them, provide systematic feedback and in turn reinforce selected behaviors and correct responses by students.

In contrast to a behavioral approach, software based on constructivist models provides the student with the opportunity to construct knowledge and understanding through interaction with the computer and its software. A program like *SimCity* (Maxis Corporation) has students manipulate different variables in an urban environment in order to create an efficient or viable city. In this case there is no precise solution to the problem addressed by the students. Students make decisions and receive feedback based on the decisions and plans they put into effect.

Blaster Learning System (Davidson & Associates)
http://www.education.com/blaster/

Word Munchers Deluxe (MECC)
http://icu.nwsc.k12.ar.us/k12/mecc2.html

Sim City (Maxis Corporation)
http://www.maxis.com/games/index.html

SimCity is an example of simulation software. This type of program makes particularly good use of the unique characteristics provided by the computer as a teaching and educational tool. Simulation programs like MECC's *Oregon Trail,* Broderbund's *Where in the World Is Carmen Sandiego?,* and Tom Snyder's *Decisions, Decisions* series, provide students with experiences they could not otherwise have by creating a limited model of a particular situation or phenomenon. Dangerous and expensive experiments can be easily undertaken. Time can be compressed. In the *SimCity* software, for example, students can see the results of their actions projected over periods of 10, 20 and 30 years, which is something that would be impossible in real time.

Oregon Trail II
http://www.hyperdrive.com/oregontrail/index.html

Where in the World Is Carmen Sandiego? (Broderbund)
http://www.carmensandiego.com/home2.html

Decisions, Decisions
http://www.teachtsp.com/products/DD.htm

Simulations are not without their problems. Theorists like Jean Baudrillard (1983) argued that by participating in a culture that is saturated with simulations (computer programs that mimic or imitate a real museum, television programs that tell us what family life should be like, and so on), we lose touch with reality. According to Baudrillard, we become increasingly engaged in a type of hyperreality, where simulations rather than the real things become our realities. Disney World in Orlando, Florida, is constructing a simulation of a Key West village that people will be able to visit, rather than actually visiting Key West, Florida, 300 miles to the south.

Although computer simulations are very useful, they are also limited. Walking through a virtual museum is beneficial, but obviously it is not the same as actually being in the museum. Likewise, listening to a recording of a musical performance is not the same as being at a live performance. Simulations can leave out vital information. They also reflect the point of view of their creators and almost inevitably have a particular perspective on the conditions being simulated. This can easily lead to biases or prejudices being introduced into the software, which need to be taken into consideration by the user.

Constructivism: view of learning that emphasizes the active role of students in learning and understanding.

Software based on **constructivist** models is by no means limited to simulations. A different type of constructivist software model is Broderbund's *Kid Pix*. On the surface, *Kid Pix* is a simple graphics program that makes it possible for children to create pictures that can incorporate text and sound. The program provides the user with a wide range of tools (brushes, fonts, color palettes, and sounds) that allow the child to experiment and create in a variety of ways. Because the program is open-ended, the children decide how to make the best use of the program and tools it provides in order to achieve their own goals.

Kid Pix (Broderbund)
http://www.broder.com/studio/atoz/kidpix.html

One final example of the constructivist model is Edmark's *Thinkin' Things. Thinkin' Things* has been released as three separate collections for students. Intended for children between 4 and 8 years of age, it encourages the development of deductive and inductive reasoning, synthesis and analysis through a wide range of activities for students.

Thinkin' Things (Edmark)
http://www.edmark.com:80/prod/tt/

Evaluating Software

Software evaluation is an essential skill for teachers using computers in their classrooms. There are many factors that must be taken into account when evaluating software. Most will fall into one of the following broad categories: content, methodology, and utilization.

Content. When looking at software in terms of its content, the first thing to do is see if it meets your instructional objectives. A well-developed piece of educational software should include specific documentation about its goals and objectives.

Unfortunately, goals and objectives that are outlined in software documentation are frequently not realized in the actual software itself. As a result, carefully reviewing a product before you purchase it for classroom use is extremely important.

When reviewing software in terms of its content, consider whether or not the concepts presented are age and developmentally appropriate, whether the software follows a logical learning sequence (e.g., does it proceed from a lower to higher level of complexity, etc.), and if the information being presented is accurate and free of bias and stereotypes?

Methodology. Once you have determined that the content of a piece of software is consistent with your curricular goals and objectives, you need to evaluate the methodology of the program. What are the methods of instruction employed within the program? Is it based on sound learning theory? Does it use behaviorist models, or does it involve the use of more open-ended and constructivist types of approaches? Does the curricular method underlying the software fit with the models of instruction you or your school are using elsewhere?

One of the authors recently talked to a principal, for example, who was interested in developing a curriculum for his school that would provide greater freedom and flexibility for both teachers and students. Believing that computers could help him in achieving his goals, but not very knowledgeable about software, he bought an integrated learning system that emphasizes programmed learning based on drill and instruction. Simply put, the software he had chosen completely negated the educational philosophy he was trying to put into effect. Avoiding this type of problem involves a clear understanding of curricular objectives and methods both at a classroom level and at the level of the software being used.

Utilization. Finally, evaluating software involves asking questions of utilization. Is the software user friendly? Can users stop at any time during the program? Can they reenter where they left off? Can children use the program without a great deal of assistance from adults (Are there picture menus? Are menus text dependent?)? Is the documentation for the program clear? Can the teacher change the parameters of the software? For example, can levels of difficulty in a game or simulation be modified, or can the spoken component in an electronic book be turned off for silent reading?

Software Evaluation Form

Check each item for the software being looked at and provide a summary evaluation.

Hardware Compatibility
___Compatible operating system
___Sufficient RAM
___Sufficient hard disk space
___Necessary peripherals such as CD-ROM drive, printer, or videodisc player

Content
___Program fits the educational goals and supports the curriculum.
___Goals and objectives of the software are clearly stated.
___Program meets its stated objectives.
___Content is accurate, dealt with in sufficient depth, and free of bias and
    stereotypes.
___Content is at a level appropriate to students.
___There is a logical learning sequence, with a low entry and high ceiling so it
    can be used across a range of ages and abilities.
___Content is suitable for multiple purposes for integration into different
    curriculum areas and classroom situations.

Methodology
___Instructional approach is appropriate. Active discovery learning is
    emphasized.
___There is a high degree of student involvement.
___Students are agents of change; there is consistent cause and effect.
___Feedback is appropriate, varied, and able to be understood by students.
___Prompts and other strategies for getting the correct answer are provided.
___Students are led through the information in a logical way. Branching
    depends on students' responses.

Utilization
___Students control the interaction and the rate of presentation and can stop at
    any point in the program.
___Teachers can change parameters, such as speed of presentation and level of
    difficulty, to fit the range of needs and interests of students.
___Students can use the software independently after initial help. Picture menus,
    simple and precise directions, and onscreen help are available.
___The software can be used in small groups or by the whole class, as well as
    by individuals. It encourages cooperation and interaction.
___Documentation includes objectives, lesson plans, resources, and other
    information for teachers, as well as clear directions for the user.
___The management or record keeping component is easy to use.

Summary Evaluation:

Sources for Software

There are many ways to learn about software, both new products and tested materials. Most larger school districts across the country have instructional resource libraries with extensive collections of software. In Dade County, Florida, for example, there is a hardware and software resource center for teachers at the district's central administration complex. All of the major computers and peripherals being used throughout the district are available. In addition, there is a collection of nearly all of the major educational software that is available. Teachers can review software titles and also see how different types of computer hardware work. In addition, every school in Dade County has a technology contact person—typically the media specialist. These individuals often have examples of software they can demonstrate and are knowledgeable about resources that might assist teachers in using computers in their classroom. Larger school districts like Dade County will also typically have extensive computer resources available online.

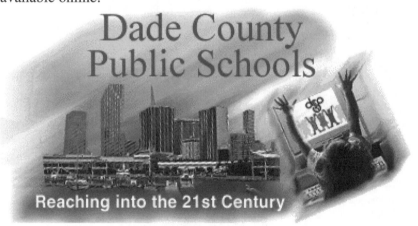

Dade County Public Schools Internet Resources
http://www.dade.k12.fl.us/internet/

Dade County Public Schools on the Web
http://www.dade.k12.fl.us/schools/

Your district may not have facilities as extensive as those of Dade County, but it is likely that there is some type of central technology office available where software and hardware can be tried out. Take advantage of teacher workdays to attend district workshops and keep an eye out for training programs provided in your area by major hardware vendors such as Apple and IBM.

Another excellent way to become familiar with software is to go to your local computer store and look at products that are for sale. Many companies like Broderbund and Edmark sell home versions of school products. You can get a general sense of many of the products that are available in this way, or by visiting their Web sites.

Broderbund
http://www.broderbund.com/

Edmark Corporation
http://www.edmark.com/

Before you purchase software, you need to preview it or get a recommendation from someone whose opinion you trust. Unfortunately, catalogue descriptions of software can be very misleading. A piece of software may look like exactly what you need, but in reality, it may not measure up to its promises.

One of the very best ways to be able to preview software is to attend one of the many regional and national educational computing conferences held around the country. At the larger conferences, software and hardware vendors will have exhibit booths where their products can be tested. In addition, they frequently have free demonstration versions of software that will allow people to try out different products at their leisure.

Most large software companies will allow software to be tried on a 30- to 60-day preview basis. If you are not sure about whether or not a piece of software will meet your needs, get a preview copy and try it. There is nothing to lose except the cost of the return postage.

Freeware: software that is given away free of charge.

A great deal of useful educational software is available in the public domain as **freeware**. Freeware is often available over the Internet, or through user groups and computer magazines. Much of it is passed informally from one person to another. Freeware frequently includes a lot of junk, but sometimes you can find just the type of program that will serve your needs. Documentation on freeware is often limited, and there is always the problem of the transmission of computer viruses through this type of material. Just keep in mind that there are hidden costs when using "free" software.

Shareware: software distributed for a free try-out, but users are expected to pay the developer if they decide to use the software.

Shareware is distributed in much the same way as freeware, but the developer of a program asks the user to send a nominal fee for using the program. In exchange for this fee, you get the right to use the program and often are put on a list for additional information about the program and even upgrades of the software. Shareware is particularly good because it allows you to try out a piece of software to see if you like it before you have to pay for it.

Computer Journals and Publications

There are a wide range of computer journals and publications of interest to teachers. Here is a list of some of the most useful. Check your local university library or district technology center for many of these titles. Wherever possible, we have tried to provide an Internet link.

American Journal of Distance Education

> Office for Distance Education
> College of Education
> The Pennsylvania State University
> 403 Allen Street, Suite 206
> University Park, PA 16801-5202

Educational Technology Research and Development

> Association for Educational Communications and Technology
> 1025 Vermont Ave., NW
> Suite 820
> Washington, DC 20005

Educational Technology

> Educational Technology Publications, Inc.
> 720 Palisades Avenue
> Englewood Cliffs, NJ 07632

Electronic Learning

> 902 Sylvan Ave.
> Englewood Cliffs, NJ 07632

Instruction Delivery Systems

Society for Applied Learning Technology
50 Culpepper Street
Warrenton, VA 22186

Journal of Computer Based Instruction

Association for the Development of Computer Based
Instructional Systems
International Headquarters
1601 W. 5th Ave., Suite 111
Columbus, OH 43212

Journal of Educational Multimedia and Hypermedia (JEMH)

Society for Information Technology & Teacher Education
c/o AACE
PO Box 2966
Charlottesville, VA 22902

http://www.aace.org/pubs/jemh/Default.htm

Journal of Interactive Learning Research (JILR)

Society for Information Technology & Teacher Education
c/o AACE
PO Box 2966
Charlottesville, VA 22902

http://www.aace.org/pubs/jilr/Default.htm

Journal of Research on Computing in Education

International Society for Technology in Education
University of Oregon
1787 Agate Street
Eugene, OR 97403

Journal of Technology Education

> *JTE*
> 144 Smyth Hall
> Virginia Tech University
> Blacksburg, VA 24061
>
> http://borg.lib.vt.edu/ejournals/JTE/jte.html

Journal of Technology and Teacher Education

> Society for Information Technology & Teacher Education
> c/o AACE
> PO Box 2966
> Charlottesville, VA 22902
>
> http://www.aace.org/site/Default.htm

Learning and Leading with Technology (Formerly *The Computing Teacher*)

> International Society for Technology in Education
> 480 Charnelton Street
> Eugene, OR 97401

MultiMedia Schools

> Online Inc.
> 462 Danbury Road
> Wilton, CT 06897
>
> http://www.infotoday.com/MMSchools/JanMMS/susan.html

School Library Media Quarterly

> American Association of School Librarians
> 50 E. Huron Street
> Chicago, IL 60611

Teaching and Computers

Scholastic, Inc.
730 Broadway
New York, NY 10003

Technology & Learning

Peter Li, Inc.
19 Davis Drive
Belmont, CA 94002

http://www.techlearning.com/

TechTrends: For Leaders in Education and Training

Association for Educational Communications and
Technology
1025 Vermont Ave., NW
Suite 820
Washington, DC 20005

http://www.aect.org/Pubs/techtrends.html

T.H.E. Journal

Information Synergy, Inc.
2626 S. Pullman
Santa Ana, CA 92705

http://www.thejournal.com/

WebNet Journal

Society for Information Technology & Teacher Education
c/o AACE
PO Box 2966
Charlottesville, VA 22902

http://www.aace.org/pubs/webnet/Default.htm

Copyright Issues

Except for freeware and public domain software, most computer programs are **copyrighted**. A copyright protects the intellectual property rights of publishers and authors. Software is sold in a number of different ways. It can be purchased as a single copy, in what is called a **lab pack** (multiple copies for a single classroom or lab), or in a network version. Typically, when you buy a computer program, unless there is another arrangement such as a **site license**, you have the right to use it on a single machine. If you have 10 students using 10 computers in a classroom, then you need to purchase a copy for each machine, or else connect the computers and get a networked version of the software.

Instead of purchasing individual software programs for each machine in a school, many school districts license the right to use a piece of software. This is called a site license. Under most arrangements, a school district agrees to pay a set fee, which is usually based on the total number of computers in a district. This fee allows the district to make as many copies as it needs for use in its schools. Such agreements are an excellent way to use multiple copies of a program at a greatly reduced rate. Publishers like such arrangements because it means their software is being used legally and they are getting a fair payment for the products they have created. When using software under a site license, keep in mind that you do not receive documentation for each site. You can often buy additional copies of documentation at a modest fee.

Some school districts elect to license all of the software from a particular publisher. Such arrangements can lead to very large savings, while making a wide range of software available at a very low cost.

In conclusion, as demonstrated with Ms. Ackerman in the case study at the beginning of this chapter, decisions about software and its use in the classroom are ultimately decisions about curriculum. Too often educators have become preoccupied with the hardware of computers and have not reflected sufficiently on what is being

Copyright: the exclusive legal right to reproduce, publish, and sell the matter and form of some type of work.

Lab Pack: typically includes five copies of a particular piece of software and the right to load it onto five computers.

Site License: when a software publisher agrees to make a software program available to be copied at a single site for a set fee.

run on the machines. Making the best use of software involves understanding the assumptions underlying a program and how it may or may not contribute to the improvement of curriculum.

QUESTIONS FOR REFLECTION AND DISCUSSION

1. What do you believe are the best uses of computers for instruction at your level? Why?

2. What is meant by operating system software?

3. What is the difference between DOS (disk operating system) and *Windows*?

4. Define what is meant by the idea of the computer being used as a *tool*, *tutor*, or *tutee*.

5. What would be an example of a behaviorist use of software? Where would it best be used in instruction?

6. What would be an example of a use of simulation software? Where can it best be used in instruction?

7. What are the good and bad points of using simulations in education?

8. What would be a constructivist model of software? Where would it best be used in instruction?

9. Where are the best places to learn about new types of software?

10. Why is copyright a subject educators need to be concerned with when using educational software?

ACTIVITIES

1. Go to the local computer store and search for software that could be used by your students. Make a list of what you think would be helpful and why. If your school district has a software library, visit it and try out the programs that are of greatest interest to you.

2. Develop a lesson plan for one of your classes that uses a simulation program like *SimCity* or *Oregon Trail.*

3. Discuss with a group of fellow teachers or students what would happen to publishing software if copyright protection were eliminated.

EXERCISE FOR FURTHER DEVELOPMENT OF YOUR REFLECTIVE PRACTICE FOR TEACHING WITH COMPUTER TECHNOLOGY

A professional teacher needs to be able to use a variety of tools to plan good teaching and learning. Computer technology is developing more sophisticated software to enable teachers to plan more sophisticated classroom experiences. Read the following presentation on digital evolution and reflect on the following issues related to teaching practice:

1. Most educational software has been developed to assist teachers in what already is occurring in schools. What types of software could be developed to teach in innovative ways?

2. As students work with computer software, how are you prepared for unintended outcomes resulting from students' learning evolving beyond traditional notions of information processing?

Digital Evolution

Researchers in artificial life have begun to experiment with establishing communities of digital organisms that are allowed to evolve and develop on their own. Tom Ray, for example, is expanding one of his programs called *Tierra*, in which complex digital organisms are set in competition with one another. The idea is to see which digital organisms will survive and evolve based on Darwinian evolutionary principles.

These digital organisms will exist online in a "Virtual Net." According to Ray, "because of its size, topological complexity and dynamically changing forms and conditions, the global network of computers is the ideal habitat for the evolution of complex digital organisms" ("Revolution in A-Life Evolution," 1994).

Ray wants to accomplish two things with his work. The first is to address the evolutionary biological question: "How does evolution spontaneously generate enormous increases in complexity?" ("Revolution in A-Life Evolution"). The second is to develop new software programs that will have useful characteristics.

Ray's idea is to watch programs evolve and develop. When they appear to have interesting characteristics, then they can be pulled out and modified for specific applications and use. This represents a very different model from traditional computer programming that comes out of a mathematical and engineering tradition. Rather than mechanically constructing a computer program, Ray is talking about planting programs in a rich developmental environment, watching them evolve naturally, and then harvesting them when they bear useful fruit.

This type of approach is more reminiscent of genetic research, in particular the early plant breeding experiments of scientists such as George Washington Carver and Luther Burbank, rather than of the work of hard core mathematicians and engineers such as John Von Neuman or Norbert Wiener.

The model is both intriguing and somewhat disquieting. Ray maintains that his digital organisms will not be able to escape from their virtual network to multiply or evolve out of control. Can we believe this to be true? If in fact what is being created is a new digitally constructed form of life, why couldn't it evolve in such a way as to prevent itself from being shut down, limited, or even eliminated? Wouldn't that be part of its evolutionary agenda that is, to survive, multiply, and proliferate?

On the other hand, a model like Ray's suggests the possibility of evolving toward more natural models of programming more in synchrony with nature. It is hard to predict what these programs might be like. The great British classicist, mathematician, and naturalist D'Arcy Wentworth Thompson (1991) outlined, in his work *On_Growth and Form,* how there are certain forms found in nature that because of their efficiency and simplicity are repeated over and over again. It is no accident, for example, that when soap bubbles, on the surface of a cookie sheet or table, are flattened with a piece of glass, the bubbles form into hexagonal shapes. When one looks at the cellular structure of a plant or animal cell under a microscope, the same hexagonal shape and structure is evident (e.g., fault lines in a dried river bed, the cracked glaze on a Tang dynasty vase). We repeat these efficient natural forms in our human constructions, as in the tile patterns for floors and the retaining walls for highway systems.

It is certainly no accident that DNA stores itself across animal and plant life in a multistrand spiral or helix. There must be some element of efficiency, of natural elegance, or evolution that causes this shape to be consistently used. If this is true then, does not Ray's idea of having computer programs and digital life forms evolve naturally make incredible sense?

Such notions suggest that we may be moving beyond traditional patterns of computing and information processing set in a typographic and modern culture. Postmodern and post-typographic models of computing may be very different from the engineering models that represent the foundations of current computer development. It is possible that competing models of computing and information processing—hard versus soft, evolutionary versus engineered—may evolve in years to come.

📖 SOURCES

Baudrillard, J. (1983). *Simulations* (P. Foos, P. Patton, & P. Beitchman, Trans.). New York: Semiotext(e).

Baudrillard, J. (1988). *Selected writings* (M. Poster, Ed.). Stanford, CA: Stanford University Press.

Revolution in a-life evolution. (1994). *Wired*, August, p. 33.

Taylor, R. (1980). *The computer in the school: Tutor, tool, tutee.* New York: Teachers College Press.

Thompson, D. W. (1961). *On growth and form.* (J. T. Bonner, Ed.). Cambridge, England: Cambridge University Press.

TECHNOLOGY AND THE CURRICULUM

Content, Language Arts and Literacy, Mathematics, Science, Social Studies, The Arts, Methodology, Utilization, Assessment With Computer-Supported Curriculum, How Do Computers Change the Work of Teachers?

To question computer use in schools is to ask what schools are for, why teachers teach certain content, how they should teach, and how children learn.

—Larry Cuban

Case Study

Ann Landers
8/3/96

Dear Ann:

I recently retired from teaching high school. During the last few years, I had a problem that was difficult to resolve.

Many of my students were producing homework essays typed on their computers. These essays were very neat. In addition, the spelling was impeccable, since the students used spell-check devices and grammar checkers.

I didn't know how to deal with this. The students with computers had a big advantage over their classmates. On the other hand, they had taken the time to become computer-literate. It was impossible to compare a painstakingly hand-written essay with spelling errors to the sanitized computer version.

It seemed foolish to forbid the use of computers, and I didn't know how to solve the problem.

Quebec Quandary

Dear Quebec Quandary:

We are going to hear more about this problem because students with computers have a definite advantage. Just as in the "olden days" when students who typed their papers had an advantage over those who wrote by hand.

Some teachers grade essays on content alone and ignore spelling, grammar and neatness. I believe teachers who want to make sure students know how to spell or conjugate a verb should give tests on those subjects. This would give all students a level playing field. Also, any student who feels a word processor would guarantee a higher grade can find a computer to use for the occasion at most libraries or copier centers.

Ann

Permission for use granted by Ann Landers and Creators Syndicate.

We agree with Ann Landers when she says "I believe teachers who want to make sure students know how to spell or conjugate a verb should give tests on those subjects." Whether through a test, or another formal or informal means of assessment, teachers need to be able to confirm what students know. To do this, however, they need to be clear about what they expect a student to learn. In other words, they need to be clear as to the purpose of the curriculum.

To discuss the use of computers, like any other teaching tools, we must consider their use in relation to the curriculum and to what a teacher actually does in the classroom. How does the use of computers improve instruction? How does it change the fundamental nature of what is being taught? Is the use of computers to deliver instruction as effective as other technologies such as textbooks, chalkboards, or the spoken word?

The fact is, the use of innovative technologies such as computers to help teachers deliver more effective curricula has always been considered desirable. Often, however, technology has failed to meet its utopian promise of transforming the classroom.

At the end of the 19th century, for example, lantern slides and victrola recordings were seen as having the potential to take learning to new levels of excellence and creativity. In the 1930s, radio was seen as holding the same promise, followed by films in the 1940s and 1950s, and television in the 1960s and 1970s.

The introduction of each of these technologies has one thing in common. Although they were successful up to a point, they have all failed to meet the promise of changing the way we teach. In the terms of Robert Taylor they have not functioned as tutor or tutee as well as tool. Why is this the case? Will computers fail to live up to their potential to change teaching?

Larry Cuban, in *Teachers and Machines: The Classroom Use of Technology Since 1920* (1986), examined in detail how new educational technologies have been adopted for use in the classrooms, and how their use has failed to meet their promised potential. While the jury is still out as to whether computers will or will not transform the classroom, Cuban believed that we can learn a great deal from how earlier technologies failed in terms of their use in the schools.

Cuban identified four possible reasons why past educational technologies failed to meet their promised potential:

- Teachers often lack the training and skills necessary to make effective use of instructional technology.
- Equipment and media are often expensive.
- Equipment is not always reliable or dependable, often it is not available when needed.
- Instructional material may not adequately fit students' instructional needs. (p. 18)

All is not lost, however! There are technologies that have been used in the classroom that have been remarkably effective. Textbooks, which were first introduced on a widespread basis in the 18th century, remain a major component of most instructional settings. The chalkboard, which was widely introduced into schools in the first half of the 19th century, still remains a major element in most classrooms.

Why have some technologies, like textbooks and chalkboards, endured? Cuban concluded that "the tools that teachers have added to their repertoire over time (e.g., chalkboard and textbooks) have been simple, durable, flexible, and responsive to teacher-defined problems in meeting the demands of daily instruction" (p. 58). This chapter examines the role of technology in the curriculum. This involves enlarging the conceptual categories used earlier in Chapter 4 in relation to evaluating software. These include content, methodology, and utilization. These categories are not only helpful in understanding how to evaluate software, they are also powerful concepts from a curriculum perspective because they connect software to the teaching and learning process in the classroom.

Content

Computers do not, in and of themselves, provide new content in the subject areas or disciplines taught in the schools. They do, however, provide a significantly different means of delivering content. This happens in two ways: First, with the explosive growth of new computer-based technologies such as CD-ROMs and the Internet, computers can bring much more information into the classroom; and second, innovative computer software is reshaping the presentation of information that influences the ways of knowing in the disciplines. This approach is most closely associated with the work of the American psychologist Jerome Bruner and his discussions of the "structures of the disciplines." Using this approach, students learn physics by learning to think and experiment like a physicist rather than by simply consuming facts about the science of physics (Bruner, 1971).

In discussing computer software, which includes masses of new information and innovative ways of presenting that same information, we will discuss how the computer can be used in the following curriculum content areas: language arts and literacy, mathematics, science, social studies, and the arts. In exploring each of these areas, we will examine how computer technology relates the content of the curriculum to the development of national curriculum standards in the content area.

National Curriculum Standards

The recent movement to establish national curriculum standards has led to the development of many different reports and sets of guidelines for different subject areas. Many of these are available on the Internet. An excellent site on educational standards with links to other Web sites is run by the Putnam Valley, New York school district.

Developing Educational Standards
http://putwest.boces.org/Standards.html

Subject area specialty and skill sites include:

National Council of Teachers of English
http://ncte.org/textindex.html

National Council of Teachers of Mathematics
http://www.enc.org/reform/journals/ENC2280/nf_280dtoc1.htm

National Council for the Social Studies
http://www.ncss.org/standards/stitle.html

National Science Education Standards
http://www.nap.edu/readingroom/books/nses/html/

National Standards in Foreign Language Education
http://www.actfl.org/htdocs/standards/index.htm

National Standards for Technology in Teacher Preparation
http://www.iste.org/index.html

Language Arts and Literacy

In the content area of language arts and literacy, technology is being used by both sides of the debate between skills-based approaches and processes approaches. This debate is popularly described as "whole language versus phonics."

Groups such as the National Council of Teachers of English and the International Reading Association argue that this debate unnecessarily polarizes and divides the field. Instead, they have worked for the development of "common ground" in documents such as *Standards for the English Language Arts* (National Council of Teachers of English, 1996). At the heart of the specific national curriculum standards are what these organizations identify as being the basis of curriculum. It involves "a focus in English language arts education on four purposes of language use:

- for obtaining and communicating information,
- for literary response and expression,
- for learning and reflection, and
- for problem solving and application." (p. 16)

In regard to each of these purposes, computer technology has the potential to contribute to their more effective implementation and use.

Purpose: For obtaining and communicating information.
In the area of reading there has been an explosion of information available for students to obtain and communicate. This has led to the development of reading/literacy software that presents reading with more tools available to the student to obtain and communicate information.

A good example of how computer technology helps students experience more than traditional reading lessons is such innovative CD-ROM software as *K.C. & Clyde in Fly Ball* (Don Johnston). Prepared for students from ages 4 to 8, this program presents language arts as an **interactive** story adventure. Students make choices that determine how a story progresses. There are 21 different paths that can be taken. The story may be read aloud to the students depending on their age. The user can select words in order to have them read again. Some words include explanations with pictures, sounds, and actions. To allow for flexible student access, single **switch**, **touch screen**, mouse, keyboard, or expanded keyboard functions are available. Computer work is supplemented with literacy learning materials including activity sheets, word cards, and bulletin board art. Programs such as *K.C. & Clyde In Fly Ball* are clear examples of how CD-ROM programs not only present information to students in innovative formats, but also provide them with large amounts of information at the same time.

Interactive: refers to the user being able to react to the computer through a command and have the system respond.

Switch: an on-off device for activating a computer and its programs.

Touch Screen: an input device for computers that is activated by touch.

K C & Clyde In Fly Ball (Don Johnston)
http://www.donjohnston.com

The ability to store masses of information has helped programs address skill-building aspects of obtaining and communicating information. *Word Munchers Deluxe CD* (MECC) uses the "Munchers" fun, interactive gameboard to expand its reading, grammar, and vocabulary skill building exercises. Students are able to return to their computer to work multiple times on skill building without some of the problems of traditional noncomputer drill and practice exercises.

Word Munchers (MECC)
http://softrack.releasesoft.com/origin/100000/info/wordmunchers/info.htm

For students whose first language is not English, software is becoming increasingly available to help them develop greater proficiency in obtaining and communicating information. CD-ROM software such as the Living Book Series which includes *Just Grandma and Me CD* (Broderbund) presents stories in more than one language. Words and the story can be read aloud.

Living Books (Broderbund)
http://www.broder.com/education/programs/livingbooks/

Just Grandma and Me (Broderbund)
http://www.broder.com/education/programs/livingbooks/grandma/

Purpose: For literary response and expression. In language arts classes students prepare book reports/reviews. This exercise of response and expression can be aided with computer technologies such as word processing. The curriculum impact can also be enhanced by other means as well. When students finish reading a book, they can enter information about it into a database. Students can tutor each other through using the database to look for a book to read. The information entered can become the basis for discussion, comparisons, and so on. Using the database, readers can make selections by subject (e.g., baseball), by page length (e.g., books less than 50 pages), or by ratings (e.g., 1, 2, 3, 4; excellent, good, fair, poor). In creating databases, the class can decide on the proper fields and the format of input. A database of fictional characters could include the fields of name, background, appearance, foibles, and other characteristics. This type of database can also be used to stimulate response and expression through creative writing assignments throughout the year.

Teachers can also encourage the development of students' understanding of expression by using the computer to record the brainstorming of adjectives or adverbs. Using word processing, a teacher can create an adjective or adverb activity. The teacher can construct a paragraph or story without any adjectives (or adverbs), putting asterisks in place of the adjectives. Students can then be assigned individually, or in groups, to insert adjectives (or adverbs). Students can print out the results and read their paragraphs/stories aloud. The class can then discuss how the tone or mood of a story changes by changing adjectives or adverbs.

Purpose: For learning and reflection. Software is also available that presents writing as more than just a mechanical activity. Many of the programs now on the market enable students to understand the thinking processes of writing by seeing "writing as a process." In these programs, the actual practice of writing becomes the means of learning writing. This is complementary to many of the approaches used in whole language.

Creative Writer 2 (Microsoft), for example, presents writing as a process with many dimensions to students as young as 8 years old. Through a multimedia world, *Imaginopolis*, students engage in a writing environment with characters, and other features that encourage creativity. Users can get ideas for stories, as well as tools, and help needed to explore a variety of writing activities. They can create banners, newsletters, greeting cards, as well as write stories and poems. The software provides many suggestions for stories and projects. It includes word processing to support desktop publishing with features such as a spell checker, thesaurus, and clip art. Its special effects include color, size, shadows, shaping, sparkle and fade, as well as borders and backgrounds. Included are dozens of sounds, over 100 pieces of clip art to illustrate stories, and more than 8,000 story starters to stimulate the reflection necessary for a budding writer's imagination. Imaginative activities such as these can lead individual learners to share with each other on the meaning of their communications.

Creative Writer 2
http://www.microsoft.com/kids/creative2.htm

Beyond prompts for outlining, story starters, and report formats, the computer can also assist in making writing a "whole" class activity. Class books can be written with a page for each student. Reflection can be encouraged through writing a class history. Information can be added on a regular basis by updating computer files about what happened that week. Software can also make it easier for students to keep journals reflecting on what they have studied and on the projects they have completed.

Purpose: For problem solving and application. Although word processing or desktop publishing software can be used to create writing activities involving the use of "descriptive language" such as composing a menu for a restaurant, students can also use spreadsheets to analyze data from restaurants. They can collect menus from local restaurants. By entering data, they can compare prices and then establish prices for class-made menu items. Many different types of data analysis can be undertaken. Spreadsheets can aid in calculating the cost of different meals. Spreadsheet software can also help in completing a nutritional analysis of meals. Comparisons can be part of cross-cultural writing activities based around data involving types of ethnic foods, origin, significance, and so on. While word processing can assist in creating questionnaires to gather information, spreadsheets can help with analyzing responses. From the analysis, a report can be written. Technology expands the scope of what goes into creating a written work, as well as assisting students in learning problem-solving techniques and making real-world applications.

Mathematics

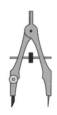

In the area of mathematics, the amount of information being made available in the classroom through the use of computer technology enables teachers to bring concepts to students earlier in their development and more often than they have been able to in the past. The information explosion also helps in creating a wider variety of experiences to assist in overcoming the drudgery of mathematics drill and practice. Computer technology enables students to think about the content of mathematics in visual ways through graphing as well as to see the presence of math across the curriculum in other subject areas.

In the 1980s, the National Council of Teachers of Mathematics (NCTM) began a continuing process of setting standards for teaching and learning in mathematics. In the development of *Curriculum and Evaluation Standards for School Mathematics* (1989), NCTM developed K–12 mathematics standards that "articulate five general goals for all students:

1.   that they learn to value mathematics,
2.   that they become confident in their ability to do

mathematics,
3.   that they become mathematical problem solvers,
4.   that they learn to communicate mathematically, and
5.   that they learn to reason mathematically (p. 5).

Computer technology is now widely available that can assist in implementing curricula and activities that address all these goals.

Goal: That they learn to value mathematics. Although this is the first of the general goals, it can only be accomplished if we are successful with the other four goals as well. Computer technology is enabling students to have more access to mathematics and to understand mathematics in more of a real-world context. Through this more "user-friendly" exposure, students can come to see the importance and role of mathematics in their world more easily. They have a better chance of learning to value mathematics rather than fear it.

Computer technology can also help students visualize mathematical information. A formula or equation can be graphed. As its values are altered and changed, the computer can automatically redraw a new graph. Similarly, in statistical areas, large data sets can be manipulated and analyzed.

Historically, we have made a distinction in the curriculum between arithmetic and mathematics. Computer technology is helping educators show the relation between these two areas by enabling educators to introduce mathematical concepts at earlier stages in a child's development alongside arithmetic concepts. There is a greater potential for student success with this increased exposure.

The potential for computer technology to incorporate mathematics into real-world contexts for students can be found in many different types of programs. An online curriculum called *Learning OnLine* (Curriculum Associates) developed by Eugene F. Provenzo, Jr., one of this book's authors, and his colleague Charles T. Mangrum II, demonstrates how the computer lends itself to developing this type of instruction.

Learning OnLine (Curriculum Associates)
http://www.curriculumassociates.com/LearningOnLine/

Learning OnLine is a series of thematically based student books designed for exploring the Internet. The audience is middle school students. Each 16-page book in the series focuses on a specific topic. The first four books in the series include *Apollo 11, The Wright Brothers and the Invention of Powered Flight, Endangered Animals,* and *Global Warming.*

After introducing each student to the thematic topic of the book, a series of online explorations are undertaken in mathematics, social studies, and language arts. Using the Internet and resources found on the World Wide Web, students address high interest thematic units, as well as practical problems using information drawn from online inquiries. In mathematics, for example, students go to a Web site at the Curriculum Associates offices in Massachusetts and connect into a *Learning OnLine* home page. There, they are able to connect directly to **Web sites** appropriate to the topic they are exploring.

Web Site: a collection of documents found on a single computer that can be linked to online via the Internet.

The "Connection to Mathematics" page in the *Apollo 11* book, for example, includes the following questions:

1. Distances in space are often reported in kilometers. Approximately how far, in kilometers, is the moon from the earth?

2. Use your answer to Question 1 to determine the distance in miles from the earth to the moon. (A mile is equal to approximately 1.6 kilometers.)

3. How many hours, minutes, and seconds passed between the launch of *Apollo 11* and the *Eagle*'s landing on the moon? To

the nearest day, how many days is this?

4. With his big backpack and heavy spacesuit, how much did Buzz Aldrin weigh on Earth? On the moon?

5. Complete this sentence with a fraction: The weight of a person on the moon is _____ that of his weight on Earth.

Each of these questions is of high interest, takes place in the real world and requires integrating math skills with electronic information gathering. Besides teaching students to value mathematics as something that is interesting and useful, the curriculum fulfills another goal of the NCTM standards to help students become more confident about doing math.

Goal: That they become confident in their ability to do mathematics. Young students can begin to become confident in their ability to do mathematics if they are encouraged to experiment with early math concepts such as patterns, shapes and sizes. Programs such as *Kid Pix* (Broderbund) provide an ideal opportunity to do so. Exploring patterns (e.g., using the stamp feature) can help young students with pattern recognition. Using the drawing tools, learners can create shapes and change sizes to learn the concepts of shape and size.

There are many math programs currently available that encourage students to become more confident by helping them to develop math skills through practice. The *Math Blaster* (Davidson) programs have become a favorite in the market for practice at math problem solving. *Math Rabbit Classic* ® (The Learning Company) focuses on developing basic number concepts and number relations. A recent updating of this program now includes digitized speech for English as a Second Language (ESL) and other students with reading problems. Besides developing confidence in the ability to use basic math skills of problem solving and computation, *Math Workshop Deluxe* (Broderbund) includes work on critical skills such as strategic thinking, estimation, recognizing equivalencies, patterns and spatial relations.

Math Blaster (Davidson)
http://www.davd.com/blaster/math.html

Math Rabbit Classic® (The Learning Company)
http://store.learningco.com/dev/product.asp?fid=0&ref_id=&sku=CMR35
44AE&mscssid=DGCPWVR3W9SH2PXG00L1R06N97B92RUM

Math Workshop Deluxe (Broderbund)
http://www.broder.com/education/programs/workshop/

Through drill and practice, creative engagement, and just plain fun, programs like these make mathematics a subject area students can feel increasingly confident about pursuing.

Goal: That they become mathematical problem solvers.
There are many types of programs now available that can help students in becoming problem solvers. The use of spreadsheets, for example, can assist teachers in helping students to learn problem solving and problem analysis. Just how rich this one type of program can be is evident in the following examples:

Statistics: A teacher can create a spreadsheet template. Students can input data from their class on variables such as height and weight, or scores on tests, or any numerical data of interest to them. From the data, the class can calculate various statistics such as mean (average), high, low, and total of all students. Going beyond data collected from their own class, students can use compilations of data from real-world situations. They can, for example, collect information about sports teams, space exploration, or geography. Using these data, they can solve problems by entering information into spreadsheets and then subjecting the information to analysis.

Geometry: Spreadsheets can be used as a tool to calculate the areas of various geometric figures. Students can input dimensions and create formulas to calculate area or perimeter. Spreadsheets can be especially effective in helping students to better understand the structure of a particular formula. They can also learn the relation between the dimensions of a figure and its formulas.

Fraction and Decimal Equivalencies: Spreadsheets can be formatted to calculate the decimal equivalents of fractions. By formatting cells with 16 decimal places, students can investigate patterns for repeating decimals. Students can also learn to see the meaning of "equivalence" by seeing the relation between fraction and decimal answers to problems.

Consumer Mathematics. Students can explore math relations by studying the relative cost of making a trip in different sized cars. The math concepts of time (length of trip) and average (miles per gallon) can be entered along with other data to derive the total cost of a trip for each type of car. Using the same type of approach, knowledge of nutrition factors can be improved by comparing how data representing diet intake can affect weight gain or loss. When comparative shopping, students can enter prices of common groceries at different stores in their neighborhood into a spreadsheet. They can use formulas to compare the cost of a meal or a day's or a week's shopping. Students can study the relative health of a company by using stock information from newspapers. They can pretend to buy stock and track its activity to see if a company is a "money maker."

Spreadsheets are just one example of how to use a computer to help students become problem solvers. Graphic visualization programs can contribute to intriguing problem-solving approaches. With *Geometric Supposer: Triangles* (Sunburst) students can select or construct a triangle of a particular size and shape. Using a menu they can then visually construct angle bisectors, segments, perpendiculars, and so on for the triangle. Students can then measure distances, angles, and areas for the shapes they have constructed. This software contributes to the problem-solving curriculum. Students can work at rewriting a problem such as the following:

> A farmer must pump water from a centrally located well to three points on his farm (the three points determine an acute triangle). Where should he locate the well to make the sum of the distances from the well to each point the shortest distance possible?

Although paper and pencil can be used to rewrite and solve this problem, computer software can be harnessed to rewrite it as well as to calculate an answer. Students are usually more willing to try alternative measurements when using the computer. If they make a mistake with the computer, it is easier to correct. Precision of measurement with computers is easier for many students than using traditional measuring tools. Students can then move on to make up their own problems. Through technology they can become problem framers, or creators of problems, as well as problems solvers.

Geometric Supposer (Sunburst)
http://www.sunburst.com:80/new_products_software.html

Goal: That they learn to communicate mathematically. Beyond the analytical use of database or spreadsheet software, learners can collect classroom data such as favorite food, favorite color, birth month, hobby, number of pets, and other information. Analysis of data can then be communicated mathematically through graphing (e.g., pie chart graphs of favorite color or birth month). Students can use graphs of data to make generalizations about which food is most liked. Graphs can enable students to understand the mathematical aspects of concepts, such as "different" and "same," by analyzing commonalities and differences.

Programs such as *Graphers* (Sunburst) can be used to enable primary age learners to select colorful picture data from sets of fruits, pets, and people to explore mathematical concepts. They can use pictures to count and take surveys. After they organize findings, students can construct and interpret graphs. Spoken instructions in the software help students with reading difficulties by making mathematical communication more accessible.

Graphers (Sunburst)
http://www.sunburst.com:80/new_products_software.html

Goal: That they learn to reason mathematically. Using their knowledge of story writing, word processing, and/or desktop publishing software, students can write their own math "stories" (i.e., problems that can be given to others in the class to solve). Using a word processor, for example, a sign maker like the one included in *The Print Shop Deluxe* (Broderbund), or a desktop publishing program such as *The Ultimate Writing Center*™ (The Learning Company), students can make up help wanted signs, items for sale or advertisements. For example:

> ### Help Wanted
> ### 10 hours of Yard Work
> ### at $2.50 per hour

Students can make up word problems to solve using the information on the signs. In doing so, they will also learn that what we have traditionally called "word" problems are actually "story" problems. Using the method for making signs or advertisements already described, students can work on time-appropriate problems. Students can solve problems involving a time when gasoline was cheaper than it is today. For example, in the late 1950s, gasoline was available at 30 cents a gallon. Using the computer, students can compare the cost of gas at that time with today's prices. Then they can compare this to the wages of the era and compute what percentage of a worker's salary went to running a car.

The Print Shop Deluxe (Broderbund)
http://www.broder.com/education/programs/printshop/home.html#disk

The Ultimate Writing Center™ (The Learning Company)
http://www.learningco.com/products/tlc/el/uwc/default.htm

Totally different approaches from those described can be used in order to help students with the process of mathematical reasoning. Pioneering computer programs such as *Logo*, developed by Seymour Papert and his associates at the Massachusetts Institute of Technology, have students learn mathematical, and more specifically, geometrical reasoning by programming in the *Logo* language. Part of the program, for example, involves students instructing a pointer called a "turtle" to create lines and shapes.

This type of mathematical reasoning process is described by Papert (1993) who explained how one day he watched a boy trying to get the turtle to write his name. He wanted an A. This required developing a little theory of the geometry of an A. It is not obvious how much the turtle should turn nor how much it should advance. This is real geometry. But it differed from School geometry in a cluster of important respects. First, it was a real problem that had come spontaneously to this boy. Of course, that can happen in regular geometry too. But it is very much more likely to happen here. Second, one visibly works toward the goal of being wrong most of the time. But one can see that one is wrong and ask oneself or someone else what happened. The movements of the turtle externalize one's conception so one can think and talk about it. One can also do some of the kinds of "problem solving" that people do in the real world, such as solve another problem instead, or borrow a solution from someone else and adapt it to fit your case (p. 177).

The Logo Foundation
http://el.www.media.mit.edu/groups/logo-foundation/index.html

Science

The National Research Council has led the way in the discussion of setting national curriculum standards for science education. In the development of *National Science Education Standards* (1996), the council stated that "the goals for school science that underlie the *National Science Education Standards* are to educate students to:

1. experience the richness and excitement of knowing about and understanding the natural world;
2. use appropriate scientific processes and principles in making personal decisions;
3. engage intelligently in public discourse and debate about matters of scientific and technological concern; and
4. increase their economic productivity through the use of the knowledge, understanding, and skills of the scientifically literate person in their careers." (p. 13)

Computer-based educational technology is being used to assist in implementing curricula and activities that address each of these goals.

Goal: Experience the richness and excitement of knowing about and understanding the natural world. Computer technology is enabling teachers to assist students at younger ages to explore basic science concepts. *Sammy's Science House* (Edmark) introduces science to students from preschool to grade 2. This software helps students build a broad range of beginning science skills through exciting experiential activities about the natural world. Five activities are available to teach them about plants, animals, seasons, and the weather. Students work with fundamental science skills like observation, classification, comparison, and sequencing. They experience the excitement of creating machines and toys, exploring weather conditions, sequencing pictures to create films, learning about the natural world by sorting the pictures of plants, animals, and minerals, as well as discovering a wealth of information about how nature and wildlife change from season to season.

Sammy's Science House
http://www.edmark.com/prod/house/sammy/

Students can experience the richness of the natural world in action through computer-generated virtual worlds on CD-ROMs. The *Eyewitness* series (DK Multimedia) provides students with opportunities to explore elements of science that reveal the mysteries of nature. This series reflects the traditional directions of the encyclopedia format in software such as *Eyewitness Encyclopedia of Science CD*. The series also includes **virtual reality** formats in software such as *Eyewitness Virtual Reality: Bird*. Scholastic's *Interactive NOVA Series* allows students in a Macintosh environment to use **videodiscs** to create scientific **multimedia** presentations, as well as to participate in visual explorations of scientific data.

Virtual Reality: refers to the idea of creating highly realistic simulations with computers.

Videodiscs: a read-only optical disc that is used to store still pictures, motion pictures, and sound.

DK Publishing
http://www.dkonline.com/dkcom/

Goal: Use appropriate scientific processes and principles in making personal decisions. Using programs like *Thinkin' Things Collection 1* (Edmark), as well as *Collections 2* and *3*, teachers can help younger students build science- and math-related critical thinking skills for effective decision making.

Multimedia: the combination of sound, animation, graphics, video, and related elements into a single program or system.

Various activities help young science students expand their memories, creativity, problem-solving and decision-making skills. This software provides activities designed to enhance auditory recognition, develop the basics of scientific and mathematical logic, sharpen the ability to identify relations and attributes, experiment with perspective and depth, test hypotheses, and demonstrate visual thinking.

Thinkin' Things
http://www.edmark.com/prod/tt/

As early as grade 3, students can begin performing science experiments with programs such as *Super Solvers Gizmos and Gadgets* (The Learning Company). On-screen simulations of experiments involving force, balance, magnetism, and electricity give students immediate information and feedback about their ability to apply scientific principles. Such software creates computer-based laboratories where simulations enable the students to "practice" science. Through probeware attached to computers, they can act like scientists doing sophisticated experimental work. These computer "laboratories" take many of the hassles out of data collection while allowing users to concentrate on hypothesis testing.

Besides software with a specific "science" orientation, graphing software related to mathematics can help students in using science processes and making decisions about natural processes in life. Just as in mathematics, database software can assist in gathering and recording the data from science study that can lead to decision making and hypothesis testing.

Word processing software so often connected to language arts work can be used by students to create and maintain science lab sheets for tracking experiments. Using information from science study and results of experiments, students can deepen their understanding of science processes by using word processing to create problems for study or "Who am I?" riddles that can be shared in class.

Using vocabulary from the study of scientific processes, students can write clues for words for crossword puzzles. Software such as *Crosswords & More* and *Crosswords & Word Games* (Expert Software) can be used to generate crossword puzzles. Students can then assist each other in working on deepening their understanding of the use of scientific terminology and processes.

Crosswords & More (Expert Software)
http://www.expertsoftware.com/edutain.htm

Word Games (Expert Software)
http://www.expertsoftware.com/edutain.htm

Goal: Engage intelligently in public discourse and debate about matters of scientific and technological concern. Computer technology is providing ways for children to enter into public discourse and debate in science. The *Jason Project* series (Jason Foundation for Education) provides a live interactive distance learning experience. In *Jason Project VII* researchers, students, and teachers joined Dr. Robert Ballard (Senior Scientist at Woods Hole Oceanographic Institution) in investigating water habitats in southern Florida (including the Florida Keys and the Everglades). A robot at the bottom of the ocean was controlled from the ship. The participants were able to interact immediately with its findings. The experiment was broadcast live via satellite to schools and students could call and ask questions. At "Dial-In" sites, students could take control of the robot using joysticks. Teaching materials and other related information from past and for future projects can be accessed through the World Wide Web.

Jason *Project*
http://www.jasonproject.org/

Using hypermedia authoring software such as *HyperStudio* (Roger Wagner), students create multimedia presentations using pictures, videos, and other information they have gathered to present points of view as well as various aspects of the debate on scientific issues. Multimedia presentations allow students to learn to communicate (participate in the discourse) in a variety of formats.

Hyper Studio (Roger Wagner)
http://www.hyperstudio.com/

Through *National Geographic Kids Network* students get to network with scientists and investigate problems in the same ways that scientists work. This international telecommunications science curriculum enables students to study real-world scientific issues such as acid rain, solar energy, nutrition, water quality, weather, and trash disposal. Through the processes involved, they learn key principles of scientific inquiry and are able to expand their knowledge of the world, as well as their ability to communicate beyond the classroom walls about the scientific debates related to these issues.

National Geographic Kids Network
http://gii-awards.com/nicampgn/28ba.htm

Goal: Increase their economic productivity through the use of the knowledge, understanding, and skills of the scientifically literate person in their careers. Using word processing software, young learners can develop their scientific literacy through activities such as writing "all about me," or letters telling about an animal they have studied (habits, diet, family, and hobbies). Collaborative projects involving groups of two or three students can encourage them to gather information on a different animal, insect, plant, and so on. The groups can then use programs such as *Creative Writer 2* (Microsoft) along with *Kid Works*™ (Davidson) to write and illustrate their reports.

Kid Works™ (Davidson)
http://www.davd.com/kid-works/deluxe/

Software can be used to create databases of information gathered by different groups of students. Learners can generate their own questions to be answered using their databases. In studying weather, students can record weather conditions over a period of time. They can then identify days with the same barometric reading, level of humidity and/or temperature. After identifying trends, students can use them to make predictions. In studying nutrition, students can bring in labels from foods they regularly eat. They can create a database or spreadsheet activity to study the number of calories or percentages of RDAs, ingredients, and nutrients.

Students can communicate with other students and classes through online programs such as the *National Geographic Kids Network* using an inquiry-oriented and hands-on science approach. Students can research, analyze, and share data with peers in problem solving and collaborative project development.

In simulation activities, students can experience virtual laboratories. *How Your Body Works CD* (Mindscape) provides students with a three-dimensional laboratory environment. Ease of access and a straight-talk approach enables students to experiment in safety and to repeat experiments at their own pace. These simulations capture the interactivity that textbook diagrams cannot.

How Your Body Works (Mindscape)
http://www.mindscape.com/

Social Studies

At the heart of its *Expectations of Excellence: Curriculum Standards for Social Studies*, the National Council for the Social Studies (1994) identified three expectations for achieving excellence in the Social Studies curriculum (pp. 5–10). In these expectations, learning in the social studies is intended to assist students in supporting the common good, adopting common and multiple perspectives, and applying knowledge, skills and values to civic action.

Expectation: Supporting the Common Good. This is a very broad expectation, but the development of the social studies as a field of study has arisen from the vision that students need to be taught to work with others and make connections in order to help them develop into good citizens. The development of new types of software enables teachers to do this in ways that have not been possible before. With programs such as *Decisions, Decisions* (Tom Snyder Productions), for example, teachers are able to gather students in working groups to learn group decision making skills through simulation programs designed to support the purpose as well as the content of social studies.

Oregon Trail and *Oregon Trail II* (MECC/The Learning Company) are some examples of this type of software. In these programs, students work through a simulation of pioneers traveling West. They experience the "common ground" that the pioneers had to share in order for the journey to be successful. They can learn about the concrete decisions that made the United States into the nation that it is today.

Oregon Trail (MECC/The Learning Company)
http://store.learningco.com/dev/product.asp?fid=0&ref_id=&sku=OTA374
4AE&mscssid=HTCPWVR3W9SH2PXG00L1R06N9XHMUD2R

For a more contemporary application of constructing a modern day city, students can engage in the activities of *SimCity 3000* (Maxis). Through the simulations of this software, students can deal with developing "common ground" in today's world.

Maxis
http://www.maxis.com/

Through sharing computers and collaborating on projects, students can learn about working together. Later in this chapter under utilization, we present ideas about the use of a limited number of computers in a classroom. Learning to work together on computer projects and with computer software, students can be taught the values of good citizenship related to sharing resources and respecting the needs of others. Teaching such an attitude has been part of social studies since long before the advent of computer technology.

Further, the chapter on ethical and legal issues identifies some concerns about values being conveyed through the computer programs we use, through the Internet, and through the ways students have access to computers. All of these issues are part of a co-curriculum to social studies. Teachers need to be alert to the values they are conveying. An inconsistency of values and/or behaviors will undermine the securing of common ground being sought in the teaching of the social studies.

Expectation: Adopting Common and Multiple Perspectives. In the social studies there is an expectation of adopting common and multiple perspectives:

> Within the school program, social studies provides coordinated, systematic study drawing upon such disciplines as anthropology, archaeology, economics, geography, history, law, philosophy, political science, psychology, religion, and sociology, as well as appropriate content from the humanities, mathematics and natural sciences. (National Council for the Social Studies, 1994, p. vii)

There are several advances in technology that support teachers of social studies in their attempts to unite various perspectives. These include multimedia encyclopedias for research, desktop publishing for report writing, and hypermedia programming for presentations.

With available technology students can create a "Book of States." Each student (or a pair) can choose a state. Using word processing they can write letters to a state travel bureau and/or chamber of commerce to request information about a state for a database they are creating. Before doing this, they can discuss what information to specify and thus understand the perspectives they are seeking to investigate. Using multimedia encyclopedias, they can do research on the state. They can then compare the two sets of data and the perspectives they represent.

Students can generate reports and make graphs by inputting their data into a database and/or spreadsheet. They can use word processing software to write commentary for a database. They can develop a presentation with hypermedia programming software in which visual images from the encyclopedias and state travel bureau or chamber of commerce can be incorporated to give readers/observers a fuller sense of the data and perspectives involved.

In a similar way, students can create a presentation on "All the Presidents." In creating a database on the presidents of the United States, students can seek to answer questions like: "What groups influenced the election of each president?" "Which state has provided the most presidents?" "Which party?" "Who was youngest?" "Oldest?" "Who had the shortest term?" In their "published" books or hypermedia presentations students can demonstrate their grasp of how the common and/or multiple perspectives of various groups have contributed to the election of our presidents.

In understanding multicultural perspectives students can use many different programs that provide information about different countries and cultures. Technology gives students opportunities to expand their understanding of factors that affect cultural perspectives. Although a program like *Zookeeper* (Davidson) may seem like a science-related program, students can learn factors through the study of animals that affect various aspects of our world. Through the simulations of the *Carmen Sandiego* series (Broderbund), students can learn the differences in cultures based on location, time period, and so on. Through the Internet, students can communicate with people of different cultures and perhaps gain an understanding of different perspectives.

Zookeeper (Davidson)
http://www.adobe.com/homepage.shtml

Where in the World Is Carmen Sandiego? (Broderbund)
http://www.broder.com/education/programs/carmenworld/

Expectation: Applying Knowledge, Skills, and Values to Civic Action. Oftentimes social studies has been taught too much on a strictly abstract or conceptual level. What has been taught is often not sufficiently concrete for young children. Clock time is typically taught to children in the early grades, but concrete chronologies are not introduced to this age group. Software like *Trudy's Time and Place House* (Edmark) provides a learning environment that enables young students to not only learn how to read an analog clock, but also to learn about the seasons. Expanding from time to geography, students have the opportunity to develop concrete understanding of concepts such as calendars, using directions, learning about world geography, and understanding map symbols.

Trudy's Time and Place House (Edmark)
http://www.edmark.com/prod/house/trudy/

TimeLiner (Tom Snyder Productions) provides students in grades K–12 with the ability to create time lines up to 99 pages long with any information as well as to display proportional relations. By charting patterns in history, recording science experiments, charting events in stories, illustrating birthdays, and/or organizing school events, students are able to visualize various forms of data. This software has four formats to address various aspects of social studies skills, permitting the creation of custom scales (e.g., distance and weight.) To assist all learners to work together, a bilingual (Spanish) version is available. Schools can also purchase *TimeLiner* data disks with information about dinosaurs, history, arts, and language arts.

TimeLiner Online (Tom Snyder Productions)
http://www.teachtsp.com/classroom/timelineronline/tlineronline.html

Computers also enable students to better experience and represent the integration of content and skills represented in the social studies. The development of multimedia encyclopedias has provided research tools for learning that immerse students in a sensory environment. Students as young as 6 years of age can conduct searches with just one word. They can browse to explore all the information and options at their finger tips. Here are three examples:

Compton's Interactive Encyclopedia (Compton's New Media) provides access to information where exact spelling is not required. It has a virtual workspace that saves all the search paths traveled through a session. Although depth of information is limited, it is a good beginner's search tool.

Compton's Interactive Encyclopedia (Compton's New Media)
http://support.intel.com/intel/software/titles/comptn_d.htm

Microsoft Encarta (Microsoft) was developed for students in grades 4–12. The higher level allows for more advanced searching techniques. Illustrations for class presentations can be pasted into a note pad.

Microsoft Encarta (Encarta)
http://encarta.msn.com/EncartaHome.asp

New Grolier Multimedia Encyclopedia (Grolier Publishing) is for older students, and provides a wealth of information that is easy to search. Learners are able to search for information through outlines, images, sounds, movies, and animations.

New Grolier Multimedia Encyclopedia (Grolier Publishing)
http://gi.grolier.com/gi/products/reference/98gme/docs/01-main.html

Students can take various sources and subjects of information and develop analytical and problem-solving skills by creating databases about states including capitals, population, area, birthrate, death rate, unemployment rate and major cities. From the database students can develop skills related to comparisons. They can find the five states with the largest population, and/or the largest areas, and/or the highest birthrates, and/or the lowest death rates, and/or the highest unemployment rates. Through discussion, groups can discover more relations among data in some of these categories.

Using word processing software, students can demonstrate their ability to synthesize perspectives in social studies by writing commentaries on social problems or analyses of historical events. Using desktop publishing software, learners can create a historic newspaper including the event and other information appropriate to the times. Students can choose an event such as the day of the landing of the Pilgrims, Paul Revere's ride, or the first landing on the moon. Multimedia encyclopedias can be used to research what happened at the event and/or around that time for inclusion in the newspaper article.

The Arts

In the last several decades concerns have been expressed about the role of the arts and arts education in the United States. In trying to situate the arts within the school curriculum, the National Endowment for the Arts suggested four purposes for basic arts education in their report, *Toward Civilization: A Report on Arts Education* (1988, pp. 14–18). These purposes include giving our young people a sense of civilization; fostering creativity; teaching effective communication; and providing critical assessment for what one reads, sees, and hears. Technology is being used to assist in implementing curriculums and activities in art, music, and other performing arts that can address these four purposes.

Purpose: To give our young people a sense of civilization. With the development of CD-ROMs there has literally been an explosion of access to arts-related information about Western Civilization. Through encyclopedias such as *Encarta* (Microsoft) or *New Grolier Multimedia Encyclopedia* (Grolier Publishing), there is much more information readily available for incorporation into the arts curriculum. Students can more easily incorporate the information into class reports and presentations. Art history is more easily seen as part of understanding history and civilization when visual images are readily available at the time and place one is studying the history.

CD-ROMs are giving students new access to art exhibitions and art museums. In 1996, an international touring exhibit of the work of Paul Cezanne was complemented by the CD-ROM product *Paul Cezanne: Portrait of My World* (Corbis). This software is an American version of what was originally a French product. It is not a replica of the exhibit, but uses works included in the exhibit as a jumping-off point to study Cezanne. Through multimedia presentations, there are over 360 entry points to engage 140 of Cezanne's works as well as close to 100 works of related artists. Not only do students get to view the works of Cezanne, they also can connect to the context and place Cezanne holds in Western civilization.

Paul Cezanne (Corbis)
http://www.cdaccess.com/html/shared/cezanne.htm

Museums can come alive through the experience of virtual museums. The hypermedia program *A Passion for Art: Renoir, Cezanne, Matisse and Dr. Barnes* (Corbis), for example, provides a personal gallery tour through the country's greatest private collection of postimpressionist art—the A. S. Barnes collection. Using the *Passion for Art* hypermedia program, students can take a "virtual" tour of the museum and its holdings. Not only can they walk through the individual galleries of the museum, but also historical timelines may be consulted, as well as archives including information on major paintings included in the Barnes collection.

A Passion for Art (Corbis)
http://www.hyperstand.com/Invision/Invision95/corbis.html

Students can visit many different types of museum sites on the Internet and the World Wide Web. Visit this textbook's Web site to see interesting examples.

Purpose: To foster creativity. Traditionally, a child's development and/or talent in the arts have limited the scope of creative expression. Programs such as *Fine Artist* (Microsoft) enable children 8 and older to paint, draw, and create multimedia projects. With the aid of tools and step-by-step projects to spur creativity, even learners with limited artistic ability can explore their own creativity. This program works with the language arts program *Creative Writer*. *Fine Artist* includes full-featured painting and drawing tools, as well as interactive lessons on basic drawing and perspective. Thus, students can explore their creativity at their own pace.

Beyond the drawing and painting, students (grades 2–12) can explore their creativity through design with *KidCAD* (Davidson). They can design and build a park, a cottage, a home, or a museum. They can do their own construction in the city, a small town, or on a farm. Students can explore their designs by navigating different views and rotating their constructions. Creations can be embellished by their choice of color and furniture. Presentations of designs can include images of people, animals, and shrubbery.

KidCad (Davidson)
http://www.davd.com/

MIDI: an acronym for Musical Instrument Digital Interface; allows for the connection of music, synthesizers, musical instruments and computers.

Before the growth of CD-ROM products, much of the use of computers in the musical arts centered on composing, editing and printing musical scores. This was done using the computer language Musical Instrument Digital Interface (**MIDI**). Building on earlier success with Macintosh CD-ROM products, Voyager's *Making Music CD* enables the student who is not a composer to create music through the "Making Music" feature. The student can create notes, modify volume and tempo, as well as alter pitch and rhythm. Sounds and instruments can be heard separately or together. Using the "Building Block" feature, students can use simple tunes to learn about structure and repetition.

Purpose: To teach effective communication. As previously identified in other content areas, art programs can enhance the ability of many students to communicate across the curriculum. Rather than function as "stand alones," fine art, music, and film are being used to enable students to communicate more effectively in the various disciplines. Programs can also work the other way around. The arts can be the main subject while language arts, and other areas, are the added dimension to communication. After using graphics and paint programs like *Color Me* (Sunburst), *Print Shop Deluxe* (Broderbund), and *Kid Pix* (Broderbund), for example, as well as other art media, students can analyze their work by using word processing to describe the steps and intentions involved in doing their art project. They can write a description or explanation of how to create the art projects they have completed. Such explanations can be gathered in a book of instructions, including samples of finished projects. Students can become peer teachers by providing directions that can be followed by others. This communication does not have to be limited to their own classroom. Students can use the Internet to send instructions to a class in another school.

Color Me (Sunburst)
http://www.sunburst.com:80/new_products_software.html

In the area of language arts, we described students using the writing process to create books and to participate in desktop publishing. Students, by including the arts in their work, can learn how integral the arts can be to communication. This can prevent the problems of the arts being marginalized in the curriculum. By integrating different aspects of the arts into various curricular areas through the use of technology, the arts can become a more apparently vital part of the basics of effective and meaningful communication.

Purpose: To provide critical assessment for what one reads, sees, and hears. Computer technology has added important dimensions to helping students develop their critical expertise. Through the wealth of information that can be stored on a CD-ROM, and with hypermedia programming, students are able to access multiple dimensions of arts information. Programs such as *Musical Instruments CD* (Microsoft) enable students to access the sounds, shapes, and images of musical instruments from around the world. In this program students can also connect to visual art pieces. Making connections enables students to cross cultures as well as the boundaries among the arts. This movement across lines can enable students to critically evaluate the relations and connections of elements within their world. *Art Gallery CD* (Microsoft) works in similar ways, but uses art rather than music as its starting point.

Musical Instruments (Microsoft)
http://www.btam.com.tr/catalog/products/MusInstr/default.htm

One of the tools of critical assessment is to be able to make judgments based on looking at things from a variety of perspectives. In addition to traditional writing, programs like *Opening Night CD* (MECC) assist students in script writing. Through this program students can compare narrative expression with the presentation in a script for the performing arts. In doing so, they can explore the meaning conveyed by different formats of expression.

Opening Night (MECC)
http://www.creativekids.com/softd/title1319.htm

Methodology

Beyond the subject areas, there are general methodological directions underlying the use of computer technology. When we analyze the methodologies that computers support, there are many that computers help deliver effectively. As noted in the software chapter, there appear to be two families of methodologies that dominate. On the one hand, some computer programs tend to support skill building, mastery learning and achieving behavioral objectives. On the other hand, some computer programs tend to support concept acquisition, critical thinking and constructivist curriculums.

Good examples of computer programs that tend to support skill building, mastery learning and achieving behavioral objectives would be the fun of drill and practice found in *Math Blasters*. Here students work on patterns and increasing skills while working with math fundamentals. Expanded to the system level, we find this mastery curriculum in integrated learning systems (ILS) such as those developed by Jostens.

We have described the other direction of methodologies that computer programs tend to support as concept acquisition, critical thinking, and constructivist curriculums. A good example of such programs would be *HyperStudio* (Roger Wagner Publishing, Inc.). Students using this multimedia authoring tool can bring together multimedia elements in the form of graphics, sound, animation, and video. Students have the capacity to capture images using AV Macs or digital cameras. In using this program teachers can facilitate a constructivist approach to learning. With such an approach, students' work on creative writing projects can be enhanced with additional media. This can be done by accessing external devices such as videodisc players; or path-based animations can be created by dragging the mouse; or graphics, sounds, and animations can be imported from other programs. The Internet can provide up-to-date information for research projects. Teachers using the program can create hypermedia stacks for instruction. But, with *HyperStudio*'s simple nontechnical multimedia authoring, an even better use of this software is student-created projects in any area of the curriculum. It provides students a means to display what they have learned. This is not just for individuals; groups can also work together, research, plan, design, and then share what they have learned through the multimedia presentations they have created.

In support of concept acquisition, critical thinking, and constructivist curriculums, *Kid Pix* programs can be seen as examples of supporting the interrelation of disciplines as a natural way of learning. If students are learning about fish, they can write about fish using word processing software. In the same unit, *Kid Pix* can help in constructing a picture story that can be narrated by recording a child's voice. With *Kid Works 2,* students can write and draw what they have learned about fish and have it read back to them. They can learn to detect errors in spelling when they hear it read aloud. They can use word processing to bring science to the class by writing letters to experts asking for information or to invite them to come to class and talk about fish.

Kid Works (Broderbund)
http://www.broderbund.com/

In these areas, problem solving, inquiry, project, and simulation are important methodologies that computer programs can support. Although we identify these two groups, it is like a spectrum with groups on either end. An example of how a teacher can use a program for various methodologies would be the ways that a program like *Where in the World Is Carmen San Diego?* can be used. A teacher can use it to teach students methods of problem solving using geography knowledge. At the same time, teachers may be using it to build students' skills at remembering geography facts. Various students can be learning in different ways with the same program.

Another example of the mastery in the constructivist spectrum can be seen with the Tom Snyder *Decisions, Decisions* series. These programs have a single problem-solving method underlying them. The use of various programs in the series can assist students to master the skills of the specific problem-solving method. At the same time, the program can be used to increase students' knowledge of the variety of problem-solving techniques. This can be done by contrasting this with other experiences of problem solving.

Utilization

As already noted, Cuban (1986) identified the difference between technologies that significantly impact the classroom and those that do not as to their utilization, or in computer terms, their "user friendliness." According to Cuban "the tools that teachers have added to their repertoire over time (e.g., chalkboard and textbooks) have been simple, durable, flexible, and responsive to teacher-defined problems in meeting the demands of daily instruction" (p. 58). In this context, the following question can be raised: How classroom friendly can computers be?

Tom Snyder, one of the founders of the educational software company, Tom Snyder Productions, seems to have clearly understood the problems teachers have had in integrating technology into their curriculums. In his software development for Tom Snyder Productions, he has tried to have computers foster great teaching. In software series such as *Decisions, Decisions* and *Choices, Choices* as well as *TimeLiners*, Snyder and his production company have tried to create software that fosters the computer as a tool in curriculum implementation. Dockterman captured this purpose in *Great Teaching in the One Computer Classroom* (1991). In the Snyder model, the computer is so simple, durable, flexible, and responsive that only one is sufficient to have it be supportive to great teaching.

Choices, Choices (Tom Snyder Productions)
http://www.teachtsp.com/products/Choices.htm

For Snyder and his colleagues, such as Dockterman, the question is not about how many computers there are in a classroom. Rather, it concerns the teaching processes and curriculum and how computers can aid in the implementation of curriculum. Teachers have to decide what type of teaching and learning they want. With that personal understanding of great teaching in mind, they can then begin to utilize the computer to implement their own best direction. Even a single computer can help a teacher implement curriculum through teaching utilizing lecture, teaching utilizing group work (small and/or large), teaching utilizing learning centers, and classroom management.

Teaching Utilizing Lecture. For the times that you decide that your curriculum implementation is best accomplished through lecture a computer can help by acting as a "smart" chalkboard. Rather than writing things on a board to aid students, you can flash outlines, keywords, or other formats on a screen. Using *PowerPoint* or other presentation software can move you from class preparation into delivery in easier ways. Students can also be taught outlining and note taking by modeling their use in lecture delivery.

Many times students can be aided to understand concepts in a lecture through visualization. Clip art or charts projected for students' visualization can facilitate the visual learner's understanding of concepts being presented in the auditory mode of lecture.

Beyond individual visual images, demonstration through simulation can enable students to understand a process being described through lecture. Computer-assisted simulated science dissections, or virtual tours, can give students a walk through process that they can also do in other ways. The program *A.D.A.M.* (Benjamin/Cummins; Mindscape/The Learning Company) can be utilized to give students a tour of the human body. You can even choose between an open-ended tour or a directed tour.

A.D.A.M. (Benjamin/Cummins)
http://www.adam.com/

A.D.A.M. (Mindscape/The Learning Company)
http://www.mindscape.com/store/health/adam/details.htm

Teaching Utilizing Group Work (Small and/or Large). With the growth in popularity of cooperative learning and other group processes and discussion-based learning techniques, teachers have increased their desire for tools to assist in facilitating such methodologies. Visual presentations can be great discussion starters. Directions or focusing questions can remain visible while groups work and discuss. Software such as *Decisions, Decisions* and *Choices, Choices* aids teachers in forming groups, pacing group movement, cross-group interactions, and competition.

Cooperative learning responsibilities and interdependence can be guided through technology assistance. The computer can aid the teacher in facilitating and monitoring the progress of various groups and individuals. Students also need to be taught the social skills of group work.

Teaching Utilizing Learning Centers. The traditional learning center can be expanded through the support of a computer. Students needing reinforcement of mathematics skills can utilize *Math Blaster* in a learning center to do the drill and practice necessary. The seemingly infinite randomization of patterns relieves the teacher from having to have multiple worksheets and activities. The various ways that computers provide stimulation can create motivating environments in a learning center. This can aid in reducing the number of times a teacher needs to monitor a student or group of students who are on-task at a learning center.

Classroom Management. An area in which computers are making changes in the way things are done has been in the area of classroom management. Programs such as *Pretty Good Grading Program* (George Beckman) and *First Class Grade Book* (1st Class Software) not only enable teachers to manage student records, grades, and attendance, they also have features that facilitate custom reports, letters, and notes to parents on student progress.

Pretty Good Grading Program (George Beckman)
http://www.pggp.com/

First Class Grade Book (1st Class Software)
http://www.interlog.com/~1stclass/

School **local area networks** (LAN) and district **metropolitan area networking** (MAN) are facilitating record keeping. In an increasing number of cases, teachers are recording information such as attendance on a computer in the classroom and, with a keystroke or two, sending the information to the school office, which in turn forwards it to the district attendance office.

Local Area Network: interconnected computers and related peripherals, such as printers and scanners in one location such as a building or office.

Word processing programs are enabling teachers to more professionally generate tests, worksheets, handouts, and displays. Although record keeping and monitoring students are important, creating curriculum materials and learning environments of good quality are the foundation of good classroom management. The

Metropolitan Area Network: a series of computers linked on a regional basis.

ability to transfer information from one program to another is enabling teachers to customize elements of the curriculum to meet the needs of individual students while making group progress. Teachers are filling disks with materials that are becoming their own interactive curriculum libraries.

Assessment with Computer-supported Curriculum

As the curriculum is redefined through the implementation of new computer technologies, so too are traditional means of student assessment changed as well. In drill and practice programs, students can be instantly evaluated as they respond to instructional materials. Well-designed programs like Davidson's *Math Blaster* can automatically direct students to additional remedial instruction should they not be adequately responding to test items provided by the program.

In many educational computing programs assessment can be largely hidden from students by integrating test functions into the overall curriculum. In a hypermedia program like *Bailey's Book House* (Edmark) students are asked to complete certain tasks (click behind a dog with their computer mouse, go through a door, etc.) based on their understanding of different prepositions. If they understand the concept, then they complete the task that is asked of them by the curriculum.

Bailey's Book House (Edmark)
http://www.edmark.com/prod/house/bailey/

This type of informal assessment is very well suited to the way that computers work. It is also closely related to, but not precisely the same, as authentic assessment.

Authentic assessment is a relatively new concept. It argues that assessment should be based on the demonstration of a specific skill being implemented. This approach is much more qualitative in nature and fits well within constructivist models of instruction. An example of authentic assessment would be to have students develop portfolios of their work. In a computer course, like the one for which you are using this textbook, this might involve your developing a portfolio that includes essays on critical educational and social issues, the development of computer-based lesson plans, and so on. Authentic assessment techniques would require students to turn in portfolios having used a word processor to generate text and even illustrations, thus demonstrating a high-level use of the computer for instructional tasks. Researching course content using the Internet would further demonstrate computer competencies.

Any assessment system has to have a set of criteria on which it is based. This can be done through informal observation and qualitative judgments, or be based on a set of rubrics and be linked to demonstrable skills.

How Do Computers Change the Work of Teachers?

We began this chapter with a letter to Ann Landers. Ann was correct to reply that the impact of computers on the curriculum will continue. Cuban (1986) was also correct when he stated that:

> teachers will alter classroom behavior selectively to the degree that certain technologies help them solve problems they define as important and avoid eroding their classroom authority. They will either resist or be indifferent to changes that they see as irrelevant to their practice, that increase their burdens, without adding benefits to their students' learning or that weaken their control of the classroom. (pp. 70–71)

Computers will change the work of teachers based on their availability to students outside the classroom. This availability raises questions of access and equity that we address in the chapter on ethics. The availability of computers outside the classroom will work in a dialectical relation to what goes on in the classroom. The more computers are used outside the classroom, the greater will be the demand for their use inside the classroom.

D. A. Dockterman (1991) believed that teachers will be able to respond to these demands only if educational curricular software support three things: teacher control, pedagogical flexibility, and accessibility (p. 136). By supporting teacher control, Dockterman meant that implementing the use of technology in a curriculum area or classroom management must reduce the difficulty of a teacher's classroom management tasks. There will be change in teachers' work when the technology reflects the classroom management needs of teachers.

By supporting pedagogical flexibility, Dockterman meant that the technology introduced must support the various ways teachers teach or are expected to teach. Only if technology goes with the flow or the direction of teaching and curriculum will it have an impact.

By supporting accessibility, Dockterman meant that teachers must have access to technology where they work, both inside and outside of the classroom. Thus the school must reflect the growing reality of home and work. The school must have computers to enable students and teachers to do the work that schools are intended to do—teaching and learning.

Our review of software related to curriculum areas and methodology is encouraging because it demonstrates that there is a lot out there to support teacher control and pedagogical flexibility.

While there is growing access, there are still questions about accessibility. There are still questions as to how well teachers are prepared to teach with technology. We hope this book prepares you to do well when teaching with technology. What still remains is a question of the accessibility of computers in schools for teaching and learning. Although the availability in schools is growing explosively, it remains unclear how much and what forms of availability are needed for teachers and students to have the access they need. What contributes to the difficulty of answering this question is the growing availability of computers outside the schools.

Computers are changing the nature and character of the curriculum at all levels of the educational system. As seen with the example from Ann Landers, what teachers can expect from students, what they are in fact receiving from them in terms of work, is being changed by the increasing availability of the computer.

Our ability to teach is also being changed. Almost every segment of the curriculum is being affected. Authors such as Lewis Perelman (1992) argued that we are moving toward a new model of education, which he referred to as hyperlearning. He predicted that schooling as we have known it is coming to an end. New technologies are making the expert lecturer obsolete. According to Perelman, as the world goes increasingly online

> schools will be transformed from a centralized architectural and bureaucratic *structure* to a dispersed information and service *channel*. Technological opportunity and economic necessity, will give the individual learner of any age at least as many choices of "schools" as the television audience now has of cable TV channels. (p. 57)

Perelman is probably correct. As this chapter has emphasized, even without going online, even without assuming models of distance education, the new computer technology radically alters the traditional presentation of curriculum and what the teacher can or cannot do in the classroom.

In conclusion, technology is increasingly part of curriculum studies. Just as the teacher from Quebec writing to Ann Landers cannot ignore how technology is reshaping his classroom, so too is it impossible for us to ignore its impact on the curriculum. We have passed a threshold grounded in technology, which brings with it a new curriculum and to a significant degree, new models of instruction for our classrooms.

QUESTIONS FOR REFLECTION AND DISCUSSION

1. What are the four reasons educational technology has failed in the past? What does that tell you for your own teaching?

2. In what ways can computer technology help teachers in whatever language arts approach their school or district is committed to?

3. How can computers help teachers to teach mathematical concepts at the earliest developmentally appropriate time?

4. How can computers help a teacher to give students an experientially rich science learning environment?

5. How can computer software assist students in developing common ground through social studies activities?

6. In what ways do computer "art" programs assist all students to develop their artistic abilities?

7. How can computer programs be used to assist students to learn higher order thinking skills?

8. Under what circumstances can a teacher use computers to improve teaching techniques?

9. In what specific ways are computers changing the work of teachers?

ACTIVITIES

1. Go online to find Internet sites that include information on curriculum standards and guidelines for the subjects and grade levels you teach.

2. Go online and find three lesson plans for teaching. Analyze them for how they would assist you in your own teaching.

3. Find a traditional lesson plan (one without computer technology). Analyze it to see how a student using computer technology at home might approach the activities and assessments differently from a student who does not have computers at home. Does Quebec Quandary at the beginning of this chapter have a point?

4. Design what could be a portfolio for the curriculum that is included in the content of this textbook. Make sure that it follows a model based on authentic assessment.

EXERCISE FOR FURTHER DEVELOPMENT OF YOUR REFLECTIVE PRACTICE FOR TEACHING WITH COMPUTER TECHNOLOGY

Teachers as professionals need to be able to teach a school's curriculum. Basic to effective teaching is a solid knowledge of the subject matter. Computer technology is giving people access to primary documents of learning. With that access comes the ability to change the data source. Read the following presentation on digital alteration of documents and reflect on the following issues related to teaching practice:

1. How does the ability of people to change accurate subject matter to inaccurate subject matter impact the ability of teachers to deliver good teaching?

2. As a teacher, how will you work to ascertain that the computer information you provide to students is accurate?

Digital Alteration of Documents

Winston Smith, the main character in George Orwell's *1984*, had a job in the Ministry of Truth that involved rewriting history. Newspapers, books, and other printed materials were recalled and rewritten by him to suit changing political trends and needs.

Offending passages and names were eliminated from existing texts.

In a predigital or pre-computer culture, rewriting history in this manner was not realistic. Rewriting a book so that "undesirable" information was edited out was extremely time consuming and not always complete or accurate. In a computer or digital context, the alteration of text becomes much simpler. Anyone who has used a word processor with a search and delete function knows how easy it is to alter data. A name can be searched out through an entire record, and then modified or eliminated with the touch of a few keystrokes.

As we proceed in a post-typographic culture, putting more and more of our information onto massive databases, it will become easier and easier to control and manipulate historical records. It is not hard to imagine how a repressive political regime such as that found in communist China might take advantage of the ability to control information to its own advantage. Any book or article could be searched for politically undesirable comments. Such comments could be eliminated from online information systems very easily. Politically suspect authors could likewise have all of their writings automatically purged from a system.

The alteration of digitally coded information is not limited to just textual sources. Photographs can easily be altered using computers. Sometimes, there are advantages to using this technology that actually protects the rights of individuals. In New York State, for example, prison inmates are required to be photographed shaven so that they can be more easily identified if they escape from prison. Rabbi Shlomo Helbrans, the leader of a small Hasidic sect, who was sentenced to 4 to 12 years in prison for kidnapping a teenage boy, called on a passage from *Leviticus* ("Ye shall not round the corners of your heads, neither shalt thou mar the corners of thy beard.") in order to keep from having his beard shaved off. He argued that his constitutional rights, under the First Amendment, required that he be allowed to keep his beard. A solution was eventually found: precise measurements being made of the rabbi's face and then photographs of him scanned into a computer. Through the use of visualization software, the rabbi's facial features, without a beard, were reconstructed (James, 1994, p. A16).

Altering digital photographic sources to distort reality and mislead the viewer, however, represents a serious problem. With digital photography it becomes a relatively simple matter to put someone at the scene of a crime who actually was not there. This is not necessarily a new phenomenon. All that is new is how easily, quickly, and professionally it can be accomplished.

Photographic sources have always been subject to alteration and manipulation. Such alterations, however, are difficult to do and relatively easy to detect. In a digital context, the alteration of photographic information is relatively easy to accomplish and almost impossible to detect. Fred Richtin (1990) refered to this whole area of digital photography as "hyper-photography" (p. 141).

Hyper-photographs cannot be trusted as historical documents. Nor can we really be sure that a historical database has not been tampered with or altered. In the *Gutenberg Galaxy* Marshall McLuhan emphasized how the transition from manuscript to print or typographic culture represented an important means of standardizing information and establishing definitive texts and sources. The ability to easily alter digital databases, whether in the form of pictures or words, means that we made it more difficult to establish definitive texts or data sets.

How can we know that a set of photographs accurately portray what they seem to be portraying? How can we know that a newspaper record, a government file, or some similar source has not been altered electronically? We have the potential, in a digital and electronic context, to live in a world in which data looks more medieval and modern, in which there is the potential for multiple texts and sources between which there can be serious discrepancies and differences. How are we to determine the real thing? Will we ever know the truth?

📖   Sources

Bruner, J. S. (1971). The process of education revisited. *Phi Delta Kappan, 52*(1), 18–22.

Cuban, L. (1986). *Teachers and machines: The classroom use of technology since 1920.* New York: Teachers College Press.

Dockterman, D. A. (1991). *Great teaching in the one computer classroom.* Cambridge, MA: Tom Snyder Productions.

James, G. (1994). "Computer replaces razor for Rabbi's prison picture," *The New York Times*, December 29, p. A16.

McLuhan, M. (1962). *The Gutenberg galaxy: The making of typographic man.* Toronto: University of Toronto Press.

National Council for the Social Studies. (1994). *Expectation of excellence: Curriculum standards for social studies.* Washington, DC: National Council for the Social Studies.

National Council of Teachers of English and International Reading Association. (1996). *Standards for the English language arts.* Urbana, IL: National Council of Teachers of English.

National Council of Teachers of Mathematics. (1989). *Curriculum and evaluation standards for school mathematics.* Reston, VA: National Council of Teachers of Mathematics.

National Endowment for the Arts. (1988). *Towards civilization: A report on arts education.* Washington, DC: National Endowment for the Arts.

National Research Council. (1996). *National science education standards.* Washington, DC: National Academy Press.

Papert, S. (1993). *The children's machine: Rethinking school in the age of the computer.* New York: Basic Books.

Perelman, L. J. (1992). *School's out.* New York: Avon.

Perkins, D. (1992). *Smart schools: Better thinking and learning for every child.* New York: Basic Books.

Richtlin, F. (1990). *In Our Own Image: The coming revolution in photography.* New York: Aperture.

TECHNOLOGY FOR INCLUSION

Adaptive Input Devices, Adaptive Output Devices, Students With Disabilities, Technology for Inclusion

A computer can be arms, legs, mouth, ears, or eyes to a disabled child.

—Tom Snyder

Case Study

Mrs. Thomas has been teaching first grade for 11 years. This year, for the first time, her class includes two children with disabilities. Carl has cerebral palsy, which has not affected his cognitive abilities, but has resulted in physical limitations. He uses a wheelchair and has little control over his fine motor skills, making writing almost impossible. He is unable to speak clearly enough to communicate with the teacher or the other children.

The other child with disabilities in her class is Shawna, who has very limited vision. She is unable to see standard size letters and words. Mrs. Thomas uses cooperative learning and thematic units in her teaching. Her goal is to have all students participate both academically and socially and she wants to find out how technology can help her reach this goal for Carl and Shawna.

When a teacher like Mrs. Thomas has students with different needs, with diverse cultural and linguistic backgrounds, and who learn in different ways in her class, she must address a variety of learning styles. She must learn what technology can do for all her students and how it can be adapted to meet the specific needs of children with disabilities.

Children with disabilities are able to take advantage of the benefits of computers and related technology through the use of **adaptive computer interfaces** and specialized software. Computer input and output devices are described in Appendix A. The standard input devices are the keyboard and the mouse. Output devices include monitors, printers, and speakers. These devices can be adapted in many ways to provide access for children with disabilities.

Adaptive Computer Interface: a computer interface that has been adapted for individuals with special needs.

Assistive Technology Viewer (Vanderbilt University)
http://peabody.vanderbilt.edu/projects/proposed/asttech/home.htm

Adaptive Input Devices

Adaptive input devices enable children with special needs to activate and send information to the computer. Standard keyboards can be modified for children who are unable to use them. In one or more of the following ways, keys used for a particular program can be marked to help children locate them more easily.

1. Caps with Braille or raised characters can be attached to the surface of keys.
2. A template or overlay can be placed over a keyboard so that only certain keys are visible.
3. A keyguard can be put over the keyboard to allow children to touch only one key at a time without accidentally activating other keys.
4. The auto repeat function can be disabled.
5. Keys can be marked with colored stickers.

Alternative Keyboard: a keyboard adapted to meet the special needs of an individual.

If modification of the standard keyboard is not sufficient to meet students' needs, **alternative keyboards** can provide access to the computer. Alternative keyboards are **input devices** that replace or work in addition to the standard keyboard and can be modified to meet the needs of individual children. Alternative keyboards are usually larger in size than standard keyboards, have large keys, greater spacing between keys, and increased sensitivity of the keys.

Input Device: a device such as a keyboard or mouse that allows information to be put into a computer.

Muppet Learning Keys (Sunburst Communications), for example, is an alternative keyboard especially designed for young children. Its numbers and letters are arranged in numerical and alphabetical sequence and the function keys are marked with pictures and colors. *Intellikeys* (IntelliTools) is a flexible and versatile keyboard that can be programmed in a variety of ways. It plugs directly into the computer and does not interfere with the regular keyboard. Different overlays can be used to create individualized keyboards geared specifically to the needs of the students and the lessons or concepts being taught.

Trackball: a type of pointing device similar to a mouse. Unlike a mouse, it is stationary and can be used in areas with restricted space.

Sunburst Communications
http://www.nysunburst.com

Intellikeys (RJ Cooper)
http://www.rjcooper.com/page4.htm

For children unable to use a mouse or **trackball**, devices such as the *SAM-JOY* (RJ Cooper) switch-adapted, mouse device, **joystick** can be used as an input device. This joystick controls a cursor in the same way as a traditional mouse. Less sensitive than a mouse, it allows children with physical disabilities to manipulate a cursor on the computer screen. *HeadMaster Plus* (Prentke Romich) allows the user's head movements to control the mouse. Mouse button functions are activated by a **puff switch**.

Joystick: a small box-like object with a moving stick and buttons used primarily for games, educational software and computer-aided design systems.

Puff Switch: a type of computer switch input that is activated by sipping or puffing through a tube.

Headmaster Plus™ (Prentke Romich)
http://www.prentrom.com/access/hdmaster.html

Sam-Joystick (RJ Cooper)
http://www.rjcooper.com/page15.htm

Voice Recognition: a computer technology that translates spoken words into commands or text in the computer.

A touch-sensitive screen, such as the *TouchWindow* (Edmark), may be less demanding than a mouse or other input device for some children. Touch input is a direct and natural way for students to interact with the computer. Students can make selections, move objects, pull down menus, and draw graphics by touching the screen. The *TouchWindow* can also be removed from the monitor and used as a single switch activated by touch.

TouchWindow (Edmark)
http://www.edmark.com/prod/tw/

Interface: the place where a connection is made between two elements. User interface is where people communicate with programs. Hardware interface is the connection between devices and components of the computer.

Voice recognition technology converts spoken words into computer input. Voice input is a much more natural **interface** than the keyboard or mouse. When a child says "Show me a lion," for example, information about lions will be presented. Spoken words can also be converted into text on the screen, making it possible for students with physical disabilities to write. Software systems such as *DragonDictate* (Dragon Systems, Inc.) can be used with DOS- and Windows-based computers to provide **voice input** capabilities. On many newer computers, voice recognition is incorporated into the standard operating system so no additional software is needed. On all of the new Apple Macintosh computers, for example, you can speak into the computer's microphone and it can be "trained" to recognize specific commands.

Voice Input: the translation of vocal instructions into executable commands in a computer.

Dragon Systems, Inc.
http://www.dragonsys.com/

Pointing devices provide a way for children who are unable to use their hands to access the keyboard. Electronic **pointing devices** allow children to operate the computer by means of a **headset** and control unit that translates eye gaze or position and head movement into cursor movements on the screen. Nonelectronic pointing devices, such as a headstick or mouthstick, can be used to strike keys on the keyboard. These can be worn on the head, held in the mouth, strapped to the chin, or held in the hand.

Pointing Device: a sensing device that translates movement into executable commands in a computer.

Headset: a head-mounted device that control devices are set in.

Switches are recommended only when no other input is within an individual's physical capabilities. A switch is an on–off device that can be easily activated. There are many different types of switches available for students with different needs. Some are activated by blowing, some by pushing an easily grasped lever, others by depressing a button. Switches are almost always used with software that displays a scanning array. A **scanning array** is a group of letters, numbers, symbols, or other choices highlighted on the computer screen, one at a time. The desired choice is selected by activating a switch.

Scanning Array: a group of letters, numbers or symbols highlighted on a computer screen that can be selected by the user, one at a time.

A **keyboard emulator** is a hardware device that connects to the computer and allows input from sources other than the standard keyboard. Keyboard emulators are capable of running regular software using alternative input devices such as switches, alternate keyboards, scanning, morse code, on-screen keyboards, and augmentative communication devices. *Discover:Kenx* (Don Johnston, Incorporated) is a keyboard emulator used to access

Keyboard Emulator: a hardware device that connects to the computer and allows input from sources other than a standard keyboard.

Macintosh computers and the *Adaptive Firmware Card* (Don Johnston Incorporated) is for Apple II computers.

Don Johnston, Incorporated
www.donjohnston.com

Adaptive Output Devices

Output Device: a device that displays information sent from a computer.

Computer output devices include monitors, printers, tactile devices, and speakers. The most common computer **output device** is the monitor, which can be adapted for students with special needs to produce enlarged text and graphics using either hardware or software.

Digitized Speech: speech that has been recorded and converted to digital format to be used by computers and electronic communication devices.

Printer output can be adapted to produce either large print or Braille. Many word processing programs and other software packages are capable of producing large bold print. Braille printers create raised dot characters that can be read tactually. Refreshable tactual output can be produced using Braille output hardware. This type of device electronically raises small pinheads on a surface emulating Braille, which then can be read by touch.

Assistive Technology: technology that assists individuals in doing something they could not do by themselves.

As described in Appendix A, speech output can be either synthesized or digitized. Synthesized speech devices can generate an unlimited vocabulary and are inexpensive, but they produce mechanical and robot-like sounds. **Digitized speech** is of higher quality because a real voice is recorded, digitized, and then played back. Digitized speech requires a large amount of memory and is limited to words that have been previously recorded.

Students With Disabilities

Adaptive Technology: is the use of computer—hardware and software—to help challenged individuals overcome a limiting condition in their lives.

Students' needs vary greatly according to their disabilities. Many students have combinations of disabilities that make adaptation of technology even more individualized. When deciding on **assistive** and **adaptive technology**, the focus should be on providing technology that will give students with disabilities the support they need to be successful in the classroom setting.

Students With Learning Disabilities. Students with learning disabilities make up about one half of all the students from age 3 to 21 who have disabilities. Learning disabled children often have problems with written or spoken language. In addition, they may have trouble concentrating, lack coordination, have difficulty with auditory or visual processing, have poor memory, and have problems with abstract reasoning.

Because children with learning disabilities find it very difficult to organize their thoughts and get them down on paper, word processing software is particularly helpful. With its capability to edit text before it is printed out, word processing helps children with learning disabilities produce neat and legible documents. Features such as **outliners**, spell checkers, **grammar checkers**, and thesauruses give them additional support for their writing. Word processing software with speech output, such as *Dr. Peet's Talkwriter* (Hartley) and *Write:OutLoud* (Don Johnston, Incorporated) help students with their writing by allowing them to hear what they have written. Word prediction software such as *Co:Writer* (Don Johnston, Incorporated) can help decrease children's struggles with spelling. Word processing software such as *Creative Writer 2* (Microsoft), which has sound effects, graphics, and a variety of typefaces and sizes of print, provides additional motivation for children who have great difficulty writing.

> **Outliner:** a type of software that assists in organizing ideas and developing outlines for projects.

> **Grammar Check:** software that checks for grammar errors.

Hartley Software
http://www.bytesandpieces.com/Publists/Hartley.html

Don Johnston, Incorporated
www.donjohnston.com

Additional support for language and literacy development can be provided for students with learning disabilities through interactive story software such as *Just Grandma and Me* (Broderbund), *K.C. & Clyde in Fly Ball* (Don Johnston, Incorporated), and *The Adventures of Ricky Raccoon* (Thomson Learning Tools). In these types of hypermedia programs students make choices that determine how the story progresses. Stories are read aloud giving students the opportunity to hear spoken words at the same time they see them on the screen. Students can select words to have read again and often have them explained with pictures, sounds, and actions. Illustrations and animations provide additional comprehension and meaning to reading experiences.

The Adventures of Ricky Raccoon
http://www.zdnet.com/familypc/content/970314/ftsw/bk07_ricky.html

Drill and Practice Software: software that drills students in a specific subject area or skill such as multiplication.

Drill and practice software such as *Math Blaster* (Davidson Associates)—with game-like formats, structured content, and immediate reinforcement—appeal to children with learning disabilities and tend to increase motivation and time on task. For help in understanding concepts, multimedia programs that present information in a variety of ways can be used to augment and clarify information.

Math Blaster (Davidson & Associates)
http://www.davd.com/blaster/math.html

Hypermedia Stacks: a hypermedia data set.

Students with learning disabilities may have difficulty demonstrating their understanding of and using traditional methods of oral and written reports. Multimedia tools can be very helpful to these children. They can develop **hypermedia stacks** using *HyperStudio*, *HyperCard*, or other multimedia authoring systems.

Adaptive Technology on Wheels

Helping teachers become familiar with new computing technologies is always a challenge. In the case of teachers of young children with special needs, learning about new technologies is even more important. Adaptive technology can help teachers reach children in new ways that have not been possible before. Problems arise, however, from the fact that technologies are constantly changing and often software and hardware must be specially adapted to individual student needs.

An exciting in-service model for working with teachers, as well as assessing the technology needs of children, is the Prekindergarten Resource Instruction Mobile for Exceptional Education

(P.R.I.M.E. Time). This modified recreational vehicle is driven out to schools by Nina Kaspar, a specialist working in the prekindergarten program for children with disabilities in the Dade County Public Schools.

Loaded onto the vehicle are two computers, an extensive software library, and a wide range of adaptive technology hardware. Nina, with her associate Sheila Miguel, goes out to different schools and tries out programs with children with special needs and models the use of specialized equipment and software for teachers.

This system allows teachers the opportunity to see state-of-the-art hardware and software and to learn how to use it from experts in the field. Even more valuable is the opportunity provided by P.R.I.M.E. to assess the needs of individual students. The P.R.I.M.E. program loans hardware such as intellikeys, switches, and communication devices for teachers to try out, as well as different software packages. As a means of modeling the use of adaptive technology for teachers in the field, the project shows great promise.

Students With Speech and Language Disabilities.

Students with speech and language disorders make up about one fourth of the five million children with disabilities. Speech and language impairment includes difficulty with articulation or voice, stuttering, or language disorders. Some children who are unable to produce intelligible speech are also unable to write or even to make their wishes known through facial expressions and gestures. Technology can provide these children with the means to communicate through **augmentative** and **alternative communication** (AAC). Augmentative and alternative communication ranges from very simple procedures like physical gestures, picture communication boards, or manual sign languages to high-technology systems that include dedicated communication devices and computer systems programmed to provide communication capabilities.

Augmentative Communication: a set of approaches, strategies, and methods used to enhance the communication abilities of individuals who do not speak or whose speech is unintelligible.

Alternative Communication: communication by other than traditional means.

Dedicated communication devices provide speech output for children unable to produce intelligible speech. Ranging in cost from fairly inexpensive to very expensive, these devices include *SpeakEasy* (AbleNet, Inc.), *Wolf* (ADAMLAB), *Say-It-All* (Innocomp) and *Liberator* (Prentke Romich Co.). In addition to cost, these devices also vary in voice (intelligibility, gender, and volume) input methods, ability to program, visual or printed output, and computer access. Selection of the most appropriate communication device for a student should be a team approach involving parents, teachers, and other professionals who work with the student.

Speak Easy (Able Net, Incorporated)
http://www.ablenetinc.com/commaids.html#SPKEZY

Wolf (ADAMLAB)
http://www.wcresa.k12.mi.us/adlab/devices.htm

Say-It-All (Innocomp)
http://www.sayitall.com/innocomp/product/say-it-all/

Liberator II™ (Prentke Romich)
http://www.prentrom.com/speech/lib.html

Speech Synthesizer: a device that takes information on the computer and translates it into speech.

Computers can also be used as communication devices. Talking word processors, as well as *Muppet Learning Keys* (Sunburst Communications) or *Intellikeys* (IntelliTools) programmed with a **speech synthesizer**, can provide communication capabilities for children with speech and language problems. The increased portability and decreasing cost of **laptop** and **notebook computers** make the use of computers as communication devices more and more feasible.

Laptop Computer: a portable computer.

Intellikeys (IntelliTools)
http://www.intellitools.com/IntelliKeys.html

Notebook Computer: a very small portable computer.

Software such as *Talk Time With Tucker* (Laureate Learning Systems) is designed to encourage speech and vocalization in children with speech impairments. Using this voice-activated program, children are able to make Tucker, the program's main character, move and talk by speaking or making sounds into the microphone.

Talk Time With Tucker (Laureate Learning Systems)
http://www.llsys.com

Children with Limited Cognitive Abilities. About 12% of students with disabilities are mentally handicapped, which is defined as significantly subaverage intellectual performance along with deficits in adaptive behavior. Adaptive computer input devices such as an alternative keyboard, touch screen, joystick, or switches can make the computer more accessible for these children.

Software that includes spoken directions and responses, as well as programs that present only one item at a time and present information in very small units, or in which information can be repeated as many times as needed, are appropriate for children with limited cognitive abilities. Software focusing on attention to a task, visual discrimination, visual and auditory memory, sequencing, discrimination, following directions, memory, or problem-solving skills is also helpful.

Programs such as *Creative Magic* (Laureate Learning Systems) introduce and reinforce cause and effect and turn taking and can be accessed through several different input methods. *Teenage Switch Progression* (RJ Cooper and Associates) for cognitively challenged teenagers uses simulations, age-appropriate music, and humor to teach cause and effect and then progresses to purposeful switch interactions.

Creative Magic (Laureate Learning Systems)
http://www.llsys.com/

Teenage Switch Progression (RJ Cooper and Associates)
http://www.rjcooper.com/

Students With Emotional and Behaviorial Disorders. Students with emotional and behavioral disorders make up about one tenth of all children with disabilities. These children can benefit from using computers with other children in small groups. Software such as *Decisions, Decisions* (Tom Snyder Productions) and *Where in the World Is Carmen Sandiego?* (Broderbund) can facilitate sharing, cooperation, and social interaction. For many of these children, behavior improves and their attention span increases when they use computers. Computers are associated with fun and can be set at levels to promote success. The machines do not make judgments. Working on the computer is a symbol of success and gives these children status.

Children With Hearing Impairments. Children with hearing impairments make up only a small percentage of all children with disabilities. Hearing loss, which can range from mild to profoundly deaf, affects children's communication skills, particularly their speech. Children with hearing problems can use standard computer input devices but may not be able to access speech and sound output.

Many hearing-impaired children have difficulty with standard written English and can benefit from software such as *Write This Way* (Don Johnston, Incorporated), which provides help with spelling, grammar, and punctuation. Software such as *Sign Language for Everyone* (IVI Publishing) helps hearing-impaired students learn sign language. This program teaches the structure of American Sign Language (ASL) and the importance of facial expression and body language. It also teaches the manual alphabet, along with vocabulary and grammar skills. Children can type in any word and see a video of how to properly communicate its meaning in ASL. The children's story *Rosie's Walk*, by Pat Hutchins, is now available on CD-ROM for both hearing and deaf children. Produced by Texas School for the Deaf, it tells the story in both ASL and Signed English. Five games reinforce the language and concepts from the story.

Write This Way (Don Johnston Incorporated)
http://www.donjohnston.com/

Sign Language for Everyone (IVI Publishing)
http://www.ivi.com/corpsite/index.htm

Telecommunications is a very promising use of technology for hearing-impaired students. The Internet and electronic mail allow hearing-impaired students to communicate on an equal footing with hearing students using written rather than spoken communication. Written interactions online provide motivation for hearing-impaired students to improve their language arts skills. They develop receptive and expressive English writing and language skills by e-mailing messages to others.

Children With Visual Disabilites. Children with visual disabilities include both low vision and blind students. Computer input adaptations for these children include Braille keyboards, scanning devices, and voice input. Adaptive output includes enlarging the size of visual materials (both video and printer output), or transforming visual information into either tactile or auditory format.

Software for children with visual disabilities includes *VisAbility* (AiSquared), which is a low vision reading system. This program magnifies print by scanning in text and having it magnified on the screen. *Zoom Text* (AiSquared) is software that magnifies the output of software on the monitor.

Zoom Text (Ai Squared)
http://www.aisquared.com

VisAbility (Ai Squared)
http://www.aisquared.com/

Screen reader software such as *outSPOKEN* (Alva Access Group, Inc.) speaks everything on the screen, including menus, text, and punctuation. **Text-to-speech** is speech output equipment that will pronounce whatever text is input. Talking word processors use this technology to convert written text into synthesized speech. Optical scanning systems can scan textbooks and other printed materials and convert them to Braille or speech output.

Text-to-Speech: text-to-speech capability converts text into speech on the computer using a speech synthesizer.

outSPOKEN (Alva Access Group, Incorporated)
http://aagi.com/docs/oswpre.htm

Students With Physical Disabilities. Physical disabilities can range from mild limitations in the ability to walk to quadriplegia with speech and cognitive disabilities. Adaptive technology for students with physical disabilities includes alternative keyboards, voice input, switch input, and eye controlled systems. Students with physical disabilities can use switch and scanning word processing software, along with word prediction, to write reports and then computers with speech synthesizers can read the reports they have generated to others. *Blocks in Motion* (Don Johnston, Incorporated) features on-screen manipulatives for students of many ability levels. It is accessible by switch, keyboard, and mouse. Students with physical disabilities can manipulate and build with blocks. It helps develop problem-solving and creativity skills.

Blocks in Motion (Don Johnston Home Page)
http://www.donjohnston.com/

Telecommunications holds promise for education, recreation, and the pursuit of vocational interests. Using adaptive computer access, these students can learn to use e-mail, the Internet and other online activities that can facilitate their integration into their local communities and the larger world.

Selected Adaptive Technology Resources Available on the Internet

AbleNet, Incorpated
www.ablenetinc.com

AbleNet, Incorporated develops and markets products and services to meet the needs of children and adults with severe disabilities.

Arkenstone, Inc.
http://www.arkenstone.org

Provider of reading machines for people with visual and reading disabilities.

Articulate Systems, Inc.
http://www.dragonsys.com

Specialists in Voice User Interface and Voice Communication technology.

AssisTech
www.assisttech.com

Company specializing in Assistive Technology.

Aurora Systems, Incorporated
www.djtech.com/aurora

Provides software to help individuals with learning disabilities and prople who require augmentative communication.

Blazie Engineering, Inc.
http://www.blazie.com/

Develops and manufactures products for people with visual impairments.

CAST, Inc. (Center for Applied Special Technology)
http://www.cast.org

A nonprofit organization whose mission is to expand the opportunities for all people through the use of innovative technology.

Closing The Gap, Inc.
http://www.closingthegap.com

Valuable information source on the use of computers for individuals with special needs.

Gus Communications, Inc.
www.gusinc.com

Computer-based communication systems.

IBM Special Needs Solutions
www.austin.ibm.com/sns/index.html

Products which enhance computer access and learning for people with special needs.

Innocomp
www.sayitall.com

Manufactures and distributes products relating to augmentative communication.

LS & S Group
www.lssgroup.com

Specializes in products for the visually impaired.

Mayer-Johnson Co.
www.mayer-johnson.com

Developer of picture communication symbols used in augmentative communication.

Microsoft - Accessibility and Disabilities Group
www.handiware.com

Solutions for adapted access, augmentative communication, and low-vision needs.

Technology for Inclusion

The purpose of inclusion is to provide an effective learning environment for students who exhibit a wide range of abilities within the context of the regular curriculum. In inclusive classrooms, students of different abilities can learn and socialize together if they are given the right support. Computers and related technologies can help provide the means to adapt classroom activities in order to provide for students' diverse needs and help make inclusion work.

Technology can facilitate interaction among students of different abilities. Technology can be integrated into the curriculum to facilitate the teaching and learning of program objectives. It can offer a range of activities that provide challenge and success for students with and without disabilities.

Students who have difficulty communicating, playing, and/or interacting with their environment can benefit from technology. Technology can provide students who are unable to speak with the means by which to communicate, and in turn, can promote social skills and interaction with peers. Technology can also provide opportunities for students with disabilities to participate in play, which is crucial for their development and learning. Students with and without disabilities can play together using adaptive input devices and computer games.

Students with disabilities can participate in the arts using adaptive technology. In spite of their inability to hold a crayon or control a paintbrush, they can create their own art using the computer with special input devices. Students of varying abilities can work together on creative projects using painting and drawing software such as *My Paint* (Laureate Learning Systems, Incorporated) and *Kid Pix* (Broderbund).

Laureate Learning Systems
http://www.llsys.com/

Technology can be used to adapt learning activities so that all students have the opportunity to participate. For example, students who are nonverbal can use communication devices or computers with adaptive input and speech output to participate in language development activities. They can take part in a play, tell a story, or provide instructions for a group game using speech output devices. Using adaptive input devices, students with diverse abilities can work together at the computer. Technology allows students of different abilities to work cooperatively on a project and allows those with disabilities to contribute at their level of competence.

Software for inclusive settings should be suitable for a wide range of ages to facilitate its use across grade levels and for multiple purposes so that it can be integrated into different curriculum areas and different classroom situations. It should include basic utilities such as spell checking, text-to-speech capability, and **word prediction** that can help students with different needs.

Word Prediction: a special software that guesses or anticipates a word that is being typed by its first letters and location in a sentence.

Teachers working with students with special needs can take special advantage of databases on the Internet, as well as use it to communicate with other teachers who are working with students with the same or similar special needs.

In conclusion, computers can be adapted for access by students of varying abilities. It is important that these adaptations allow students to experience control and to actively participate in the learning process. Adaptive technology needs to be available not only in classrooms, but on the playground, at home, and across all environments. It needs to be simple enough for students and their families to use. Adaptive technology should promote increased independence for students and should not draw attention to their disabilities.

Technology for students with disabilities is becoming more powerful and more transparent because of miniaturization. Advances in technology, along with legislation to support its use in classrooms, should make technology more available for students with disabilities.

The cost of technology can be a major barrier for students with disabilities. But cost is not the only concern. Even when funding is available and the technology is obtained, it may not lead to successful use. Time needs to be spent assessing students' needs and capabilities, helping students and families become comfortable with the technology, and with installation, troubleshooting, and maintenance of the equipment.

QUESTIONS FOR REFLECTION AND DISCUSSION

1. What is meant by the term *adaptive technology*?

2. How does adaptive technology empower children with disabilities?

3. What are some of the problems, both ethical and financial, associated with the use of adaptive technology?

4. What is the current legal status of the use of assistive and adaptive technology in schools? Describe the legislation that led up to the current status.

5. What are the implications of the cost of adaptive technology for children with disabilities?

6. Describe how input devices can be adapted to provide access to computers for children with a variety of abilities.

7. How can word processing software support the writing process for students with learning disabilities?

8. Describe some of the unique capabilities of the Internet for students with disabilities.

9. How can technology help children with disabilities learn, play, and communicate with other children in the classroom?

10. Describe how technology can augment abilities and compensate for disabilities.

11. How can a desktop publishing program be used to include children of varying abilities in the creation of a class newspaper?

12. Should students who need adaptive technologies to learn be guaranteed access to computers?

ACTIVITIES

1. Visit an inclusive classroom where children are using technology. Observe how technology is being used and what adaptations are being made to the standard input and output devices.

2. Visit Web sites of adaptive hardware and software vendors listed in the chapter and find out more about their products.

3. Visit Web sites of organizations such as Alliance for Technology Access (http://marin.org/npo/ata/), Closing the Gap (http://www.closingthe gap.com), Council for Exceptional Children (http://cec.sped.org), and Trace Research and Development Center (http://www.trace.wisc.edu/). Find out about the purpose of each organization, whom they serve, and what services they provide, particularly as related to technology.

4. Interview a student with a disability who uses technology. Find out his/her perceptions of the ways in which technology affects his/her life.

EXERCISE FOR FURTHER DEVELOPMENT OF YOUR REFLECTIVE PRACTICE FOR TEACHING WITH COMPUTER TECHNOLOGY

Teachers as professionals need to be able to teach all students in relation to their level of human development and learning. Computer technology helps us reach such a goal by facilitating inclusion. Read the following presentation on "Wireheads" and reflect on the following issues related to teaching practice:

1. How can a teacher work with students and parents to ensure that they have the computer technology assistance that they need and to which they are entitled?

2. How can technology go beyond assisting students to navigate through learning and move to the point of shaping them to be simply docile and compliant students?

Wireheads

In Samuel Delaney's novel *Nova* the characters are fitted with sockets on each of their wrists and at the base of their spines. These sockets connect them to a series of devices that they operate through psychoneural energy. Such a system, which is described at length by other science fiction writers such as John Brunner and William Gibson, represents the ultimate human–machine interface.

Underlying the desire that some people have to link their consciousness to a machine is a complex merging of humans with the mechanical world. In popular television programs such as "The Bionic Man," "The Bionic Woman," and "Mantis," humans are merged with machines. In doing so, they are given superhuman powers, becoming part human and part machine.

This desire to merge with machines is reflected in much of the romanticism underlying cyberspace. In novels such as Gibson's *Neuromancer* and *Count Zero*, "counsel cowboys" jack directly into the matrix and cruise through vast graphic representations of information and, ultimately, power.

Jacking into a computer and into cyberspace is compelling because it suggests the possibility of being immortal. If an individual's consciousness is transferred to a computer network or memory bank, then in theory as long as the computer or network exists so too will the human consciousness. Even if a network is destroyed, back-up copies will guarantee that an entity will not perish.

Just how far-fetched is this notion? Hans Moravec (1988), one of the country's leading robot researchers and a professor at Carnegie Mellon University, argued in his book *Mind Children* that in the next generation we probably will have the capability of downloading a human consciousness into a computer where it will be able to control robot mechanisms.

The idea of wiring humans to machines is not totally new. Pacemakers represent a merging of humans and machines at a basic physical level. Biofeedback mechanisms do so at the level of human consciousness. Approximately 7,000 people worldwide have cochlear hearing implants, which are surgically implanted devices that work through the placement of tiny electrodes within the inner ear. These devices are substituted for the lack of cochlear hair cells that normally transmit sounds into bioelectrical impulses in the inner ear. Although these devices work imperfectly, they suggest how sensing devices may eventually be wired directly into the brain.

Neural plugs that allow individuals to jack into computers are commonplace in science fiction. Not only can they be used for work, but for pleasure as well. In Gibson's *Neuromancer*, for example, a male character interfaces through a computer link with the body and consciousness of a female character.

Whereas such a possibility may seem a bit far-fetched, it is not difficult to imagine other comparable scenarios. One of the authors studied introductory psychology as an undergraduate student over 20 years ago, and remembers discussions of rats having very small electrical wires set in the pleasure centers of their brains. By touching an electrical device on a press bar in their cages, they were able to stimulate themselves. The rats would press the bar until they were totally exhausted.

It seems plausible that humans could be wired in a similar way and an electrical neural stimulator could be activated as a plug-in-drug—what is referred to elsewhere as a "dildonic." Sophisticated electronic stimulation systems could conceivably take the place of illegal narcotics and hallucinogens.

There are major moral and ethical issues that will have to be addressed as it becomes more and more possible to wire people into computers and mechanical systems. Is it right to wire a quadriplegic to a computer robot construct to give them mobility?

The science fiction writer Anne McCaffrey, in her story "The Ship that Sang," described a future in which children born with massive physical deformities, who would otherwise die, have their brains surgically separated from their bodies and interfaced with the computers of a space ship. Is this type of life preferable to no life at all? When is a human no longer a human? These are questions that almost certainly will have to be addressed in one form or another in years to come.

📖 Sources

Anderson-Inman, L., Knox-Quinn, C., & Horney, M. (1996). Computer-based study strategies for students with learning disabilities: Individual differences associated with adoption level. *Journal of Learning Disabilities, 29*(5), 461–484.

Brett, A., & Provenzo, E. F. Jr. (1995). *Adaptive technology for special human needs.* New York: State University of New York Press.

Brunner, J. (1990). *Shockwaverider.* New York: Ballantine.

Closing the Gap. Published bi-monthly. Closing the Gap, P. O. Box, Henderson, MN, 1993. See: http:www.closing the gap.com

Daiute, C., & Morse, F. (1994). Access to knowledge and expression: Multimedia writing tools for students with diverse needs and strengths. *Journal of Special Education Technology, 12*(3), 221–256.

Delany, S. (1991). *Nova.* New York: Bantam.

Ferretti, R., & Okolo, C. (1996). Authenticity in learning: Multimedia design projects in the social studies for students with disabilities. *Journal of Learning Disabilities, 29*(5), 450–460.

Gibson, W. (1984). *Neuromancer.* New York: Ace.

Gibson, W. (1987). *Count Zero.* New York: Ace.

Grabe, M., & Grabe, C. (1996). *Integrating technology for meaningful learning.* Boston: Houghton Mifflin.

Hebert, B., & Murdock, J. (1994). Comparing three computer-aided instruction output modes to teach vocabulary words to students with learning disabilities. *Learning Disability Quarterly, 9*(3), 136–141.

Larsen, S. (1995). What is "quality" in the use of technology for children with learning disabilities? *Learning Disability Quarterly, 18*(2), 118–130.

Lewis, R. (1993). *Special education technology: Classroom applications.* Pacific Grove, CA: Brooks/Cole.

Lindsey, J. (Ed.), (1993). *Computers and exceptional individuals* (2nd ed.). Austin, TX: Pro-Ed.

Male, M. (1994). *Technology for inclusion* (3rd ed.). Boston: Allyn & Bacon.

McCaffrey, A. (1993). *The ship who sang.* New York: Ballantine.

Moeller, B., & Jeffers, L. (1996). Technology for inclusive teaching. *Electronic Learning,* 16 (3), 44.

Moravec, H. (1988). *Mind children: The future of robot and human intelligence.* Cambridge, MA: Harvard University Press.

Okolo, C., Bahr, C., & Rieth, H. (1993). A retrospective view of computer-based instruction. *Journal of Special Education Technology,* 12(1), 1–27.

Phillips, M. (1996). Beyond the best CDs list. *Electronic Learning, 15*(6), 16.

Walker, D., & Williamson, R. (1995). Computers and adolescents with emotional/behavior disorders. *Closing the Gap, 14*(2), 10–11, 16–17, 29.

Wetzel, K. (1996). Speech-recognizing computers: A written communication tool for students with learning disabilities*? Journal of Learning Disabilities, 29*(4), 371–380.

Wissick, C. (1996). Multimedia: Enhancing instruction for students with learning disabilities. *Journal of Learning Disabilities,* 29(5), 494–503.

MULTIMEDIA AND HYPERMEDIA

What Is Multimedia? Hypertext and Hypermedia, Multimedia Authoring Tools, Mathematical Processors, Videodisc Technology

The printed book...seems destined to move to the margin of our literate culture. The issue is not whether print technology will completely disappear; books may long continue to be printed for certain kinds of texts and for luxury consumption. But the idea and ideal of the book will change: print will no longer define the organization and presentation of knowledge, as it has for the past five centuries.

—Jay David Bolter

Case Study

Louise Smithson is a second grade teacher whose school is in a working-class suburb of Chicago. Very few of her children are interested in reading on their own. However, they love to have someone read to them. While visiting a local computer store, Louise came across a number of CD-ROM hypermedia programs that added read-aloud functions to storybooks, as well as animations and a read-aloud hypermedia dictionary. She wonders if there are more programs like these available and if she could integrate them into her classroom's reading program so that children could read stories by themselves while she worked with individual reading groups.

What features should she be looking for in materials like these? Are some hypermedia programs designed better than others?

Ms. Smithson's needs can be met by a wide range of educational and commercial programs currently available on the market. Broderbund, well-known for distributing games like *Where in the World Is Carmen Sandiego?* and *Myst*, has produced a "Living Books" series that includes titles such as: *Three for Me Library Volume 1*™; *Three For Me Library Volume 2*™; *Arthur's Birthday* ®; *Arthur's Teacher Trouble*®; *The Berenstain Bears Get in a Fight*; *The Berenstain Bears in the Dark*; *Dr. Seuss' ABC*; *Dr. Seuss' Green Eggs and Ham*; *Harry & the Haunted House*; *Just Grandma & Me*; *Little Monster*™ *at School*; *The New Kid on the Block*; *Ruff's Bone*; *Sheila Rae, the Brave*; *Stellaluna*; *The Tortoise & the Hare*. These programs have a special read-aloud function and clever animations included in almost every screen. In addition, read-aloud functions are available in Spanish and other languages.

Broderbund
http://www.broderbund.com

Living Books ®
http://www.broder.com/studio/livingbooks.html

In *Green Eggs and Ham*, the classic Dr. Seus story and its main character Sam, who does not "like green eggs and ham", can be read silently by its user or listened to. Fun animations make the program into more of a television cartoon than a book. This tendency is reinforced through the inclusion of three clever games. The first is a color matching game, the second a word completion game, and the third a word rhyming game. Users can select different languages to hear the program in.

Ruff's Bone, for example, follows the valiant canine Ruff in a far-flung search for his lost bone. He travels to a distant jungle, an ancient sunken ship and other far-off places. Along the way, he meets a playful monkey, tap dancing jeans, a friendly robot and dozens of other charming characters. Finally, he recovers his bone and returns home in a passing UFO. The book reads aloud in either Spanish or English and is an excellent example of an innovative hypermedia book for younger children.

Ruff's Bone
http://www.broder.com/studio/captures/rb1.html

For children interested in history, Scholastic, Inc. has created programs as part of their "Smart" Books series such as "...*If Your Name Was Changed at Ellis Island.*" This program is based on a handsomely illustrated book by Ellen Levine. It provides an electronic tour of Ellis Island, stories about famous immigrants and information about contemporary immigration. Other *Smart Books* include titles on Malcom X, Greek Mythology, and the Titanic.

Scholastic Corporation
http://www.scholastic.com/

More traditional instruction can be provided through the use of a program like Steck Vaughn's *World of Dinosaurs.* This program is based on a 10 book (16 pages each) reading series that includes titles such as *The Dinosaur Battle*, *What Happened to the Dinosaurs?*, and *Plant Eaters and Meat Eaters.* In addition to full speak-aloud dictionary functions in which any word on the screen can be clicked on and activated, the program includes extensive animations; a database on dinosaurs, animals, and plants; video clips from documentaries; and a testing and student management system. It even features an animated character named "Dr. Dino," who leads students through the program, asks them questions, and provides advanced organizers and reviews.

World of Dinosaurs (Steck Vaughn)
http://www.steckvaughn.com/c/@5iKUuVE.sfOq2/product.html?record@88

Programs like these are examples of computer-based multimedia educational software. In this chapter, we look at different types of multimedia software, and in particular hypermedia, and discuss their potential to transform traditional models of instruction and literacy.

What Is Multimedia?

Multimedia is the combination of sound, animation, graphics, video, and related elements into a single program or system. Until recently, computer-based multimedia programs have been extremely difficult to use in the school and very expensive. With the introduction of increasingly inexpensive high-speed computers and greatly improved software, multimedia has become a feasible educational technology for schools.

Mathematical Processor: a type of computer system that graphs different mathematical formulas and equations.

Scientific Visualization Program: a computer program that visually represents scientific information and concepts.

Multimedia includes many different things. Although a film strip with an accompanying audiotape is a type of multimedia program, **mathematical processors**, which graph different formulas and equations, and **scientific visualization programs** and simulators, are also different types of multimedia. A CD-ROM-based video game is a multimedia program, as is a read-aloud hypermedia book.

Multimedia programs require fast machines, large **hard drives**, and high-speed CD-ROM players. They are almost always interactive. This means that users can do something and the program will respond to their actions. This may be as simple as users striking the wrong command and having the computer correct them, or a user telling a character to go in a certain direction in a virtual adventure game or simulation.

Hard Drive: a mass storage device for a computer.

The most useful multimedia programs in education are those that branch, or take users to a different level. These programs are typically based on a **hypertext** or hypermedia model.

Hypertext: a model for presenting information in which text becomes linked in ways that allow readers to browse and discover the connections between different sets of information.

Computers and the Movies

Computers have been in the movies since the 1950s. In 1957, Spencer Tracey and Katherine Hepburn starred in the comedy *Desk Set* with a computer called EMARAC (Electromagnetic Memory and Research Calculator). Many of these movies talk to social and cultural issues that we are increasingly facing or will have to face in the near future. The list of films included below should be both entertaining and provide insights into some of the challenges posed by the new technology.

1965 *Alphaville.* A disturbing look at a future in which humans are controlled by a machine that dislikes art and makes sorrow illegal.

1968 *2001: A Space Odyssey.* A malfunctioning computer destroys its users as it attempts to literally fulfill its mission assignment.

1977 *The Demon Seed.* A computer tries to impregnate a woman in order to create a new life form.

1982 *Tron.* A fantasy film by Walt Disney, Inc., whose action takes place inside of a giant malevolent computer.

1983 *Brainstorm.* The military abuses computer technology through its use of virtual reality devices.

1983 *War Games.* Kids hacking a military computer network almost set off the end of the world.

1992 *Lawnmower Man.* A mentally retarded handyman is made into a genius through interfacing with a virtual reality program.

1995 *Johnny Mnemonic.* A human messenger carries vast electronic databases in his head. Based on a short story by William Gibson, the author of *Neuromancer.*

1996 *The Net.* The capacity of the Internet to be used for unethical purposes is demonstrated.

Strange Days. Computer users "jack in" to other people's experiences to get high.

Hypertext and Hypermedia

Hypertext, or "hypermedia," is a concept that dates back to at least the end of the World War II and the work of the computer pioneer Vannevar Bush (1890–1974). In 1945 he described a publishing system called a "memex." According to Bush, the memex would be:

a sort of mechanized private file and library… a device in which an individual stores his books, records and communications, and which is mechanized so that it may be consulted with exceeding speed and flexibility. It is an enlarged intimate supplement to his memory. (Nyce & Kahn, 1991)

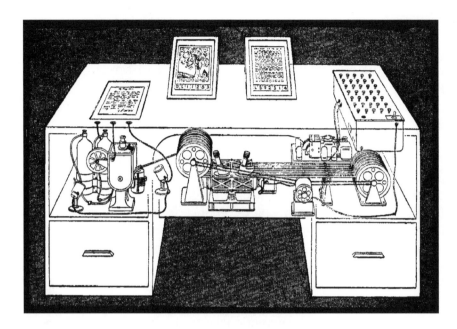

The memex was an awkward photomechanical hypertext and hypermedia system. Yet despite this fact, it brilliantly anticipated the possibility of hypermedia systems such as those commonly found on electronic computers today. The illustration above, from a 1946 issue of *Life* magazine, shows a desktop memex unit with a translucent screen for viewing images. (*LIFE 19* (11), p. 123)

The memex was a desk-sized device. It would store massive amounts of microfilm so that even if the user inserted thousands of pages of material a day it would take him or her hundreds of years to fill the system's storage capacity. Most of the content of the memex could be purchased on microfilm ready for insertion. Books, pictures, periodicals, and newspapers could be dropped into the system. Personal notes and materials could be entered as well. An index would be included that would allow the user easy navigation through the system.

The memex was mechanically awkward, if not almost totally impractical. Conceptually it was brilliant in that it anticipated the integration of sophisticated word processing systems with microcomputers, databases, imaging devices (scanners), and laser videodisc systems. The memex was, in effect, a hypertext or hypermedia system.

Hypertext does not lend itself to a simple definition. Ted Nelson (1987) defined it as *"non-sequential writing*–text that allows choice to the reader, best read as an interactive screen" (p. 0/2). Popularly conceived, this represents "a series of text chunks connected by links which offer the reader different pathways" (p. p. 0/2).

Jeff Conklin (1987) described hypertext as a system that makes possible "direct machine-supported references from one textual chunk to another; new interfaces provide the user with the ability to interact directly with these chunks and to establish new relationships between them" (p. 17). He pointed out that "the concept of hypertext is quite simple: Windows on the screen are associated with objects in a database and links are provided between these objects, both graphically—(as labeled tokens) and in the database (as pointers)" (p. 17). Hypermedia, when employed in appropriate ways, is a revolutionary tool for educators. It is a confusing technology for beginning computer users because it can be used in so many different ways. In this context, a comparison with traditional books is helpful.

Books can be presented in many sizes and shapes. They can be short or long, use graphics or be text based, be in color or in black and white, and so on. Students can read books or they can be made by them.

Likewise, hypermedia has many different formats and can be used by students in many different ways. For a high school or college student, a hypermedia text can present a literary classic and include buttons or hyperlinks that will connect the user to related works of literature or sources of criticism. A hypertext or hypermedia system can make it possible for elementary school children learning to read a text to have instant access to a dictionary that will speak aloud to them and provide other explanations of complex or difficult materials.

What are some examples of hypermedia software that are currently being used in the schools? We have already described in this chapter some examples of elementary level reading programs. For reference use, there are many different types of hypermedia programs that can be used effectively in the schools.

The control screen on the right of the memex allowed the user to input marginal notes and comments that would be linked to the document projected on the left. This function is achieved on today's computers by using a mouse, a keyboard or a drawing tablet. (*LIFE 19* (11), p. 124)

Reference books, such as dictionaries and encyclopedias, are ideally suited for a hypermedia format. Large and awkward for students to use, and quickly outdated, reference sources become much more accessible to students when placed on a computer. Searches for information are more easily conducted, cross-references are automatic and sound and animation can lend a new dimension to the information being presented. An example is *Compton's Interactive Encyclopedia*. This program includes the complete 26-volume *Compton's Encyclopedia* with over 9 million words and 32,000 articles. Enhanced sound and visual features, as well as powerful search and cross-referencing functions, make this, and similar multimedia encyclopedias such as Microsoft's *Encarta* very appealing.

Compton's Interactive Encyclopedia
http://store.learningco.com/dev/product.asp?fid=0&ref_id=&sku=CIED38
44CE&mscssid=BC9UEJQPVESH2PXG00L1R06N9PB0VD3M

Encarta (Microsoft)
http://encarta.msn.com/EncartaHome.asp

Dictionaries also lend themselves well to hypermedia and hypertext formats. The *Macmillan Dictionary for Children* (Macmillan New Media), for example, includes over 12,000 word entries, 1,000 illustrations, and 400 sound effects. A guided tour of how to use the dictionary is included with the program, and an animated character appears throughout the program to provide special help to the user when needed.

My First Incredible Amazing Dictionary, which is available from Dorling Kindserley Multimedia, includes more than 1,250 screens and pop-ups, 1,100 illustrations, 850 animations, 2,500 pronunciations, and 3,000 individual sounds. Its lively music, sound effects, and charming graphics make it very appealing to young children learning to read and spell.

Other multimedia programs from Dorling Kindersley that are well-suited for use at the elementary and middle school level include *Encyclopedia of Science, Cartopedia, The Ultimate World Reference Atlas, The Way Things Work, Stowaway, Encyclopedia of Nature, History of the World, The Ultimate Human Body,* and *P. B. Bear's Birthday Party*. Each of these programs makes extensive use of sound and graphics to create unique interactive and electronic books.

Dorling Kindersley
http://www.dkonline.com/dkcom/

The Way Things Work
http://www.dkonline.com/dkcom/dk/4cat5.html

Hypermedia/CD-ROM-based programs are not just interactive books. Curriculum Associates, for example, has developed an interesting program called *Postcards*, in which students can visit and learn about four different countries: Mexico, Ghana, Japan, and Turkey. In *Postcards,* students tour each country. They are presented with photos, videos, music, and illustrations, charts, and maps for each of the countries they are visiting.   A travel log allows students to take notes as part of their travels. "Scaffolded" postcards that they write and can actually print off the computer, introduce them to narrative, compare/contrast, persuasive and descriptive modes of writing.

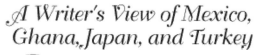

A program like Curriculum Associates *Postcards* provides students a framework and set of experiences for classroom writing assignments by allowing the opportunity to visit people and places within the program, and then to write postcards based on their experiences.

A program like *Postcards* suggests the wide range of uses multimedia/hypermedia can be put to in the classroom. Students can do more than just use multimedia and hypermedia programs, however, for they can actually create them for themselves—thus becoming creators and organizers of knowledge rather just recipients of it.

Curriculum Associates
http://www.curriculumassociates.com

Postcards
http://www.curriculumassociates.com/demos.html#pc

Multimedia Authoring Tools

Authoring Program:
software for coordinating
the graphics, video,
animation, text, and sound
in the development of
multimedia.

There are many different **authoring programs** currently available for use in developing hypermedia projects and multimedia programs. Most are for professional developers. Gifted high schoolers may want to explore programs such as: *Authorware Professional* (Macromedia), which is an object-oriented program that allows nonprogrammers to develop extremely sophisticated hypermedia and multimedia programs; *Macromedia Director* (Macromedia), which is one of the most sophisticated multimedia authoring tools currently available that allows for the creation of sophisticated animations, with full sound and graphic resources; and *Toolbook* (Asymetrix Corporation), which is one of the first hypermedia programs for MS-DOS and Windows computers.

Director (Macromedia)
http://www.macromedia.com/software/director

Toolbook (Asymetrix)
http://www.asymetrix.com/

Simpler, and as a result less powerful authoring programs include *Digital Chisel* (Pierian Software), which is an extremely flexible multimedia authoring program that teachers and students can use to develop hypermedia programs by clicking on and then "dragging" items onto master templates included in the program; *HyperCard* (Apple Computers), which is a tool kit for creating hypermedia software; *HyperStudio* (Roger Wagner Publishing), which is a hypermedia program that because of its simplicity particularly lends itself for use at the elementary and middle school level; and *LinkWay Live* (IBM/Eduquest), which was one of the very first hypermedia programs available on MS-DOS machines.

Digital Chisel (Pierian Springs Software)
http://www.pierian.com/multimed.htm#DC2

Hypercard (Apple Computers)
http://www.apple.com/hypercard

HyperStudio (Roger Wagner Publishing)
http://www.hyperstudio.com/abouths/index.html

Mathematical Processors

As mentioned earlier, multimedia and hypermedia are not limited to just electronic books. Mathematical processors are coming into widespread use at the high school and college level. These programs are used to create symbolic manipulations of mathematical information. Some of the tasks they can handle include the factoring of large polynomials, symbolic and numeric differentiation and integration, real and complex trigonometry and hyperbolic functions, symbolic and numeric matrix and linear algebra, and graphing solutions in two and three dimensions.

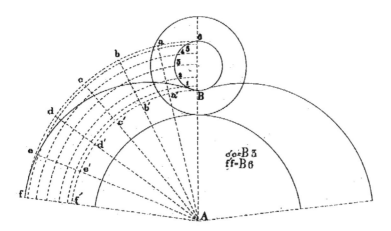

For students who struggle to visualize the meaning of a formula or an equation, these programs are ideal. Examples of mathematical processors and related mathematical tools for instruction include: *MATHLAB* (The Math Works), which is an interactive mathematics processor; *Mathematica* (Wolfram Research), which is an interactive calculation program for numeric, symbolic, and graphical computing; and *Maple* V (Maple Software), which like *Mathematica,* provides a total mathematical environment for performing symbolic, graphic, and numerical computations.

Wolfram Media (Mathematica)
http://www.wolfram-media.com/

Waterloo Maple (Maple)
http://www.maplesoft.com/

Programs like these, as well as scientific visualization programs that can simulate atomic level processes or complex chemical reactions, have a tremendous potential for use at the secondary and college level. The extent to which such programs are integrated into the general curriculum, not just the most advanced courses, remains to be seen. Such programs may, in fact, be an important means of enhancing learning at many different levels in the future.

Videodisc Technology

As mentioned earlier, **videodisc** technology is a transitional computer-based technology that can still be found in many schools. A videodisc typically measures 12 inches in diameter and can hold, depending on its format, 30 to 60 minutes of television or film per side. It creates the image of motion by projecting still images in rapid succession.

Each videodisc has up to four discreet audio tracks that can be used for music or voice. Programming is encoded on a videodisc in the form of millions of tiny nonreflective pits on a reflective surface. As in CD-ROM technology, a beam of low powered laser light hits either the pits or the reflective areas between pits, producing a high-frequency signal which the player converts to television and stereo.

There are numerous educational programs available on videodisc. Such programs have been particularly successful in areas such as foreign language instruction and film study where large amounts of video or film material needs to be presented. As mentioned earlier, however, videodisc technology is a transitional storage medium that does not seem likely to survive beyond another 5 or 10 years.

In conclusion, multimedia and hypermedia are technologies that hold enormous promise for curriculum development in the future. As computers become more powerful and inexpensive, and as multimedia and hypermedia programming systems become more accessible, educators are likely to increasingly adapt this technology for use in the classroom. When combined with other computer-based technologies such as the Internet and the World Wide Web, we believe that multimedia and hypermedia have the potential to transform traditional learning and instruction. In the following chapter, we explore the potential of the Internet and the World Wide Web for use in the schools.

QUESTIONS FOR REFLECTION AND DISCUSSION

1. Is the printed book in danger of disappearing?

2. What is the difference between hypertext and hypermedia?

3. How does hypermedia change the meaning of literacy?

4. If the concept of hypertext was invented by Vannevar Bush as early as 1945, why has it not been more widely discussed and used?

5. What are the advantages or limitations of students using a printed encyclopedia versus a multimedia encyclopedia?

6. Why might the use of a mathematical processor be more important for certain types of learners compared to others?

7. Why are videotapes more commonly used in our culture than videodiscs, which have better quality and hold more information? Is cost the only factor?

8. How does multimedia potentially change traditional instruction?

9. How do libraries potentially change with the introduction of multimedia resources?

10. What is the future of CD-ROM technology as the Internet and the World Wide Web become more widespread and powerful?

ACTIVITIES

1. Using a hypertext program like *HyperCard* or *Toolbook,* create a simple hypermedia curriculum that can be used in a school setting.

2. Go to a local computer store or school district computer curriculum center and make a list of hypermedia and

multimedia programs that you think would be useful for instruction.

3. Visit a local museum that is of interest to you and think about how it could be redesigned as a hypermedia exploration.

EXERCISE FOR FURTHER DEVELOPMENT OF YOUR REFLECTIVE PRACTICE FOR TEACHING WITH COMPUTER TECHNOLOGY

Teachers, as professionals, need to be able to teach all students in relation to their diversity and the diversity of student learning styles. Computer technology helps us reach such a goal by assisting in presenting information in diverse ways. Read the following presentation on digital theme parks and reflect on the following issues related to teaching practice:

1. How does "theme park" technology encourage people to expect more diverse forms of dealing with information in everyday life?

2. How can technology assist students in experiencing a more diverse sense of community?

Digital Theme Parks

No one personifies the idea of the modern theme park as much as Walt Disney. Beginning with the opening of Disneyland in 1955 on a 182-acre orange grove in Anaheim, California, Disney theme parks have spread throughout the world to include sites in Orlando, Florida, Tokyo, Japan, and Paris, France.

The Disney theme parks represent an attempt on the part of Disney to create a total experience for his visitors that would keep them occupied not for just a day or two, but for an entire vacation. The Disney theme parks were designed for families. They were also supposed to be on the cutting edge of technology EPCOT

(Experimental Prototype Community of Tomorrow), for example, was intended by Disney to be an experimental community where the most innovative and advanced models of community and social planning could be tested.

Despite its impeccable neatness, EPCOT has a strangely dated quality to it. In fact, all of the Disney theme parks seem outdated. In many respects, the design and layout of the Disney theme parks are reminiscent of the international expositions and amusement parks of the late 19th and early 20th centuries. In EPCOT, for example, one can visit foreign pavilions—a model taken directly from the exhibits of foreign people that were so much a part of the world's fairs. The roller coaster and other amusement rides that are so much a part of Disneyland and Disney World replicate early 20th-century amusement parks such as Coney Island.

Disney's theme parks take up enormous amounts of space and have a huge financial overhead. They will probably disappear or be reinvented in years to come. The Evans & Sutherland Company, a computer company famous for its military flight simulators, has developed a program called *The Loch Ness Adventure*. The adventure takes place inside a command vehicle—in this case, a submarine—on the famous lake in Scotland after which the monster is named. The adventure scenario has eight people in the command vehicle attempting to save the recently discovered Loch Ness monster from extinction by protecting its eggs from evil bounty hunters.

The eight players pilot the submarine through the water viewing what is going on through polarized glasses on a large screen, or "window," at the front of the command module. The commander of the submarines gives orders to his or her crew, including a navigator and a periscope operator.

The *Loch Ness Adventure* is appealing as an interactive and participatory adventure. It has been designed to be nonviolent and to appeal to people interested in sharing a gaming activity and adventure. Amusements and adventures like the *Loch Ness Adventure* may very well replace theme parks like Disney World in the future. Virtual rides and amusements can be moved anywhere in a trailer. They do not need a parklike setting to operate. One can easily imagine a carnival circuit developing where trailers full of interactive equipment pull into a mall parking lot and open for business.

Interest can be maintained by constantly updating and enhancing programs. The *Loch Ness Adventure* is played in a control room. It simulates a submarine bridge, but can quickly be reprogrammed to be the bridge of an intergalactic spacecraft. New programs and scenarios can be introduced and technology updated with minimal revamping of equipment.

In a post-typographic culture, it seems reasonable to assume that theme parks like Disneyland and Disney World will become corporate icons and headquarters. Symbolically, it may be important for them to continue to exist, but the main business of tomorrow's theme parks will be in the digital arena in trailers parked at malls in the suburbs, or in the homes of those people who can afford the necessary equipment.

Disney has already experimented with early prototypes of this type of technology and incorporated them into their theme parks. In the future, however, it will probably have to be the main thrust of their theme park programs, or they will no longer be competitive in a field that they have dominated since the 1950s.

📖 Sources

Barrett, E. (1985). *Text, ConText, and Hypertext: Writing with and for the computer.* Cambridge, MA: MIT Press.

Birkerts, S. (1994). *The Gutenberg elegies: The fate of reading in an electronic age.* Boston: Faber & Faber.

Bolter, J. D. (1991). *Writing space: The computer, hypertext and the history of writing.* Hillsdale, NJ: Lawrence Erlbaum Associates.

Bush, V. (1945). As we may think. *Atlantic Monthly, 176*(1), 101–108. Reprinted in part in Nelson's *Literary Machines*, pp. 1/39-1/54. A full reprint of the article can be found in Irene Greif, Ed., *Computer-Supported Cooperative Work*, pp. 17–34.

Carr, C. (1988). Hypertext: A new training tool. *Educational Technology*, August, pp. 7–11.

Conklin, J. (1987), "Hypertext: An introduction and survey," *Computer, 20* (9), pp. 17-41.

Delany, P., & Landow, G. P. (Eds.). (1991). *Hypermedia and literary studies.* Cambridge: MIT Press.

Englebart, D. (1963). A conceptual framework for the augmentation of man's intellect. In P. W. Howerton & D. C. Weeks (Eds.), *Vistas in information handling: Vol. 1. The augmentation of man's intellect by machine.* (pp. 1–29). Washington, DC: Spartan Books.

Greif, I. (Ed.). (1988). *Computer-supported cooperative work: A book of readings.* San Mateo, CA: Morgan Kaufmann.

Hardison, O. B. (1989). *Disappearing through the skylight: Culture and technology in the twentieth century.* New York: Penguin.

Heim, M. (1993). *The metaphysics of virtual reality.* New York: Oxford University Press.

Landow, G. P. (1989). The rhetoric of hypermedia: Some rules for authors. *Journal of Computing in Higher Education, 1*(1).

Landow, G. P. (1992). *Hypertext: The convergence of contemporary critical theory and technology*. Baltimore, MD: Johns Hopkins University Press.

Lanham, R. A. (1993). *The electronic word: Democracy, technology and the arts*. Chicago: University of Chicago Press.

Nelson, T. H. (1997). *Dream machines*. Redmond, WA: Microsoft Press.

Nyce, J. M., & Kahn, P. (Eds.). (1991). *From Memex to hypertext: Vannevar Bush and the mind's machine*. Boston: Academic Press.

Tuman, M. C. (Ed.). (1992). *Literacy online: The promise (and peril) of reading and writing with computers*. Pittsburgh: University of Pittsburgh Press.

NETWORKING AND TELECOMMUNICATION

What Is the Internet? The World Wide Web (WWW), Multicultural Education and the Internet, Protecting Students Using the Internet, Establishing an Acceptable Use Policy

At one level, the computer is a tool. It helps us write, keep track of our accounts, and communicate with others. Beyond this, the computer offers us both new models of mind and a new medium on which to project our ideas and fantasies.

—Sherry Turkle

Case Study

Eveleen Wright teaches fifth grade in an inner-city school in Charlotte, North Carolina. Her students are a mix of African Americans and rural White southerners whose parents have moved to the city seeking jobs in the service sector. Her school has a very small library. There is little money available in the school's budget for supplementary classroom materials.

As part of a program to "wire" classrooms throughout the state, Ms. Wright has access to the Internet. The two computers in her classroom, bought with Chapter II funds, have had high-speed modems installed in them. She has attended several workshops on how to get access to the Internet and she is excited about the fact that it can literally bring a world of information and ideas to her children. Ms. Wright is confused, though, about how to integrate the Internet into her curriculum. How can she use its resources to help her cover required material? What is the best use of this remarkable new technology?

Ms. Wright's dilemma is one of the most interesting problems currently facing educators. The Internet holds enormous promise as a resource for teachers and students, but the question of how to make the best use of it is open to considerable debate.

As a source for supplemental activities, the Internet could be used by Ms. Wright and her students to talk to other students around the country or around the world. Through the Global Schoolhouse Project, for example, students can connect to other students not only throughout the United States, but in Asia, Africa, Australia, and Europe as well.

Global Schoolhouse Project
http: /k12.cnidr.org/gsh/gshwelcome.html

Download: to transfer data from one computer to another.

Suppose Ms. Wright's students are interested in space exploration. The Internet would make it possible for them to see and **download** photographs from outer space and the archives of the National Aeronautics and Space Administration (NASA). Her students could visit the Shuttle Countdown Status Home Page to get daily information about the space shuttle, its payload status, weather reports from Cape Kennedy, and other types of information.

Shuttle Countdown Status Home Page
http:// http://www.ksc.nasa.gov/shuttle/countdown/

If students are interested in museums, they can visit such places as the Louvre in Paris, France, the Exploratorium in San Francisco, or the National Air and Space Museum in Washington, DC.

The Louvre
http://mistral.culture.fr/louvre/

Exploratorium
http://www/exploratorium.edu

National Air and Space Museum
http://k12.cnidr.org/gsh/gshwelcome.html

Through the Internet students can visit the home page for the White House and learn about the executive branch of the government, hear a message from the president, take a virtual tour of the President's home, and even leave their names in an electronic guestbook.

The White House
http://www.whitehouse.gov/

There are even special tours of the White House on the Internet just for kids!

The White House for Kids
http://www.whitehouse.gov/WH/kids/html/home.html

Using the Internet this way is the equivalent of an electronic field trip. Although it may be a wonderful experience for children, it still does not address Ms. Wright's problem of how to integrate the Internet with the more traditional curriculum.

There are several solutions to her problems. Curricula need to be—and almost certainly will be—developed that encourage children to draw on Internet resources to learn traditional subject content. Mathematics could be taught, for example, by students going to the Home Page of the National Aeronautics Space Administration on the World Wide Web where they can find files on the Apollo 11 moon landing in July 1969. They could be asked to find the mean distance of the Earth to the moon (238,857 miles) and then to determine the minimal total distance that had to be completed by the astronauts for the round trip (2 x 238,857 miles = 477,714). Many other similar types of problems could be constructed that require students to gather information from selected Internet sites and then to use those data to solve a specific problem.

National Aeronautics and Space Administration
http://www.nasa.gov/NASA_homepage.html

After using the Internet, students could be asked to write a history of moon exploration, the history of a particular mission, or a biography of an astronaut. Another activity could teach students scientific vocabulary based on Internet sources. The possibilities are almost unlimited. Art posters could be drawn commemorating specific space flights. Students could write and act in plays based on information they collected about space flights.

As mentioned earlier, such curricula will almost certainly be created in the near future. They integrate the Internet with its extraordinary informational resources along with traditional curriculum content. Before we go any further, however, we need to define exactly what the Internet is and how it works.

What is the Internet?

The origins of the Internet can be traced to the Cold War. In 1969, research scientists working for the U.S. Department of Defense connected computers in Utah and California so that they could exchange information. In doing so, they created what is called a network.

ARPANET: a predecessor to the Internet funded by the Department of Defense.

This first network was called the **ARPANET** after its military sponsor, the Advanced Research Projects Agency (ARPA). In 1990, the ARPANET was shut down and the Internet took its place. Today the Internet connects tens of millions of people not just across the United States, but around the world. The Internet has been called the "information superhighway." Just how true this is will become clear as you begin to discover and explore its extraordinary resources.

History of the Internet

The Internet is a direct outgrowth of the Cold War. Shortly after the launch of the Russian satellite Sputnik in 1956, the U.S. Department of Defense formed the Advanced Research Projects Agency (ARPA) in order to compete with the Soviets in technological development. During the early 1960s, this group became concerned with creating a computer system that could withstand nuclear attack. Rather than centralize computer resources, it was determined that a decentralized system with many computers connected to one another would have a much better chance of surviving. This decentralized system, known as ARPANET, was first tested in 1969.

In 1972, the first e-mail program was used on ARPANET, sending and receiving messages across the network. Use of the network grew during the 1980s. By 1987, the number of computers connected to the ARPANET had reached over 10,000. The first educational use of the program, an Internet mailing list for children called Kidsphere, went into operation in 1989. In 1990, ARPANET ceased to exist and the system that took its place was renamed the Internet. In 1991, the first Internet search and navigation tools were released.

In 1992, World Wide Web technology (WWW), which provides the Internet with visual or graphic interface technology, was released. By 1993, the number of users on the Internet had grown to more than 20 million. Information on Internet use can be found at:

Computer Industry Almanac Inc.
http://www.c-i-a.com/

A detailed timeline on the history and development of the Internet can be found at:

Hobbe's Internet Timeline
http://info.isoc.org/guest/zakon/Internet/History/HIT.html

The World Wide Web (WWW)

The Internet has been difficult for many people to explore because it required the use of complicated and often confusing search tools. This changed with the introduction of the World Wide Web, which greatly simplified the use of the Internet.

The World Wide Web (WWW) was introduced to the computing community in 1992 by researchers at the European Laboratory for Particle Physics in Switzerland. It is so important because it connects different Internet sites using a very simple visual interactive format.

Web Browser: graphical user interface used to view documents on the World Wide Web.

This is done through what is called a **Web browser**. Perhaps you have heard of or used Web browsers like Microsoft's Internet Explorer, MacWeb, Mosaic, or Netscape. These are programs that allow you to browse the World Wide Web taking full advantage of its graphic functions and connections.

Hyperlink: is a highlighted graphic such as a button or illustration, or piece of text, that connects a user to another Web site or source of information or file on the Internet.

Every World Wide Web site has a home page that includes **hyperlinks** that can instantly connect you to other parts of the document you are in, or to other Web sites on the Internet. These are the same types of hyperlinks that are used in the multimedia programs described in chapter 6. Instead of referencing material on a CD-ROM or a hard drive, they can reference information from anywhere on the Internet.

On the following page is an illustration of the home page from the Library of Congress's American Memory Project. It outlines the basic elements included on a Web page along with major browser functions.

American Memory Project
http://lcweb2.loc.gov/ammem/ammemhome.html

Elements of a Web Page (Viewed Through a Netscape Browser)

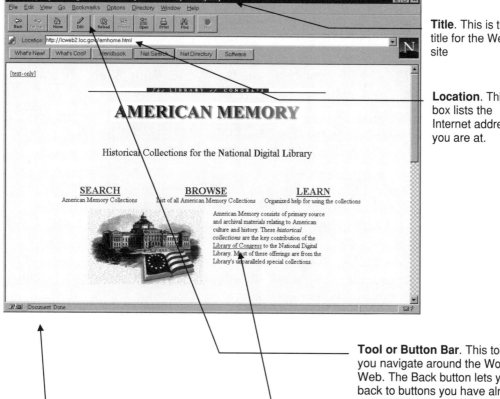

Title. This is the title for the Web site

Location. This box lists the Internet address you are at.

Tool or Button Bar. This tool bar lets you navigate around the World Wide Web. The Back button lets you go back to buttons you have already visited. The Forward button moves you in the other direction. Clicking on the Open button gives you a blank box for typing in a new address to visit. Print sends the Web page on your screen to your printer.

URL Link. This box shows the address or home page you will go to if you click on a hyperlink or link.

Hyperlinks or Links. These highlighted buttons and words will take you by means of a hyperlink to another site.

Multicultural Education and the Internet

In efforts to bring multicultural perspectives and diversity into the classroom, there are many computer programs available to assist teachers in their efforts. Word processing and spreadsheet programs can easily be used in projects related to multicultural education. However, for us, the most powerful new tool in multicultural education is the Internet and the World Wide Web. Through the Internet and the World Wide Web, students with different cultural experience can more easily share with each other. Students can reach out across the globe, learn about different cultures and people, exchange materials, and develop a broader understanding of the world around them.

Such efforts are not new. Earlier educational movements, such as global education outreach projects, have experimented with exchanges since the beginning of this century. In the early 1920s, for example, the Modern School Movement was begun by Célestin Freinet (Cummins & Sayers, pp. 123–125). His program was based around three separate techniques. The first of these techniques involved his students going on "learning walks" through their village and local neighborhoods. Students would gather information about community life that would become the basis for subsequent classroom activities. As a follow-up to these walks students would then create "free texts," which would be turned into "pretexts," or documents that addressed problems or needs in their local communities.

As a result of their community-based walks, students became involved in projects such as building a new village fountain and constructing a small hydroelectric dam on a local stream. Initially reports were collected in a folder. In order to disseminate these reports more widely, Freinet introduced his second technique, which involved students typesetting their reports and distributing them among themselves and their families and friends. The third technique introduced by Freinet was to have students establish interschool networks. This was done originally with Rene Daniel, a teacher in a neighboring province. In October 1924, they exchanged "culture packages" and writing between their students (p. 125).

The model that eventually evolved had two teachers in distant schools matched in a partnership. Cultural packages were exchanged between classes, along with examples of individual student work. Eventually, Freinet's program led to team-teaching partnerships among 10,000 schools throughout the world (p. 126).

Freinet's model emphasized the development of cooperative learning models and the development of a broadly based and experiential cultural and social literacy. His schools continue to operate today in France and around the world. For schools using their model of curriculum, computers and the Internet are extraordinary resources. But, the lack of a practical technology for the exchanges has limited the feasibility of implementing this model as widely as it deserves. Students using the Internet can exchange "cultural packages," write letters to one another and work together on collaborative projects. The Internet and the World Wide Web can be a vehicle for deeper and more meaningful multicultural exchanges.

There are many sites on the Internet where teachers and students can go to learn more about international exchanges, as well as about other cultures. These situations provide positive experiences of "learning walks" in the spirit of Freinet. From our perspective, the true wealth of these Internet and World Wide Web sites for multicultural education will be of use to students when they are able to engage in the second and third technique of Freinet (i.e., sharing perspectives and finding and networking).

Opportunities for "learning walks," the sharing of perspectives and findings, as well as student networking can be found at many Web sites. The Global SchoolNet Foundation, for example, sponsors through its Web site a wide range of programs involving student and teacher exchanges.

Global SchoolNet Foundation
http://www.gsn.org

All About Education is a Web site that will help teachers, students, and parents set up e-mail exchanges.

All About Education
http://www.shadetree.com/~rplogman/

KidLink is a similar program that connects students from around the world with over 60,000 people having participated in their programs.

Kidlink
http://www.kidlink.org/kidlink/listmail.html

Explore the following list of addresses for examples of multicultural educational sites and resources:

The African-American Mosaic
http://lcweb.loc.gov/exhibits/African.American/intro.html

African-American history and cultural resources.

Asian Arts
http://www.webart.com/asianart/index.html

Resources on Asian art and culture.

An Electronic Field Trip to the United Nations
http://www.pbs.org/tal/un/

Visit the United Nations online.

Global Democracy Network
http:/www.gdn.org/

Information about protecting human rights.

Global Show and Tell
http://www.manymedia.com/show-n-tell/

An international show-and-tell forum for students.

K-12 Electronic Guide for African Resources on the Internet
http://www.sas.upenn.edu/African_Studies/Home_Page/AFR_GIDE.html

African cultural resources.

Nativeweb
http://web.maxwell.syr.edu/nativeweb

A site devoted to indigenous people from around the world.

Educational Native American Network (ENAN)
http://oiep.unm.edu/enan/home.html

Sources on Native American education and culture.

Protecting Students Using the Internet

Bringing the Internet and the World Wide Web into classrooms presents a number of potential problems for educators. The fact that the Internet allows virtually unlimited access to information means that students can visit sites inappropriate for them. Using the search engine on a Web browser, students can type in words as simple as "sex" or "erotic art" and connect into a huge number of sites that include adult information.

There are various software packages such as *CyberPatrol*, *Surf Watch*, and *Cyber Sitter,* that will block students from getting access to most inappropriate sites on the Internet. These programs are not totally foolproof, but can help avoid many problems.

Inappropriate sites for children can also include adult chat lines. One of the wonderful things about the Internet is that it provides children with the opportunity to go online and talk with adults. Children need to understand that because they make an acquaintance or friend online, it does not mean that they should not be cautious. These people are essentially strangers. In the past several years there have been several well-publicized national incidents involving children being contacted by adults via the Internet and subsequently being lured away from their homes.

In this context, children should be warned not to provide photographs of themselves, telephone numbers, or addresses to strangers over the Internet. They need to be made aware that someone who seems friendly on the Internet may in fact not have their best interests at heart. Useful child safety information is provided at a wide range of sites on the Internet.

Child Safety and Censorship on the Net
http://www.voicenet.com/~cranmer/censorship.html

Child Safety Online
http://www.omix.com/magid/child.safety.online.html

Child Safety on the Information Highway
http://www.larrysworld.com/child_safety.html

Acceptable Use Policy (AUP): an agreement signed by students, parents, teachers, and administrators concerning the agreed on rules for using the Internet in a particular school.

A major step toward making Internet use in your school safe is the establishment of an **acceptable use policy**.

Establishing an Acceptable Use Policy

What is an acceptable use policy? It is a contract signed by students, parents, teachers, and administrators that agrees to specific rules about using the Internet and its resources.

What is acceptable and appropriate use of the Internet in schools? An acceptable use policy should include at least four separate elements:

1. The policy should explain how the Internet is connected to the teaching and learning expected in the classroom. This includes who will have access to the Internet and how access will be managed.

2. The policy should explain student responsibilities while online. This often includes description of etiquette on the Internet commonly called "netiquette."

3. The policy includes the consequences that will result from the violation of the policies.

4. The policy is written and agreed to by students and parents.

Chapter 10 explores in detail the ethical ramifications of an acceptable use policy. This chapter emphasizes the importance of an acceptable use policy as a means of regulating the use of the Internet in order to protect students. Acceptable use policies already exist in other parts of the educational system. It is an unacceptable use of a school library for students to misuse sexually explicit anatomical drawings from a biology or anatomy textbook. By clearly defining an acceptable use policy for students on the Internet, educators can contribute to students' understanding of the mature and appropriate use of research and reference material.

There are many sources of information on acceptable use policies available on the Internet. Among the very best models in the country is the one created by the Bellingham Public Schools in Bellingham, Washington. Their acceptable use policies are available online at:

Bellingham Public Schools Internet Policies
http://www.bham.wednet.edu/policies.htm

Other valuable sites dealing with Internet use and acceptable use policies include:

Acceptable Use Policies Houston Independent School System
http://chico.rice.edu/armadillo/Rice/Resources/acceptable.html

Mankato (Minnesota) Area Public Schools Acceptable Use Policy
http://www.isd77.k12.mn.us/guidelines.html

State of Indiana Requirements for Public School Internet Acceptable Use Policies
http://ideanet.doe.state.in.us/LearningResources/aupreg

Community High School (Ann Arbor, Michigan) Internetwork Policy Statement
http://communityhigh.org/about/CHS_policy.html

Internet and Electronic Mail Permission Form - 1995

 Bellingham Public Schools

We are pleased to offer students of the Bellingham Public Schools access to the district computer network for electronic mail and the Internet. To gain access to e-mail and the Internet, all students under the age of 18 must obtain parental permission and must sign and return this form to the LIBRARY MEDIA SPECIALIST. Students 18 and over may sign their own forms.

Access to e-mail and the Internet will enable students to explore thousands of libraries, databases, and bulletin boards while exchanging messages with Internet users throughout the world. Families should be warned that some material accessible via the Internet may contain items that are illegal, defamatory, inaccurate or potentially offensive to some people. While our intent is to make Internet access available to further educational goals and objectives, students may find ways to access other materials as well. We believe that the benefits to students from access to the Internet, in the form of information resources and opportunities for collaboration, exceed any disadvantages. But ultimately, parents and guardians of minors are responsible for setting and conveying the standards that their children should follow when using media and information sources. To that end, the Bellingham Public Schools support and respect each family's right to decide whether or not to apply for access.

District Internet and E-Mail Rules

Students are responsible for good behavior on school computer networks just as they are in a classroom or a school hallway. Communications on the network are often public in nature. General school rules for behavior and communications apply.

The network is provided for students to conduct research and communicate with others. Access to network services is given to students who agree to act in a considerate and responsible manner. Parent permission is required. Access is a privilege - not a right. Access entails responsibility.

Individual users of the district computer networks are responsible for their behavior and communications over those networks. It is presumed that users will comply with district standards and will honor the agreements they have signed. Beyond the clarification of such standards, the district is not responsible for restricting, monitoring or controlling the communications of individuals utilizing the network.

Network storage areas may be treated like school lockers. Network administrators may review files and communications to maintain system integrity and insure that users are using the system responsibly. Users should not expect that files stored on district servers will always be private.

Within reason, freedom of speech and access to information will be honored. During school, teachers of younger students will guide them toward appropriate materials. Outside of school, families bear the same responsibility for such guidance as they exercise with information sources such as television, telephones, movies, radio and other potentially offensive media.

As outlined in Board policy and procedures on student rights and responsibilities (3200), copies of which are available in school offices, the following are not permitted:

- Sending or displaying offensive messages or pictures
- Using obscene language
- Harassing, insulting or attacking others
- Damaging computers, computer systems or computer networks
- Violating copyright laws
- Using another's password
- Trespassing in another's folders, work or files
- Intentionally wasting limited resources
- Employing the network for commercial purposes

Violations may result in a loss of access as well as other disciplinary or legal action.

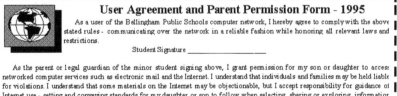

User Agreement and Parent Permission Form - 1995

As a user of the Bellingham Public Schools computer network, I hereby agree to comply with the above stated rules - communicating over the network in a reliable fashion while honoring all relevant laws and restrictions.

Student Signature _____

As the parent or legal guardian of the minor student signing above, I grant permission for my son or daughter to access networked computer services such as electronic mail and the Internet. I understand that individuals and families may be held liable for violations. I understand that some materials on the Internet may be objectionable, but I accept responsibility for guidance of Internet use - setting and conveying standards for my daughter or son to follow when selecting, sharing or exploring information and media.

Parent Signature _____ Date _____

Name of Student _____ School _____ Grade _____ Soc. Sec.# _____

Birth Date _____ Street Address _____ Home Telephone _____

Internet and Electronic Mail Permission Form, Bellingham, Washington Schools.

The Future in Perspective

Estimates for 1999 are that the worldwide installed base for personal computers will increase to approximately 303 million machines and Internet access will number approximately 184 million of these machines. This means that through 1999 the compound annual growth of personal computers with Internet access will increase 68.4%, or four times as fast as the overall installed base of personal computers (Wilde, 1996, p. 21F).

In conclusion, the Internet and the World Wide Web have the potential to literally "bring the world to the child." More so than any other recent educational innovation, the use of online resources can radically change the activities of students in the schools. Through online exchanges with people around the country and the world, and as a result of having virtually unlimited access to reference sources and materials, a whole new universe of learning is within a student's reach.

Before the potential of the Internet and the World Wide Web can be fully realized, however, new models of instruction that take advantage of the Internet's resources and integrate themselves with traditional curricula will have to be developed. This is a significant challenge, which may or may not be adequately met by the educational system.

QUESTIONS FOR REFLECTION AND DISCUSSION

1. How are the Internet and the World Wide Web hypertext or hypermedia systems?

2. What is the difference between the Internet and the World Wide Web?

3. What are the advantages of the Internet for multicultural education?

4. How is the exposure of students to potentially unsuitable materials on the Internet potentially different from their exposure to similar materials via television or film?

5. What is an acceptable use policy? How does it protect schools and teachers?

6. What are the advantages versus disadvantages of a student researching a paper on the Internet versus the library?

7. How do the Internet and the World Wide Web potentially change the work of teachers?

8. Can the Internet and the World Wide Web contribute to greater equity in the educational system? If so, how?

9. Is the world becoming a "global village" as a result of the Internet and the World Wide Web?

10. What are the implications of the fact that the great majority of activities on the Internet are in English?

ACTIVITIES

1. Develop a classroom lesson using information resources drawn from the Internet.

2. Visit a chat room or discussion group for a subject that is of interest to you on the Internet.

3. Read one of the science ficition novels by William Gibson such as *Neuromancer* or *Mona Lisa Overdrive* that deals with some of the ways the Internet may evolve in the future.

EXERCISE FOR FURTHER DEVELOPMENT OF YOUR REFLECTIVE PRACTICE FOR TEACHING WITH COMPUTER TECHNOLOGY

Teachers as professionals need to be able to teach all students in relation to their communication with students. The use of computer technology is impacting the ways we communicate. Read the following presentation on digital counseling and reflect on the following issues related to teaching practice:

1. How does the emulation of human thinking with computer technology lead us to believe that using computers is interpersonal communication?

2. In what ways can a proper communication role for computer technology be found in schools?

Digital Counseling

Rogerian counseling is a method developed by the psychologist Carl Rogers. It involves the counselor asking a question when a client or patient makes a statement. If you were to say, for example, that "the weather outside today is beautiful," someone using this technique would respond by asking what you meant by beautiful.

When interjected into day-to-day conversations the effect is to have a pseudo-dialogue. In fact, what the process does is isolate the person who is asking the questions from engaging in a genuine conversation or dialogue. Perhaps this is a good way for counselors to insulate themselves from the emotional stress and problems of a client, but it is ultimately a false and dehumanizing technique if there is to be genuine and meaningful dialogue between people.

In his book *Computers, Power and Human Reason*, the computer scientist Joseph Weizenbaum (1976) described his development of an experimental computer program called ELIZA. The program, which was named after the character Eliza in the George Bernard Shaw play *Pygmalion,* was created in the mid-1960s. The program was designed on a two-tier level, the first was a language analyzer and the second was a script (Wiezenbaum, 1976, pp. 2–3). For his first experiment with the program, Wiezenbaum gave the program a script that allowed it to play (or as Wiezenbaum insisted "parody") the role of a Rogerian psychotherapist.

An example of the ELIZA program at work can be seen in the following segment of a conversation between a young woman and the ELIZA program. The interaction begins with the woman speaking. The responses made by the ELIZA program are in capitals:

Men are all alike.

IN WHAT WAY

They're always bugging us about something or other.

CAN YOU THINK OF A SPECIFIC EXAMPLE

Well my boyfriend made me come here.

YOUR BOYFRIEND MADE YOU COME HERE

He says I'm depressed much of the time.

I AM SORRY TO HEAR THAT YOU ARE DEPRESSED... (*Ibid*, p. 3)

ELIZA was widely experimented with at MIT and it quickly became known in the international computer community.

The ELIZA program, with its Rogerian script, was called "DOCTOR" by Wiezenbaum. Wiezenbaum was shocked at the extent to which people became emotionally involved with the ELIZA/DOCTOR program and the fact that many psychiatrists and psychologists actually thought the program could eventually be used in clinical settings.

Wiezenbaum had not expected the program to be taken seriously by the psychological community. For him, it was simply an interesting experiment. His assumption had been from the beginning that "as a prerequisite to the very possibility that one person might help another learn to cope with his emotional problems, that the helper himself participate in the other's experience of those problems and, in large part by way of his own empathic recognition of them, himself come to understand them" (Wiezenbaum, 1976, pp. 5–6)

I suppose that my objection to the conversations that I have with my colleague who speaks to me as though I were in Rogerian counseling, has to do with the fact that he is not engaging with me in a human and genuine dialogue but is simply processing knowledge.

I come from a tradition of narrative description and dialogue. Storytelling, and what ethnographic theorists refer to as "thick description," is essential to my knowing and interacting with the world. Rogerian counseling, although developed as a technique outside of the computer, is in fact based on an information-processing model, which explains in large part why it was so well-suited to be used with a computer.

As we move farther into a post-typographic and postmodern culture, models of a similar type are likely to become more and more common in our human interactions. They represent what Wiezenbaum referred to as a "mechanical conception of man." The model is a disturbing one—one that suggests sacrificing genuine dialogue for a pseudo and false engagement.

📖 SOURCES

Armstrong, S. (1996). *A pocket tour of the Kidstuff on the Internet.* San Francisco: Sybex.

Benedikt, M. (Ed.). (1992). *Cyberspace: First steps.* Cambridge, MA: MIT Press.

Cerf, V. G. (1991). Networks. *Scientific American, 265*(3), 72–81.

Classroom Connect. (1991). *Educators' world wide web tour guide.* Lancaster, PA: Wentworth World Wide Media, Inc.

Cummins, J. and Sayers, D. (1997). *Brave new schools: Challenging cultural illiteracy through global learning networks.* New York: St. Martin's Press.

Frazier, G. G. & Frazier, D. (1994). *Telecommunications and education: Surfing and the art of change.* Alexandria, VA: National School Boards Association.

Gibson, W. (1984). *Neuromancer.* (New York: Ace.

Gibson, W. (1996). The net is a waste of time, and that's exactly what's right about it. *The New York Times,* July 14, pp. 30–31.

Harris, J. (1996). *Way of the Ferret—Finding and using educational resources on the Internet.* Eugene, OR: International Society for Technology in Education.

Provenzo, E. F., Jr. (1998). *The educator's brief guide to the internet and the world wide web.* Princeton, NJ: Eye on Education.

Rheingold, H. (1993). *The virtual community: Homesteading on the electronic frontier.* Reading, MA: Addison-Wesley.

Ryder, R., & Hughes, T. (1997). *Internet for educators.* Upper Saddle River, NJ: Prentice-Hall.

Turkle, S. (1995). *Life on the screen: Identity in the age of the internet.* New York: Simon & Schuster.

Wiezenbaum, J. (1976). *Computers, power and human reason: From judgement to calculation.* San Francisco: W. H. Freeman.

Wilde, C. (1996). The Internet and electronic commerce: A revolution begins. *The New York Times*, March 24, p. 21F.

ETHICAL AND LEGAL ASPECTS OF TEACHING WITH TECHNOLOGY

A Specific Case of Ethical and Legal Issues, General Ethical and Legal Issues in Teaching With Technology, Use of Computers as Instructional Tools, Responsible Use of Computers in the Classroom, Individual Responsible Use of Computers, Problems Arising From Computer Access, Questions of Personal Responsibility and Safety, Public Nature of Computer Use in the Classroom, Copyright Protection, Privacy Rights, Hackers and Viruses

Some are tempted to think of life in cyberspace as insignificant, as escape or meaningless diversion. It is not. Our experiences there are serious play. We belittle them at our risk. We must understand the dynamics of virtual experience both to foresee who might be in danger and to put these experiences to best use.

—Sherry Turkle

CASE STUDY

Ms. Robards is the librarian at a high school in suburban Los Angeles. The students attending her school are economically and socially privileged. As part of the library's new "media lab" there are not only high-speed links to the Internet and the World Wide Web, but also high-quality color printers for the students and faculty to use in the preparation of reports and projects. Mrs. French—a mother of one of the 11th graders—called the school's principal, Dr. Zemecki, this morning. She was livid about pornographic pictures her son had brought home from school.

Evidently he had gotten access to them through the school's Internet link and had printed them off on the school's printer. Dr. Zemecki wants Ms. Robards to either adequately police the lab or shut it down. As she explained to her, "We never had this type of problem when we had the students just using textbooks and library materials."

The introduction to this book made reference to Bowers' work and his argument that computers are not a neutral technology. As discussed earlier, every computer program has a particular perspective from which it is written. Computers and their software also radically change the access people, including students, have to different types of information. In a tightly controlled library environment, the materials students have access to can be carefully managed. Giving them access to the Internet means losing that control.

As a result of the introduction of computers into the learning environment, teachers and administrators find themselves faced with a whole new series of ethical and legal problems. The following chapter discusses the ethical and legal issues that have arisen as a result of the introduction of computers into the schools.

For us, the specific ethical and legal issues found in the section on acceptable use policies for the Internet are a concrete example of the general issues related to teaching with technology.

A Specific Case of Ethical and Legal Issues: Acceptable Use Policies for the Internet

In Chapter 8 we presented an example of an acceptable use policy. When talking about "acceptable use," questions arise such as: What is acceptable and appropriate use of the Internet in schools? Who should decide the policies underlying its use? What obligations do teachers and administrators have as a result of introducing the Internet into their schools?

As is evident in the case study that introduces this chapter, the use of the Internet brings these questions out into the open. Prior to the Internet, a librarian like Ms. Robards believed that she could control access to materials in her library. However, the introduction of the Internet demonstrates how students can use school-based technologies and materials for their own purposes.

The phenomenon of acceptable use policies has grown up as a way to manage the use of the Internet in schools, as well as to educate students, teachers, administrators, and parents about responsible Internet use. If effectively implemented, it addresses the type of problems faced by Ms. Robards by clearly defining acceptable use for school-sponsored technologies such as the Internet.

In fact, acceptable use policies already exist in many schools. Using school phones to conduct private business affairs, for example, is generally considered unacceptable for most administrators, students, and teachers. Likewise, at the senior high school level, cars intended for use in driver education are not to be used by a teacher to go to the bank after school, or by a student needing transportation to the senior prom.

In the case of the Internet and the schools, what are the essential characteristics of an acceptable use policy? We believe that it should include the four following parts:

1. The policy explains how the Internet is connected to the teaching and learning expected in the classroom. This includes who will have access to the Internet and how access will be managed. Here the *use of computers as instructional tools* is the ethical and legal issue.

2. The policy explains student responsibilities while online. This often includes description of etiquette on the Internet commonly called "netiquette." Here *responsible use of computers in the classroom* is the ethical and legal issue.

3. The policy includes the repercussions that will result from the violation of policies. Here *problems arising from computer access* is the ethical and legal issue.

4. The policy is written and agreed to by students and parents. Here the *public nature of computer use in the classroom* is the ethical and legal issue.

An acceptable use policy that includes the types of elements outlined earlier is essentially a statement of ethical and legal intent. It is important because it recognizes that the use of computers on the part of students, teachers, and administrators carries with it both ethical and legal obligations and duties. These obligations and duties are part of a more general set of issues that must be addressed by those making appropriate, or "acceptable" use of computers.

General Ethical and Legal Issues in Teaching With Technology

Are computers simply toys with bells and whistles, or are they powerful instructional tools? What responsibilities do students and parents have when computers are used for instruction? Who has access, and what type of access do they have to computers in schools? How can that access be abused? Are the limits of a student's freedom, and in turn responsibility, different in schools than when they use the machines on a private basis? The experience of problems with the Internet acts as a mirror for the teacher to observe the ethical issues related to instructional computing. This experience delineates the following four areas of ethical and legal issues: use of computers as instructional tools, responsible use of computers in the classroom, problems arising from computer access, and public nature of computer use in the classroom.

Computer Ethics

1. Never harm anyone through your use of a computer.
2. Never interfere with someone else's work using a computer.
3. Never use a computer to do something illegal.
4. Never use illegally obtained software.
5. Never use another person's ideas without proper credit.

Use of Computers as Instructional Tools

Because we are talking about computers in schools, we need to understand that "appropriate use" must always be related to teaching. Including computers in classrooms should be based on their merit as instructional tools. Computers are a new technology, but they are being introduced into a curriculum originally designed without them in mind.

Teachers tend to have problems with technologies that do not assist them in what they already are trying to do. The attractiveness of computers should never overpower the purpose of teaching (i.e., student learning). With or without computers, exciting things should be going on in classrooms. Students should be engaged in activities that stimulate their learning. Computers should not be viewed as a way to change teaching methods. Rather, they should be assessed in relation to how their inclusion improves the learning being sought. According to Larry Cuban (1984):

> No longer should the central issue about instruction be: how should teachers teach? Based upon my experience and study of classrooms over the last century, I believe the central question is simply: how can what teachers already do be improved? (p. 268)

Cuban came to this position from researching how American teachers have taught in this century. This does not mean that using computers will not change classrooms. Nor does it mean that they will not necessarily bring with them new means of delivering instructional materials. They will. But the change will be in relation to the improvement of the delivery of the curriculum that teachers are already committed to teach. We see it as ethically wrong to provide computers simply to change teachers or to make classrooms "teacher proof." We see it this way because research on teaching shows this cannot work. What does work and is appropriate is to have computers work as instructional tools within a direction that is desired for its own sake.

Although we feel that computers should not be used mainly to change teaching, we strongly believe they change the learning environment of classrooms and schools. A classroom with computers represents a different set of values and commitments than one without them. C. A. Bowers (1980) identified the inherent value impact of putting computers in classrooms as recognizing their "non-neutrality." Including them is not a neutral act.

This view does not solely apply to computers, but it is involved when any technology is introduced into the teaching process. Larry Hickman (1991) saw the value-laden reality of including technology as being understood by the philosopher John Dewey in the early part of this century. For Hickman, Dewey's notion of technology rejects the view that "neutral tools are brought to bear on ends that are valued for reasons external to the situations within which those tools have been developed" (p. 202). According to Hickman, Dewey held the view that "tools and artifacts are no more neutral than are plants, non-human animals, or human beings themselves: they are interactive within situations that teem with values" (p. 202). Teachers need to reflect on the value judgments they are making in either including or not including computers in their teaching.

The close linking of technology values and curriculum values not only strengthens the consistency of messages, but can also make the use of computers a tool in creating a more equitable classroom atmosphere. In assessing access to computer technology, the Office of Technology Assessment of the U.S. Congress (OTA, 1988) observed that "there has been much concern over the apparent tendency for school computer use to be dominated by male students. OTA has found that this phenomenon is abated when application of technology is linked to curriculum" (p. 36).

Earlier we identified that an Internet acceptable use policy should have an explanation of the curricular purpose of using the Internet through computers. In reality, this should only be a reflection and recording of a specific piece of the overall picture and purpose of using computers and computer-related technology in a school and classroom. If schools and teachers are going to use computers to support teaching and learning, then there is an ethical responsibility to identify "why" they are being used. That answer must have a curricular purpose that justifies the expenditure of time and effort given over to their use.

Responsible Use of Computers in the Classroom

Although the Office of Technology Assessment identifies linking to curriculum as a means to overcome some equity problems, equity issues are varied. Who gets access to computers? Boys or girls? Rich or poor? People with special needs versus the general population?

Teachers need to be aware of how computers are or are not reinforcing desired patterns of access. As early as its 1988 report, the Office of Technology Assessment found that "in absolute terms, small schools have fewer computers than large ones, but smaller schools have *proportionally* more computers than large schools" (p. 35). Analyzing their data further, they observed that "because minority students are more likely to attend large urban schools, their access to computers has been worse than that of white students" (p. 35). Access has been related to acquisition policies and "wealthier schools have acquired technology more rapidly than schools with students of predominantly low socio-economic status" (p. 35).

In terms of computer sophistication and access, 1988 was a long time ago. In a 1995 study, the Office of Technology Assessment found that to assess fully the responsible use of computers by schools we must look at aggregate numbers. As they pointed out: "Conventional data on infrastructure—numbers of computers in a school, student-computer ratios, and school ownership of various kinds of video and telecommunications equipment—are insufficient measures of access to technologies" (p. 122).

To assess equitable access in a school or classroom they identified three factors that need to be determined:

1. Availability of computers

2. Organization and arrangements of computer access

3. Computer support of teaching

In the area of availability of computers, OTA reported that "key factors include the age and power of hardware and the kinds of peripherals and software the equipment can support," as well as "the presence of connectivity hardware and software" (p. 122). Number of computers can hide the power of computers to assist students in their work. Students may have access to computers, but the power necessary to do moderately sophisticated work may be unavailable. It is possible that a teacher with a Pentium PC and Windows 95 at home may be told that her classroom already is equipped with computers because there are two Apple IIEs in it—even though these computers were obsolete by the mid-1980s.

Beyond physical availability, responsible (i.e., equitable) use involves the organization and arrangement of computer access in "a way that is conducive to frequent and effective use by teachers and students" (p. 122). This means their real questions are not how many computers does a school or school district have, but how many computers are in a classroom readily available to students and how often they are being used? Possession tells only a small part of the story. Responsible use in the classroom is the real story.

As already noted, essential to effective teaching with technology is the support of teaching through the use of computers. As the Office of Technological Assessment reported, for students to have real access teachers must be ready "to use technology in their everyday teaching, to use technologies for two-way communication, and to use technologies to encourage the best instructional practices" (p. 122). Because teachers are at different levels of computer literacy and usage, we can only conclude that student access is at different levels in different classrooms. Again, the real assessment of this type of equity is at the classroom level rather than at the school or district level. Schools and local districts, however, should be using their resources to make the differences less dramatic. Inservice training should not be conducted without a goal of improving the computer support of teaching for each classroom, as well as the whole school where the instruction occurs.

Individual Responsible Use of Computers

Any technology brings with it specific problems related to classroom management. Computer technology is no exception. While students may believe they are working alone on a computer, they are not. Whether, for example, working on or off a computer network, the machine a student uses is communal property and should be treated with appropriate care and respect. When on a network, students need to know they are connected to an unseen, virtual community.

In networked settings, students need to understand that there are appropriate rules of behavior or etiquette. The rules of "netiquette" include:

1. Being polite. Users should not "flame," that is, write or send abusive messages to others. USERS SHOULD NOT WRITE IN ALL CAPITALS. It is like shouting. Users should have tolerance

for neophytes. A private message would be better than a public notice.

2. Using appropriate language. Users should not swear, use vulgarities, or use any other inappropriate language.

3. Protecting your privacy. Users should not reveal their personal addresses or phone numbers.

4. Protecting the privacy of fellow users. Users should not reveal the personal addresses or phone numbers of other users.

5. Respecting the property of others. Users should respect copyrighted software and other materials.

6. Recognizing that electronic mail (e-mail) is not private. Users should realize that the privacy of e-mail is not guaranteed. System operators have access to all mail. Messages relating to illegal activities may be reported to authorities.

These points all relate to common courtesy and respect. Sometimes we forget because computers are machines that there are other human beings connected to them. We respond to a message that comes on the screen in an impersonal manner, letting down our inhibitions because we do not necessarily have to reveal ourselves to the user on the other end of the computer line.

Because they are at a physically safe distance on a computer does not mean that we do not have to treat people with courtesy and respect in an online context. Courtesy and respect are more than a convention. They are signals of the respect we have for each other as human beings. Users need to be taught to extend these face-to-face ethical considerations to the virtual world of networked or online use.

Besides ethical concerns related to individual use, we have made the point that good ethics demand that we be concerned about equity of access to computers for each student. However, we also need to identify, in addition to the benefits, the ethical problems attached to such general equitable access.

Problems Arising From Computer Access

Case Study

Mr. Renfrow teaches junior high school science in a working-class neighborhood in Pittsburgh. He has been terrifically successful at getting his students into computing by having them share computer games with one another. A lot of the games are violent and sexist. One of the most popular games the students like to play is called NightTrap. The game's story line revolves around a group of coeds who are staying overnight in a house in northern California. They are mysteriously disappearing and being murdered. It turns out that the kidnappers/murderers are alien vampires who drain all the blood from their victims. Although he does not let his students play the game in class or during the school's after hours program, they talk about it frequently in class. What should he do?

When we give access to students, we need to be sure that we understand that not all access to computers is positive. Mr. Renfrow's problem arises from the world of computer video games that exists outside the classroom. Ethical issues unaddressed outside the classroom need to be addressed inside the classroom. In the case of video games, for example, their computer-based technology is a source of media that both entertains and teaches students specific values.

Video games are important because most students' primary contact with computers is through video game systems such as Nintendo or Sega. Rather than being neutral, these games include specific themes (i.e., social texts) that are often violent, sexist, and racist. In the case of the Nintendo game system, research on the social content of the games from the early 1990s indicated that of the 47 most popular games included in the system, 13 involved scenarios in which women were kidnapped and had to be rescued (i.e., the idea of women as victims). This represents 30% of the games, a number that is even more revealing when we take into account that 11 of the 47 games were based on sports themes such as car racing or basketball. Women were always rescued by men. Although men were rescued in the games too, they were never rescued by women (Provenzo, 1991, pp. 109-110).

From an ethical point of view, are we just talking about trivial games, or is this something with which educators and parents need to be concerned? There is clear evidence to suggest that while girls are very interested in computers and video games, they are not interested in games whose main themes focus on women being victimized. Such themes are described as being "dumb" or "boring." They also discourage girls from using video games and in turn computers because they are activities "only for boys." What are the consequences for women in terms of developing computer skills that can be used in their professional and work careers, when they are so actively discouraged from using video games and computer games when they are younger? We believe that commercial video games do in fact have an important potential influence on students and the attitudes about computing they carry into the schools.

Questions of Personal Responsibility and Safety

Case Study

John Roberts is a 15-year-old freshman at a rural high school in Colorado. John's family is deeply religious. He is also gay, but has told no one but his math teacher, Mr. Swensen. Mr. Swensen has quietly provided him with counseling and advice. Recently, John stopped by after school to talk with Mr. Swensen. He was excited because he had discovered a chat line for gay teenagers. He has been invited to go to Denver to meet some of the people he has been talking to in the chat room. He has told his parents that he is going to be gone on a school trip for the weekend, instead of telling them that he is going to meet with his new friends.

For John, this is a simple situation. Surely Mr. Swensen understands the difficulties and will help John see the problematic situation he is getting himself into. While students are on a computer, they may not realize that the world they have entered is more complex than they are imagining. While they are on a computer, they are connected through the Internet to millions of other computers around the world. Although they may feel alone and protected, users of the Internet are in a public place. The Internet has risks attached to it. These risks are similar to those found in playgrounds, on school buses, and even in schools themselves.

While most people in society are respectful and well-intentioned, not all are. The Internet is not different. There are users who are rude, mean, and even exploitive and predatory. Parents and schools should teach students to keep themselves safe. One way is to acknowledge that some Internet users are unsavory characters. To help students keep themselves safe, here are some rules to follow:

1. Users should never give out in an e-mail message, or online posting, personal identifying information such as home address, telephone number, age, or physical location.

2. Student users should never arrange a face-to-face meeting with another Internet user without parental permission.

3. Users should never respond to threatening or obscene e-mail messages. Student users should forward a copy of these messages to a teacher or parent so that they can be dealt with.

4. Because the Internet is a "virtual" rather than a real world, users should remember that online users may not be who they appear to be. An Internet contact who says "she's" a "teenage student" may in fact be a 35-year-old man posing as someone else.

5. In school, computers should be in a central part of the classroom. They should be placed where the teacher and other students can keep an eye on each other.

The National Center for Missing and Exploited Children (NCMEC) has additional information on this subject.

The National Center for Missing and Exploited Children
www.missingkids.org

In addition to the problems of unethical Internet users, there is also the problem of access on the Internet to material inappropriate for student users. A technique for taking action to limit access to such material has been the development of software that blocks inappropriate material. This software is designed to keep students away from inappropriate, adult-oriented, and/or explicit materials found in Web sites, newsgroups, ftp sites, gopher sites and IRC channels. The premise is that anything with an Internet address can be blocked. Examples of this software include *CyberPatrol*, *CyberSitter*, *Internet Filter*, the *Internet WatchDog*, *KinderGuard*, *Net Shepherd*, *NetNanny Parental Guidance*, *Rated PG*, *SPECS for Kids*, *SurfWatch*, and *Web Track SE*. The software provides lists of restrictable material as well as regular updates. Some allow for the creation of custom lists by allowing additions and subtractions. Some also facilitate control of the time of access during a day and the length of access by individual users.

This type of software is helpful, but it is not totally foolproof. People putting inappropriate material on the Internet are finding ways around software, as well as adding material at a rate that makes it a challenge to keep up with additions. You should warn parents and other responsible parties that blocking the software is not foolproof. It will certainly lessen problems, but it cannot totally eliminate them. Do not oversell the power of this software. Overselling it can give the impression that you have taken total responsibility for protecting users. Given the increasing growth of the Internet, no one is capable of following through on that type of promise.

Public Nature of Computer Use in the Classroom

Case Study

Mrs. Goldman is a middle school teacher in St. Louis who runs an afterschool computer program for gifted inner-city students. Her star pupil is Joey, a 12-year-old programming whiz who has just discovered multimedia. He has outlined an elaborate multimedia program he wants to create using the authoring program *Director*. The school does not own the program, but her husband, who is a professor in communications at a local community college, has a copy of the program for his work. There is no money in the budget to buy the program, which is extremely expensive, and Joey is the only student skilled enough to use it. Mrs. Goldman's husband has said he would be glad to make a copy of the program for Joey.

This scenario raises ethical issues about teachers' involvement in copyright infringement. It also raises issues about the private work of a student and possible privacy rights. Finally, Joey is a gifted student, but is he being encouraged to circumvent proper rules and laws? Such circumventing has encouraged hackers and viruses. While this may seem to be a private relationship between a teacher and a student, it is public because the school use of computers involves public acts and public concerns. Among these concerns are copyright protection and privacy rights, as well as the impact of hackers and viruses.

Copyright Protection

The legal protection of the intellectual property rights of authors and publishers is called copyright. This protection covers computer software as well as written materials. The Software Publishers Association has printed guidelines on fair use of software, which they distribute as a free service. The copyright of owners is protected by federal law (Copyright Act, Title 17 of the U.S. Code) from the time of its creation. Because it is easy to duplicate, software has special problems related to copyright. Unlike other media, a copy of software is as good as the original. Copiers are liable, whether or not they know they have violated the law.

Schools and other educational institutions are not exempt from obeying the laws related to copyrights. Because of the influence schools have, teachers should be educating students about their legal and ethical responsibilities to respect copyrighted material. Schools may have limited budgets, but this does not lessen their responsibility to pay for services and equipment. Books and equipment are bought at fair market prices. Software, by law, is given the same protection.

In fact, publishers provide schools with special arrangements to evaluate and purchase software at discount rates. Schools can evaluate software through demonstration ("demo") programs. These are programs that give a feel for the software but usually have some features disabled. When a school decides to buy specific software, there are several arrangements that are available to have "legal" software in schools. The regular means for purchasing software is a single user/single machine license. This is the way you find software in a computer store. A single user is able to make a backup/archival copy in case of disk failure.

To assist schools further, there are multiple user/multiple machine arrangements. These arrangements protect the author's right to compensation while trying to make programs more affordable for group usage. The typical arrangements are "lab packs" and "site licenses. In a lab pack there are several users/machines licensed— usually 5, sometimes 10. For larger groups such as 50, 100, or 250, there are "site licenses" that provide materials for the multiple users. These "site" arrangements usually allow schools to make a specified number of copies for one location at a reduced price per copy. The Software Publisher's Association, the main industry group concerned with protecting software copyright, provides guidelines on copyright and fair use of computer software at their Web site.

Software Publisher's Association
http://www.spa.com

Privacy Rights

Students need someplace to store their work. Ease of access often dictates that this will be on the school's computers. Although they may believe that these machines are private, the privacy of their work may not be protected. They need to be taught to work knowing they will not have privacy.

The 11th grader in the vignette at the beginning of this chapter probably thought he was working in private. After his mother and Dr. Zemecki's response, he is probably disabused of that belief. While this student may see the reaction as censorship, he needs to learn that he has used public property in a public setting and must face public reaction.

One area of computer usage in which students and parents should expect privacy rights is the area of the privacy of student records. The "Buckley Amendment," legally known as the Family Education Rights and Privacy Act of 1974 (FERPA), was enacted to safeguard students' and parents' rights to correct problems in the collection and maintenance of public records. Besides the right to inspect records, this law limits access to school records, such as test scores, to those who have a legitimate educational need for the information. Written consent is required for the release of this information. With the increasing power of computers to store data and to provide information for analysis, means of access to restricted information is increasing. Teachers and schools must strengthen their vigilance to control access. Students and parents have a legal and ethical basis for expecting such protection of their privacy. A major source for information about privacy and intellectual freedom and computing is provided by the Electronic Frontier Foundation.

Electronic Frontier Foundation
http://www.eff.org/

Privacy on the Internet

Privacy on the Internet is becoming an increasing problem as new technologies develop that make it possible to capture information about users when they visit Web sites. Software known as "Cyber-Cookies" makes it possible for a computer with a Web site on the Internet to capture very specific information about anyone who visits. A demonstration of this is provided by the Center for Democracy and Technology's web privacy site.

Center for Democracy and Technology
http://www.13x.com/cgi-bin/cdt/snoop.pl

When one of the authors visited this web site, it generated the following report:

Your computer is a PC running Windows 95.
Your Internet browser is Netscape.
You are coming from slip166-72-131-84.fl.us.ibm.net.

Information of this type is of enormous interest to merchandisers. Imagine selling real estate and being able to capture the names and addresses of the people who visit your web site. Often such sites ask for specific information about the type of house you are interested in buying, as well as the price range in which you are interested. This type of information can be enormously valuable to retailers interested in capturing information about individuals whom they can target for marketing campaigns.

Do retailers and others have the right to this type of information about you? Should they know what sites you have visited on the Internet? In the nonelectronic world, one can enter a library or store without revealing one's name, one's interests, or one's buying habits. Should the same principles apply in cyberspace? Commercial online service providers can use special types of software to track every online site that you visit. Do they have the right to this information? Do they have the right to resell or make it available to others?

Of course, how this information is used is critical. As the Center for Democracy and Technology explains: "if your repeated visits to web sites containing information on cigarettes results in free samples, coupons, or even e-mail to you about a new tobacco product, you may not be concerned. However, if your visits to these web sites result in escalating insurance premiums due to categorization as a smoker—now you're beginning to get concerned."

Privacy in cyberspace and on the Internet will become a more and more important issue as technologies become more sophisticated and surveillance and the collection of data more systematic. It is an issue that deserves very careful thought and attention.

Hackers and Viruses

Hacker: a computer expert; person for whom extending the computer's capabilities is a consuming interest.

It seems as though from the inception of modern computing, some computer users have sought to invade other people's computers with the intention of doing harm. People who break into other computers through electronic means are called "**hackers**." Programs and program extensions or hidden files that damage computers and their contents are called "viruses."

"Hackers" sometimes gain admiration because they are individuals gifted with a technical ability who are able to think in creative ways about computer programs. But there should be no mistake that they are illegally breaking into networks, stealing software and data, disrupting services, creating chaos for users, or fraudulently misrepresenting who they are. The problem of hacking has direct consequences for the Internet that allows remote access. Two-way computer connections with servers permitting entrance to a system are prey to hacking. The ways that hackers are excluded are various solutions such as "firewalls." A firewall is a system that allows access to only some areas to unauthorized users. Given the mentality of hackers, this is an area where Internet users need to keep constant vigilance. Each time a prevention scheme is established, it becomes a challenge to the hackers. Students need to be educated to be alert to what can happen to their work and computers in the hands of hackers. Students who are gifted at using computers need to be educated about their responsibility to respect the rights and property of others.

"The Millennium Bug"

Seemingly trivial decisions can have enormous long-term consequences in a field like computing. An example can be seen in the case of the "Millenium Bug."

In the late 1960s, software was abbreviated to save expensive space in computer programs. Instead of writing out the full year for a program date (e.g., 1969), just 69 was used instead. By January 1, 2000, it is predicted that as many as 30% of the computers in the United States may crash or simply not work.

Every standard date on a computer will be set back to the year 1900. People born in 1950 will for the purposes of the computer not exist yet. The potential for havoc is enormous. Older government computer programs, such as those found in the Social Security Administration, will have to be reprogrammed to make sure that people are not dropped from their lists. New people could receive checks and support they are not due for many years. For example, a child born on January 1, 2000 could appear to be a 100-year-old retiree fully qualified to collect retirement benefits.

The problem on the surface is a simple one, yet it is enormously difficult to solve. Every program using a two-digit date for a year rather than a four-digit date will have to be reprogrammed. Some people estimate that the total cost of fixing the problem worldwide could run as high as $600 billion—a huge figure if it is true.

The crisis will not affect newer computers. Because it will cost hundreds of dollars on average for every person living on the face of the Earth to solve the problem, the "Millenium Bug" provides an interesting case study. It does suggest the extent to which computers can have unexpected consequences for our economy.

Computer viruses can destroy data or hardware on your computer. At times they are only irritating and somewhat harmless. They take their name from biological viruses. Such viruses attach themselves to "well" cells and take them over. Computer viruses attach themselves when they are copied onto programs or come with downloaded programs. Computers or disks can become infected when programs or media are moved from one machine to another. Because some viruses are programmed maliciously, users need to be careful about the programs they share and the files they put on their machines. It is best to install new software whose packaging is still intact. Antivirus software that is regularly updated can help to set the necessary protections. Again, students need to be educated to be alert to what can happen to their work and computers from viruses.

We began this chapter with a vignette about Ms. Robards, a high school librarian. We also conclude it by examining her case. Because of student access to pornography on the World Wide Web, she faced difficulties that can result from student access to the "power of computing." She was forced to face some of the ethical and practical issues facing almost every teacher, administrator, and school system interested in using computers.

Ethical issues in computing must be addressed. As we have seen, these can arise in many different contexts. Who has access to the power provided by this new technology? What is appropriate use of materials? What rights do people have in terms of privacy and not having their work compromised? These are very real challenges faced by anyone interested in using computers in the schools. Although the problems are not simple, we believe the power of computer technology in enhancing education is well worth the struggle needed to deal with them.

QUESTIONS FOR REFLECTION AND DISCUSSION

1. How does the idea of an acceptable use policy help us understand the ethical and legal issues of using computer technology? What are four major areas of ethical and legal issues of using computer technology?

2. What are some basic computer ethics?

3. Why do teachers have problems with technology that does not assist them in their teaching?

4. What are the factors that need to be assessed to determine equitable use of computers in a school or classroom?

5. What is "netiquette"? What are some basic rules of "netiquette"?

6. How can access to computers be seen as a gender issue?

7. What are some rules for personal safety in using the Internet?

8. In what ways do students and teachers need to respect copyright laws with computer technology? Why?

9. While computer users may seem to be working alone, how is computing not a private affair? What ways should students know that what they do on the computer is not private?

10. What is a "hacker"? What problems do they present to computer users?

11. What is a computer "virus"?

12. What types of problems do computer viruses present to computer users?

ACTIVITIES

1. Take the box and other packaging in which a computer program comes. Read the license agreement. What are you committing to in using the program?

2. Find an antivirus program. Check your disks with it. What does it tell you? Why does it need to be updated regularly.

3. Find a video game. Play it. Analyze the type of human relationships it portrays.

EXERCISE FOR FURTHER DEVELOPMENT OF YOUR REFLECTIVE PRACTICE FOR TEACHING WITH COMPUTER TECHNOLOGY

Teachers as professionals need to be able to teach students the ethics involved in working with computer technology. Computer technology is impacting our legal and ethical rights and responsibilities. Read the following presentation on visual copyright and reflect on the following issues related to teaching practice:

1. How does computer technology blur an author's intellectual property rights?

2. How can a student be taught what plagiarism is in an era when what we see can so easily be altered?

Visual Copyright

Copyrights were not an issue during the Middle Ages. A scholar such as St. Thomas Aquinas wrote a text, a limited number of copies were made by scribes, and those manuscripts were distributed. People listening to Aquinas lecturing would listen to his ideas, remember them, and retell them throughout their travels. The tradition of the medieval wandering scholar developed because those seeking knowledge would have to hear a thinker lecture or come to the place where manuscript copies of his books were available.

As Marshall McLuhan (1962) pointed out, "Scribal culture could have neither authors nor publics such as were created by typography" (p. 130). Ownership of ideas, as in the modern notion of copyright, was not possible. This could only happen with the mass production of books. Copyright, in the post-typographic world of the computer, becomes increasingly obscure. The computer allows the user to sample and choose parts rather than wholes. What happens in photography, for example, when an image is sampled and combined with another? Suppose that, using some of the types of image processing software that we have described earlier in this book, someone was to use dozens of photographs of a single model—let's say for the sake of argument, Cindy Crawford. Let's further suppose that these photographs constituted the work of 10 different photographers. Merging these images together could create a single composite image of Crawford. This would be done by sampling small parts of individual photographs and merging them with one another using a morphing program. Would this be considered fair use? The general rule in the book world is that I can quote between 250 and 400 words from any text without having to seek permission for its use. Can I sample 200 pixels from a photograph by Scuvallo or Newtson? Is 300 too many? If I am doing this artistically, is it any different than looking at many different photographs of Crawford and composing my own pen and ink portrait of her?

Important issues of copyright arise in the context of hyperphotography. What are the rights of the original photographer who took an image? Does an editor have the right to do cosmetic or aesthetic alterations to a photograph? What rights does a photographer have to a composite picture in which his work is included? What happens to the integrity of photographs as historical documents? These are issues that the computer is creating for us that we will have to address in the immediate future. Visual copyright is increasingly obscured as new digital technologies allow us to recreate the world as we see it.

📖 SOURCES

Bowers, C. A. (1980). *The cultural dimensions of educational computing: Understanding the non-neutrality of technology.* New York: Teachers College Press.

Cuban, L. (1984). *How teachers taught: Constancy and change in American classrooms 1890–1980.* New York: Longman.

Hickman, L. A. (1991). *John Dewey's pragmatic technology.* Bloomington: Indiana University Press.

McLuhan, M. (1962). *The Gutenberg galaxy: The emergence of Post-typographic man.* Toronto: University of Toronto Press.

Provenzo, E. F., Jr. (1991). *Video kids: Making sense of Nintendo* Cambridge, MA: Harvard University Press.

U.S. Congress, Office of Technology Assessment. (1988). *Power on! New tools for teaching and learning* (Report No. OTA-SET-379). Washington, DC: U.S. Government Printing Office.

U.S. Congress, Office of Technology Assessment. (1995). *Teachers and technology: Making the connection* (Report No. OTA-EHR-616). Washington, DC: U.S. Government Printing Office.

Vistica, G. (1997). I'm sorry, sir, but the 20th century just disappeared. *Newsweek*, January 27, p. 18.

CONCLUSION

Complaining about computers is about as smart today as complaining about the printing press would have been in in the 1500s.

—Tom Snyder

Imagine for a moment that it is not the end of the 20th century, but instead the end of the 15th century. Imagine that you are a teacher—perhaps a humanist scholar—reflecting on the importance of the new technology of movable type. What will the world look like in the future? How will scholarship and teaching be transformed by this new technology? Will it change the way people learn? How much will it cost? Will we have to teach people new skills to use this technology?

Think about the fact that in the year 1500 there were no novels. Novels as a type of writing are an outgrowth of the technology of movable type and the book. In 1500, there were no reference books as we know them. Memory was limited largely to what you could remember in your head. Very few people were literate. Books made it possible to disseminate new ideas. Textbooks did not exist for teaching. They literally were invented in the 15th century. How did schools and instruction change as a result of their introduction? Without printing, the Protestant Reformation probably would not have taken place.

The parallels between the beginning of the 15th century—the Renaissance—and our own era are obvious. We are in the first phases of a profound revolution in technology whose consequences for teaching and learning are enormous. Our culture will never be the same again.

At the beginning of this book, we referred to the idea of the computer and its associated technologies as being a "Singularity." Essentially, a Singularity implies that everything that follows it will be different. We believe that this is essentially the case with computing and contemporary culture. It is not that we will not be able to recognize the new world that is emerging as a result of computer technology, but it does mean that the world we are familiar with will change dramatically—and so will education and learning.

What issues will educators face in the future as a result of the increasing use of computers in our culture and the classroom? Throughout this book, we have tried to begin to answer this question, while at the same time providing readers with a basic background for using computers as an effective part of their instruction.

We are not totally without direction. It is clear to us that the use of computers in classroom instruction must involve a process of reflection. We must consider how computers contribute to the process of instruction, how they carry certain values and assumptions into the educational setting, and how they can potentially limit and enrich the process of instruction and learning.

The rules used to critically evaluate traditional printed curricula in many respects work well for evaluating computer-based curricula. It is easy to be overwhelmed by flashy new computer technology. In the end, the issue is whether or not the new technology contributes to the improved delivery of instruction. In other words, does the use of the computer in the classroom facilitate your work as a teacher and ultimately your students' work as learners?

We are confronted by uncertainty about the future. No one can precisely predict where we will be in terms of computing even 5 or 10 years from now. We know, for example, of almost no one who predicted the widespread proliferation and use of the Internet that has taken place since the early 1990s. New computer technologies rapidly make old predictions obsolete. For example, during the mid-1980s, there was a great deal of discussion in the computer literature about the development of supercomputers. Japan was taking the lead in this field, when suddenly American researchers developed the idea of linking hundreds of small computers (i.e., parallel computers) together to run as a single machine. New models of software had to be developed, new engineering technologies had to be invented, but the result was that a new model for computing evolved that was far more powerful than anyone could have predicted just a few years earlier, and that made the supercomputer obsolete.

In a similar vein, several years ago one of the authors speculated with a colleague at the university's computer center that it might be possible to grow computers from protein. He was laughed at for proposing anything so absurd. Recently, researchers have demonstrated the feasibility of this idea using a strand of DNA. Theoretically, such machines/organisms have the potential to be enormously fast and cheap. Will they be part of our future? We almost certainly think so.

The future of educational computing will continue to change the models of instruction used throughout the educational system. Will students learn on computers more at home than in school? Will learning be much more of a lifelong process?

What will be the long-term teaching and learning impact of computing functioning as an augmentor or enhancer of intelligence? How will this change the way we teach and what we teach? What will happen to students who have been traditionally labeled disabled and who are now enabled through computer technology? Will the curriculum become more generic and less tailored to individual needs as the computer is used to facilitate individual applications in the educational process?

Who will have access to computing? What type of computing? How will we train teachers to work in new computer-rich environments? These are all-important questions. Like Prospero in Shakespeare's *The Tempest*, we must come to terms with a "brave new world," one that is in the process of being created through the introduction of new computer-based technologies. We hope you find the challenge both interesting and worthwhile.

QUESTIONS FOR REFLECTION AND DISCUSSION

1. How do you think art, literature, and music will change in the years to come as a result of the introduction of new computer technologies?

2. How do you think schools will change?

3. What are the implications of the new technology for how we train teachers in the future?

4. Are we going through a "Singularity" with the introduction of new computer technologies in education? Argue for and against.

5. How will the curriculum potentially change as a result of the introduction of new computer technologies?

📖 SOURCES

Dery, M. (1996). *Escape velocity: Cyberculture at the end of the century.* New York: Grove Press.

COMPUTER HARDWARE BASICS

Machines that Count, Digital Calculating, Types of Computers, Input Devices, Output Devices, The Central Processing Unit, External Storage

Computers in the future may...perhaps only weigh 1.5 tons.

—*Popular Mechanics Magazine*, 1949

Case Study

Mrs. Garcia is a second-grade teacher who works in an inner-city school in Miami, Florida. Most of the children she works with are recently arrived immigrants from Cuba and Nicaragua. She wants to find ways to help motivate her students to read more.

While attending the annual statewide reading conference she visited the computer exhibits and saw a hypermedia program on a CD-ROM that was perfect for her students. It was a reading program designed for second and third graders that not only had a read-aloud function, but allowed children to click on any word and have its meaning read aloud in both English and Spanish. The program had interesting animated sequences, among other features. She was convinced it would be ideal for her students.

Mrs. Garcia has several computers in her classroom and one has a CD-ROM drive, but she has been a little intimidated by it. She uses a computer to do word processing for her research papers and other assignments at the local university, where she is working on a masters' degree However, she really does not understand the difference between a hard drive and a CD-ROM drive. She wants to make the reading program available to her students, but is

CD-ROM Drive: a device that reads the data from a CD-ROM into a computer.

Hard Drive: a mass storage device for a computer.

RAM: an acronym for random access memory.

worried about whether or not it will work on her machine. Should she order the program? How can she be sure that she is making the right decision?

Mrs. Garcia's problem is fairly typical of many teachers across the country. Although she thinks computers could be useful in working with her students, she has limited understanding of how the machines actually work. New technologies like CD-ROM just add to her confusion. What is the difference between a double speed **CD-ROM drive** and a quad speed drive? How do you install a CD-ROM program on the directory of your **hard drive**? What is the difference between a CD-ROM and a CD-audio? Can you copy a CD-ROM the same way you copy a floppy disk? These are just some of her concerns.

Unlike some of the younger teachers in her school, Mrs. Garcia, who is in her early forties, did not have access to computers when she was an undergraduate. She is a bit in awe of Miss Verlin, who is only in her second year of teaching but who has been using computers since she was in elementary school. For Miss Verlin, computers are a natural, almost an automatic, part of her work.

Having a good grounding in how hardware and software works, however, is not all you need to know about computers. There is the constant problem of keeping up to date. Even a teacher who had courses on computers and their use in the classroom in the early or mid-1980s today faces a wide range of new machines and software that have significantly changed the nature and possibilities of educational computing. While this can be very exciting, it can also be overwhelming. When the authors of this textbook got their first computers, the machines were Apple+ computers and Apple IIEs with 64 kilobytes of **RAM**. The machine on which this book is being written has 8 megabytes of RAM (these numbers are explained later), which is 125 times more than the earlier machines. By the time you read this information, computers of this size and memory will already be outdated.

When we first began to work in the field of computer education, we dreamed of being able to switch from one word processing file to another. This would make it possible to have access to two manuscripts or text files at once for the purposes of comparison or merging text. The word processors we are using to write this book (WordPerfect 6.0 and Word 6.0) can display dozens of separate files at once—many more than any average user would ever need. These same word processing programs include a spell checking system, a grammar checking system, a spreadsheet, a **calculator**, and a painting or drawing system. Sound files can be imported into these programs. They can even be used to set type. The result is a word processing system that is, in fact, a highly sophisticated multitask tool system far more powerful than anything most users could have imagined during the late 1970s or early 1980s.

Calculator: any device that performs arithmetic operations on numbers.

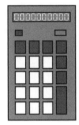

With increasingly expanded possibilities, however, come increasing complexity and the need to learn more and more. A serious issue for many teachers is figuring out how much they really need to know about computer hardware and software to do their job well. Is there a point where learning a new software system or learning how to use a new machine becomes counterproductive? When people in the past learned to type, they were able to transfer their skills from one typewriter to another. They did not find their skills quickly outdated. With rapid developments in hardware and software in computing, it is almost inevitable that much of what we know today is already becoming obsolete.

Until recently, for example, videodisc players were the only means to incorporate high-quality full motion video into computers. Many people have invested heavily in learning videodisc technology. It seems clear now, however, that advances in CD-ROM technology are rapidly superseding videodisc technology. New digitizing and compression techniques, along with advances in laser technology, are making it possible to put large amounts of full motion video on CD-ROMs. In the next few years it will be possible to access several hours of video and sound on a single 5 and 1/4 CD-ROM. Videodiscs will almost certainly be obsolete—similar to what happened to phonograph records following the introduction of CD-audio.

This chapter tries to make the concepts underlying hardware as clear and as straightforward as possible. For many of you this information may be new and perhaps even a bit intimidating. If this is the case, think of yourselves as visiting a new country where you do not know anything about its history, language, or people. At first you may feel very uncomfortable. The food may taste funny, the language may sound strange, and things may seem impossibly complicated and mixed-up. Once you have had some time to learn about the place and to get used to it, you will probably discover that things that seemed foreign are now becoming familiar.

Machines That Count

Any computer, no matter how complicated, is a machine that computes or counts numbers. Actually, we have used such machines for thousands of years. Our earliest computing devices were our fingers, which we can use to help keep count of numbers in our head. We all know the term digit, a noun describing a finger or toe. In mathematics, a digit is any of the figures 0, 1, 2, 3, 4, 5, 6, 7, 8, 9. Obviously, the two uses of the word suggest that fingers or toes were used to keep track of numbers.

Of course it did not take long for people to run out of fingers or toes when they had large numbers to count. It is not surprising, therefore, that they began to use markers or counters to help them record the numbers. The earliest counters were probably pebbles or sticks, perhaps even the bones of animals. What people used is not so important as the fact that they were substituting something physical to represent the number or quantity they wanted to remember.

Once people learned how to represent numbers with objects they could move the objects around to represent different quantities. By doing so, they could calculate or compute new numbers to represent the mathematical functions of addition, subtraction, multiplication, or division. It was not long before people began to invent mechanical devices that would help them keep track of their calculations.

One of the earliest such devices was the abacus. The earliest abacus was simply a series of holes scooped in the ground to hold pebbles that were used to represent numbers. Eventually, the abacus evolved into a frame that held rows of counters or beads strung on wires or rods. The different positions of the beads on the wires indicated the numbers they represented.

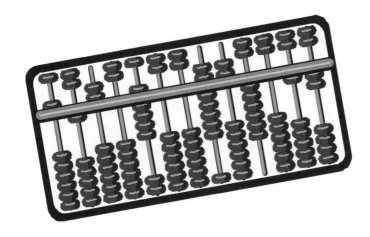

The Abacus
http://www.ee.ryerson.ca:8080/~elf/abacus/

An actual "working" or electronic abacus on the Internet.

The abacus can probably be considered the first modern calculating machine. Many other calculating devices or machines have been developed over the centuries by different cultures. In medieval England, a counting board or cloth was used to do calculations. In 1614, the Scotsman John Napier published a book about his discovery of **Logarithms** containing tables of numbers that made multiplication and division much easier. Logarithms provided the basis for the English mathematician William Oughtred's invention of the slide rule, a calculating device widely used until the 1960s, when pocket calculators were introduced.

Logarithm: in mathematics, the power to which a base must be raised to equal a given number.

Texas Instruments Calculator History
http://archive.ppp.ti.com/calc/docs/calchist.htm

Digital Calculating

Analog: continuous variable qualities such as voltage fluctuations. Signals of continuous nature that vary in frequency and amplitude.

The slide rule is an **analog** calculating machine. This means that it calculates by converting numbers into a physical quantity such as the measured units on a slide rule. A pocket watch with hands is another example of an analog device. Measurements of time are presented by points arranged around its face. Early attempts at computing employed analog systems, but were eventually superseded by digital technologies.

Analog Computer: processes continuously variable data such as that created by voltage fluctuations.

There are two types of computers: *analog* and *digital*. **Analog computers** represent computational values by using a continuously variable physical property such as voltage. Digital computers use binary code 0s, and 1s, to represent values. Analog computers are mostly used for specialized types of scientific research. Digital computers are what most people think of as computers.

Another type of calculating device uses digital information. A digital watch is a good example. It tells time in digits or distinct units. An analog watch measures time with the sweep of its hands. A digital watch records a precise number. As a result, digital timing mechanisms, when broken down into very small units, are much more accurate.

A digital computer is a computer that performs calculations and operations with quantities that are represented electronically as digits. By using a binary number system, only two digits need to be represented (0 and 1) to create any number. The digit 0 is represented by the absence of an electrical charge and 1 by the presence of a charge. Thus, by turning on a series of *on* and *off* switches, any character and therefore any word or number, can be represented. By simply activating a series of *on* and *off* switches, it becomes possible to create or represent what is being written, or to copy Shakespeare's plays or Tolstoy's novels. Similarly, paintings and photographs can be digitized and represented inside the computer.

All of us are familiar with the decimal system, which is based on 10 digits (0–9), place value, and powers of 100. The value of each digit in a number is based on its position in the number and is 10 times the value of the digit to its right. In contrast, the binary system uses only two digits, 0 and 1, is based on place value, and powers of two. The value of each digit in a number is based on its position and is two times the value of a digit on its right.

For example, the decimal number 107 is represented in the binary number system as 1101011. Using comparative place value charts, you can see how the number 107 is derived in the binary system.

Decimal to Binary

```
0...........      0
1...........      1
2...........      10    (1 two 0 ones)
3...........      11    (1 two 1 one)
4...........      100   (1 four 0 twos 0 ones)
5...........      101   (1 four, 0 twos 1 one)
6...........      110   (1 four, 1 two, 0 one)
7...........      111   (1 four, 1 two, 1 one)
8...........      1000 (1 eight, 0 fours, 0 twos, 0 ones)
9...........      1001 (1 eight, 0 fours, 0 twos, 1 one)
```

Therefore 107 in the decimal system is 1101011 in the binary system, which means:

1 in the sixty fours place
1 in the thirty twos place
0 in the sixteens place
1 in the eights place
0 in the fours place
1 in the twos place
1 in the ones place

ASCII: stands for American Standard Code for Information Interchange. It is a common standard used in computer programs for converting 0s and 1s into letters of the alphabet, digits, and punctuation marks.

The American Standard Code for Information Interchange (**ASCII**) is a coding system that assigns numerical values to numbers, letters, punctuation marks, or other characters. These numbers are then represented in the computer in the form of binary numbers. The capital letter A, for example, is assigned the decimal number 65, which is the binary number 1000001. The capital letters in the Alphabet (A–Z) are represented by the decimal numbers 65–90. A space is indicated by the decimal number 32 (100000). A period is 46 (101110) and an equal sign is 61 (0111101). Can you translate your age into binary? What about the number 2,000?

Computer Timeline

1642 Blaise Pascal invents the first mechanical adding machine known as the Pascaline.

1822 Charles Babbage completes a model for the "difference engine," widely considered the first modern computing device.

1837 Samuel Morse patents the telegraph.

1876 Alexander Graham Bell invents the telephone.

1896 The first telephone dialer is introduced. Telephone operators are no longer necessary to place a call.

1904 The vacuum tube is invented.

1930 Vannevar Bush builds the first analog computer while working as a professor at MIT.

1936 Alan Turing, a British mathematician, publishes an essay describing a "universal machine" that can solve any mathematical problem.

1941 Konrad Zuse demonstrates a working programmable calculator to German military authorities.

1946 The *ENIAC*, the first automatic electronic computer, is built at the University of Pennsylvania.

1947 The experiment that leads to the invention of the transistor is conducted at Bell Laboratories.

1956 *FORTRAN*, the first computer programming language, is introduced.

1962 Telstar I, the first commercial communications satellite, is launched.

1968 Burroughs creates the first computer using an integrated circuit.

1969 An experimental computer network known as the ARPANET is set up by the American Defense Department.

1972 *Pong*, the first home video game, is introduced by the Atari Corporation.

1977 Apple Computer, Inc. introduces the first personal practical computer, the Apple II.

1981 IBM introduces its first personal computer and an industry wide operating system—DOS.

1984 Phillips and Sony develop the first compact discs or CD-ROMs.

1991 The first Internet search and navigation tools are released.

1992 World Wide Web technology (WWW), which provides the Internet with visual or graphic interface technology, is released.

Types of Computers

What is a computer? *A computer is a device that can accept input (i.e., information or data in a prescribed form), process the data, store the data, and finally produce output.* A computer system includes hardware and software. Hardware is the machinery, the physical components of the computer system that can be seen and touched. Software is the set of logical instructions that control the hardware. Unlike hardware, software is not visible. It is typically stored on a medium such as a floppy disk or a CD-ROM.

Computer hardware is dependent on two types of software. The first is systems software or operating systems, and the second is applications software. The systems software controls the workings of the computer. Applications software enables the computer's hardware to perform specific tasks. Operating systems and applications software are explained in greater detail in Chapter 4.

Until recently, when the term *computer* was used, most people thought of a large mainframe machine that took up enormous amounts of space. These were the only types of computers that existed until the late 1970s. Because they were large does not mean they were very powerful compared to today's machines.

Basically, there are three types of computers in widespread use today. There are mainframe, mini, and micro, or personal, computers. Most micro, or personal, computers run faster and have more storage capacity than the largest mainframes of 10 or 15 years ago. Mainframes are still used because they have massive storage and can be accessed by multiple users doing many different tasks.

Terminal: a device consisting of a video adapter, a keyboard, and a monitor where data can be input or output.

In a large school system, for example, a mainframe computer can be used for storing student records, keeping payroll accounts, or providing a master library catalogue. Mainframes are typically accessed through **terminals**, which can keep costs down when there are many users needing computer time. Mainframes work particularly well when large numbers of people need to have access to the same data and programs.

Minicomputers function very much like mainframes, except that fewer users can access their resources. The distinction between a mainframe and a minicomputer is often unclear. What used to require a mainframe can now often be done by minicomputers, and in many instances, even by personal or microcomputers.

Minicomputer: a midlevel computer whose capabilities are between those of a mainframe and a microcomputer.

Microcomputers, also called personal computers, are intended for the use of one person at a time. They are built around a single chip microprocessor, and can be connected or networked to other computers. When the term is capitalized (Personal Computer) or referred to as a "PC" in capitals, the reference is to a specific model of microcomputers introduced by the International Business Machine Corporation (IBM) in the early 1980s.

Microcomputers can be further classified as desktop, laptop, notebook, or palm-sized. Typically, a laptop computer weighs 8 to 15 pounds and runs on current or batteries. A notebook computer weighs between 2 and 8 pounds, and a palm-sized machine weighs under 2 pounds. The computing power of a notebook is often as great as that of a desktop machine. Toshiba's 1996 notebook computer, for example, has a 90-megahertz Pentium processor, a 720-megabyte hard drive, and 8 megabytes of RAM expandable to 40 megabytes with an active-matrix color screen. Weighing 4.8 pounds with a battery, this computer is as powerful as almost any desktop computer available today. Compactness and portability, however, are expensive—the price of the machine can be two to three times the price of a comparable desktop machine.

Tomorrow's personal computers will almost certainly leave today's mainframe and minicomputers in the dust in terms of speed and storage. The distinctions between types of computers become even less clear if we take into account that you can use a personal computer to connect to a mainframe or minicomputer. From a functional point of view, by connecting through a modem or network, a personal computer can essentially function as a terminal, bringing the desirable features of the mainframe into the personal computer's environment.

Moore's Law

In 1964 Gordon Moore, the co-founder of the Intel Corporation, argued that the number of transistors put on electronic chips would double every 2 years. This means that in the case of computers, computing power would double every 24 months. In fact, "Moore's Law" has been revised as chips have become more sophisticated at an ever-increasing rate. Now the law states that the number doubles every 18 months, meaning that computing power is currently quadrupling every 3 years. Translated, this means that the computer you buy today is four times more powerful than the one you purchased 3 years ago.

Moore's Law
http://www.intel.com/intel/museum/25anniv/html/hof/moore.htm

Input Devices

In order to get information into a computer it is necessary to have an input device. The input device on a telephone for calling a number is the rotary dial or touchpad. When you want to dial a number you input it through the telephone's "dial," or "touch keys." There are many ways to input data into a computer. Early mainframe computers used paper tapes or punched cards on which information was coded and mechanically read. Today, the most frequently used input devices for computers are keyboards and mice. Other input devices include touch screens, joysticks, optical scanners, digital cameras, analog to digital converters, and voice recognition systems.

A computer keyboard is similar in many of its functions to a typewriter keyboard. It includes **alphanumeric** characters, punctuation, and other printable characters along with a number of nontext keys. Nontext keys such as Shift, Option, Command, Control, Clear, Delete, and Escape are typically used by themselves or in combination with other keys to perform specific functions. There are many variations of the standard computer keyboard. The *Muppet Learning Keys* and *Intellikeys*, for example, are enlarged and colorful keyboards appropriate for young children. Alternative keyboards are discussed in more detail in Chapter 6.

Alphanumeric:
pertaining to letters, numerals, and symbols.

The mouse is an input device that allows you to manipulate information on a computer screen. Moving the mouse on a surface, such as desktop or table, controls a cursor on the computer screen. Commands are initiated by pointing and clicking.

A trackball is a type of computer mouse. Unlike the standard computer mouse whose tracking ball is dragged over a surface, the housing of the trackball remains stationary and the ball is rolled with the tip of a finger. Trackballs require less desk space than the standard computer mouse to use and are commonly found in laptop and notebook computers. Other variations of the standard computer mouse include GlidePoint, which is a flat glass surface that senses movement of the user's finger moving over its surface.

Resolution: the clarity or detail of a monitor or image.

A touch screen is a computer screen that recognizes the location of a touch or pressure point on its surface. Information is entered into the computer by directly touching the surface of the monitor. Touch screens are typically used with computer information kiosks or as an input device for young children. This method of input is quite tiring, and does not provide high **resolution** for input.

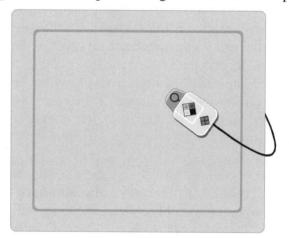

A graphics tablet, also called a digitizing tablet, translates the movement of a pointing device, usually a pen or stylus, on a tablet to specific on-screen cursor positions. It is most widely used in engineering and design applications. The touch pad is a variation of a graphics tablet that uses pressure sensors. A popular touch pad is the Koala pad, which is used in graphics software for children.

A joystick is a pointing device used to control movement of objects on the computer screen. It has a stem that can be moved in all directions and buttons to activate various features of the software. Joysticks are most commonly used in computer games.

They can also be used by individuals with physical disabilities, because they can be adjusted to be touch sensitive and require minimal fine motor skills to operate.

An optical scanner is an input devce that uses light sensing to translate text or graphics into digital form so they can be used as data in a computer program. There are three widely used types of scanning devices: flatbed, feeder, and handheld. Using a scanner, a page of text or a picture can be scanned into word processing or graphics software and manipulated just like data entered through the keyboard, mouse, or other input device. **Optical character recognition** software can translate printed or specially prepared bar code patterns into data for the computer.

Optical Character Recognition (OCR): computerized scanning technology that can interpret characters on the printed page.

Bar code technology is widely used in commercial settings such as grocery, hardware, and department stores. It is also used in libraries. Basically, a **bar code** is a series of printed bars and spaces in which binary information is encoded. Black bars and white spaces represent 0's and 1's. These are read by running an optical scanner (a laser light beam) across them.

Bar Code: a linear coding system that can be read by an optical scanning device.

Digital cameras store images as digital/electronic information instead of on traditional film. This type of camera can be directly connected to a computer and its images stored on the computer's hard drive. Images can then be incorporated into a wide range of software programs.

Analog to digital converters (A/D converters) are input devices that record and analyze analog measures such as temperature, barometric pressure, wind speed and direction, humidity, rainfall, light, force/weight, elapsed time, speed, motion, and many other things. Sensors read temperature, motion, heart rate, blood pressure, and so on. These devices are widely used in scientific applications and most commonly show up in the classroom as part of specially designed science microbased laboratory software systems.

Finally, data can be entered into the computer through speech recognition devices. These devices allow the spoken word to be translated into commands and data for the computer. Using these devices allows you to talk into the computer and digitally encode a command ("Save file!") or spoken text (a dictated business letter). Speech input devices are particularly useful for people with physical disabilities and those with keyboard-related stress injuries.

Output Devices

Speakers: output devices that allow the computer to generate sound.

Besides providing for the input of data, computers output data as well. Output, which is the result of the computer processing data or information, is typically sent to a computer display, a printer, a set of **speakers**, or to a transmission or storage device.

Liquid Crystal Display (LCD): uses liquid compound positioned between two sheets of polarizing material squeezed between two glass panels.

Display Devices. There are two major types of display devices used with computers: a monitor and a **liquid crystal display**. Monitors, which are also called video displays, computer screens, or **cathode ray tubes** (CRTs), can be monochrome or color. Early in the microcomputer revolution monitors were all monochrome. By the mid-1980s, most computer monitors were color. Color computer monitors require sophisticated video adapters or video boards that generate the signal that is sent from the computer through a cable to the screen or monitor.

Cathode Ray Tube (CRT): the basic element used in a video terminal or television.

Different computer monitors have different screen resolutions. Resolution is the number of **pixels** per unit of measurement on the screen. As you might expect, higher resolution screens cost significantly more than low-resolution screens. Resolution determines the clarity of detail on the screen or monitor. If you are doing a lot of graphics or visual imaging, then it is probably important that you get a higher resolution monitor for your computer. The quality of the image you get on your monitor will

Pixel: one dot on a computer's screen; the smallest element a scanner can detect on a monitor.

also depend on the quality of your video card or board. Giving precise guidelines is difficult to do, because products in the computer field change so rapidly. What was a top-of-the-line monitor a year or two ago is standard, or perhaps even below the standards of acceptance now. Consult with a knowledgeable hardware specialist in order to make the best decision before buying a computer monitor.

The final variable affecting the quality of output you get on a monitor is the size of the monitor itself. The larger the monitor, the greater the cost. If you are doing page layouts for desktop publishing, a larger monitor will make it possible for you to work with and see two-page spreads and other large-format projects. Very large monitors can be used as display systems for group instruction in the classroom, thus taking the place of the traditional overhead projector.

Another important type of display device that takes the place of, or can be used along with a computer monitor, is the liquid crystal display (LCD) panel. Liquid crystals with a polar molecular structure are sandwiched between two transparent electrodes. A message is sent from the computer to the display panel and an electrical charge causes the crystals to align themselves positively or negatively in such a way that letters and graphics can be displayed. LCD panels are most widely used as displays on laptop and other portable computers, as well as on the faces of computer watches and calculators. Semi-transparent LCD projection panels can also be placed on overhead projectors in order to project images from a computer onto a wall or screen.

P*rin te rs* . There are many different types of printers used with computers. Initially, dot matrix printers, which use very fine pins to impact on a ribbon, were widely used. More finished printing was done with a **daisy wheel** printer, which worked much like an electric typewriter wheel. Dot matrix printers can still be found in many schools and businesses, but they are not usually used for work that requires high-quality printing. Daisy wheel printers have been completely superseded by laser and ink-jet technology.

Daisy Wheel: an impact-type printer that produces characters when a wheel with type characters strikes a ribbon.

Dot matrix and daisy wheel printers are based on impact technologies. Like typewriters, they strike a ribbon and leave an impression. Laser, thermal, and ink-jet printers use nonimpact technologies to print.

Laser printers use the same processes as photocopiers. Basically, a focused laser beam and a rotating mirror are used to draw an image of the page being printed onto a photosensitive drum. The image is then converted on the drum into an electrostatic charge, which attracts and holds toner. A piece of electrostatically charged paper is then rolled against the drum and then pulled away from the drum onto the paper.

Thermal printers use heat sensitive paper that comes in contact with pins that are gently heated to produce an image on the paper. Thermal imaging is widely used with inexpensive fax machines, but is not particularly practical for most computer applications.

Ink-jet printers fire tiny drops of ink at the paper to form the images sent from the computer. These devices are less expensive than laser printers, but can produce images of virtually the same quality. They are more expensive to run and also are much slower than laser printers. They have the advantage, however, of providing images not just in black and white, but also in color at a very low cost.

So *u n* **d.** Sound output is provided in computers through speakers connected to a sound board or card. Depending on the quality of the sound board and the speakers attached to it, the quality of sound generated by a computer can rival the best stereo system available. Sound output is still at a relatively early stage of development as compared to monitor and print output.

High-quality sound output is particularly important for educators. Human speech in language and literacy programs, for example, needs to be as clear and lifelike as possible. Much synthesized speech is too robotlike to be used for instruction in these areas. This is because only the phonemes, or the phonetic representation of the language, are recorded and stored in the computer. When words are produced they are pronounced phonetically and they lack variation in rhythm and pitch normally found in spoken language. As a result, such systems sound artificial and sometimes even mispronounce words. For example, the word "hands" in synthesized computer speech is often pronounced as "handez."

Digitized speech produces a much higher quality of speech output by recording actual utterances and then converting them from analog waveforms into a digital format. This is then stored on a disk. The computer converts the digital information back into sound. Digitized speech requires a large amount of storage space. Its potential has become much greater with the widespread use of CD-ROM technologies.

The Central Processing Unit

The most important part of any computer is the central processing unit. A central processing unit (CPU) is the computational or control unit of the computer. In a micro, or personal, computer it is a single silicon chip—often no larger than one centimeter across. The central processing unit can be thought of as the computer's "brain," or logic center.

Microcomputers and their central processing units evolved from the integrated circuits used in electronic calculators. Basically, today's personal computer is a greatly enhanced integrated circuit that contains the equivalent of millions of transistors packed onto a single chip.

Microprocessors are designated by different numbers. On **DOS**-based machines (IBMs and IBM clones), the lower the number, the earlier the model and hence the lower its computational power. An 8088 is a processor that was manufactured by Intel Corporation in

DOS: an acronym that stands for disk operating system communication devices.

286, 386, 486, 586: the different numbers that accompany the descriptions of most computers refer to various types of microprocessors.

the mid-1970s. It was superseded by the 80**286**, which came out in the early 1980s; the 80**386**, which came out about 1985; and the 80**486**, which was introduced onto the market in the late 1980s. You have probably heard the term *Pentium chip*, which would have been Intel's **586**, but was given a name for copyright and trademark purposes. By the time this book is published, there will almost certainly be a new generation of more powerful processors. In the case of Apple Computers, a similar system exists that uses processors manufactured by the Motorola Corporation.

Processing Speed: the speed at which data are manipulated within a computer.

Processing speed, or how fast the computer runs, is measured in megahertz (MHz) or millions of cycles per second. A hertz is a measure of frequency. In computers, it is a unit of measurement equal to one cycle of electricity per second. A megahertz is one million cycles per second. This means that one megahertz is equal to an electrical charge cycling through a chip or the computer's circuitry one million times per second. Thus, a 100-megahertz computer would cycle electricity at twice the speed of a 50-megahertz machine, at a speed of 100 million cycles per second.

Disk Drive: an electrical and mechanical device that reads and writes data to a disk.

A computer's speed is primarily a combination of what generation of microprocessor is being used by the machine in conjunction with its processor or clock speed (megahertz). Other factors such as speed of the **disk drive** and the amount of RAM in the machine will affect speed as well.

Me *m o ry* ▪ Random access memory (RAM) is the amount of space available to the user for data and programming. It is measured in megabytes. Random access refers to the fact that the microprocessor can go directly to any information in RAM. In other words, it does not have to access the information or data sequentially.

RAM is made up of internal memory chips, and the amount of RAM in your computer will determine what size program you can load onto your machine. Early computers measured RAM in kilobytes. Now it is measured in megabytes. And, it is conceivable that before too long, it will be measured in gigabytes. Newer computer programs make massive demands on RAM and have made most earlier machines obsolete. The trend of programs to use larger and larger amounts of RAM is almost certainly going to continue. RAM can be upgraded on most machines. The general rule is to buy as much RAM as you can reasonably afford in a new machine. RAM is volatile, which means that if the power supply to the computer is shut off, then whatever program or data is in RAM is lost.

Read-only memory (ROM) functions as the computer's permanent memory. It stores the information that the computer needs when it is first turned on. ROM can only be read by the computer. Nothing can be written or stored on ROM. ROM contains the instructions to the computer to make its system operational when the power is turned on.

External Storage

Technically, storage in a computer includes random access memory (RAM), as well as devices such as floppy disks, hard disks or drives, and optical discs. Floppy disks, hard disks, and optical disks are referred to as secondary memory systems, whereas RAM is a primary memory system. Although built into most computers, floppy disks, hard disks, and optical disks can be described as external storage.

Early computers used punched paper tapes and then punch cards to store and input data. Disks, including floppy disks and hard disks, and tape drives have become the most common type of storage device. The floppy disk, which is a mylar surface with a magnetic coating, comes in many different sizes—with the 3-inch disk becoming the standard for the industry. High-density (HD) 3-inch floppy disks can store 1.44 megabytes of data. These floppy disks are used to transfer data and programs and sometimes used to back up data. Hard disks are now standard components of computer systems. Data stored on a hard disk can be accessed much faster than information stored on floppy disks. The capacity of hard disks has increased from the original one megabyte (one million bytes) of early systems to one or more gigabytes (a billion bytes) of storage space.

With the increasing use of visual and sound files, massive storage of data is necessary. Even the largest hard drives cannot always manage the storage demands that are placed on them. In order to provide greater storage capacity, there are various removable hard disk drives available that allow the user to insert a cartridge or disk on a single drive. Thus, the amount of storage available is unlimited, provided that the necessary blank cartridges or disks are available.

Backup: copy of a file, disk, or program as a safeguard against loss.

Tape drives are mass storage devices that use mylar magnetized tape to store large quantities of information. These drives are used to back up or duplicate a hard drive and are used almost exclusively for archival purposes. They are a slow, but effective way to make **backup** copies of programs and data.

All of the storage devices described are magnetic. Information can also be stored on laser disks or optical discs. These are disks in which beams or pulses of light are used to encode and transmit data. The two major types of optical discs are CD-ROM (Compact-Disc Read Only Memory) and the videodisc. These two types of discs are read only and cannot be written to in most configurations.

One type of optical disc coming into widespread use is the WORM. WORM is an acronym for "Write Once, Read Many." This type of disc can have data or programs written to it, but cannot be erased and rewritten over like a magnetic disk.

In summary, hardware represents the nuts and bolts of computing. Hardware is virtually useless, however, without the software that runs on it. Dealing with hardware is one part of the larger computing picture.

QUESTIONS FOR REFLECTION AND DISCUSSION

1. Why is it helpful to understand the historical development of computers? Should students be required to learn about the history of computers?

2. What is the relation of the binary number system to digital computers?

3. How did the invention of the microcomputer affect access to computing and change the nature of computer use?

4. How do factors such as processor speed, amount of RAM, hard disk space, and peripherals affect the way computers can be used by students and teachers?

5. How does the type of input device used change the nature of the interaction between the user and the computer?

6. How does the type of output device change the nature of the interaction between the user and the computer?

7. Is it essential to have a printer as part of a computer system for children with disabilities? Why or why not?

8. If you are buying a computer system, how much RAM should it have? How much storage capacity should the hard drive have? What peripherals should it include? How do you determine what you need?

ACTIVITIES

1. Collect several advertisements for computer systems from the newspaper. Compare information on the processor, speed, hard drive capacity, amount of RAM, and peripherals, such as CD-ROM drive, external storage device, and printer. Compare capabilities and prices and try to determine which computer system is the best value.

2. Look at the computers in your school setting. Try to find out the brand, operating system, processor, speed, amount of hard disk space, amount of RAM, and peripherals for the computers in that school.

3. Use a software catalog or visit a store that sells computer software. Choose five pieces of software of interest to you and make a list of hardware requirements for each program. Which of the computer systems identified in Activities 1 and 2 would meet the requirements of the software you selected?

EXERCISE FOR FURTHER DEVELOPMENT OF YOUR REFLECTIVE PRACTICE FOR TEACHING WITH COMPUTER TECHNOLOGY

Teachers as professionals need to be able to teach with the hardware of technology. Knowledge of hardware either expands or limits our ability to teach with computer technology. Read the following presentation on interactive television and reflect on the following issues related to teaching practice:

1. How does computer technology hardware's continuing development present challenges to successful teaching?

2. How does the continued development of interactive video games, fostered by computer technology, increase the demand for teachers to teach more interactively?

Interactive Television

Science fiction and utopian writers have been predicting the emergence of interactive films and television for over half a century. Aldous Huxley, in his 1932 novel *Brave New World,* described a type of interactive movie—the "Feelies"—in which viewers could literally feel what took place on the screen. In a love scene on a bear rug, for example, you could sense the fur with what Huxley's character Henry Foster described as "the most amazing tactual effects" (p. 23). In Ray Bradbury's (1989) *Fahrenheit 451*, televisions with giant screens are installed so that they surround you on all four sides. Programs allow you to participate in—not just view—adventures being broadcast.

There is a very basic human desire to participate in what is happening on a television or movie screen. The extraordinary popularity of the Home Shopping Network, for example, may be a result of the fact that you can interact (i.e., you can tangibly be connected to) with what you see take place on your television screen.

Other models already found in our culture suggest the desire to interact with and control television. Video games, for example, are a type of crude interactive television. Perhaps a careful look at video games will give us significant insight into the direction that interactive television may take in the years to come.

Video games reflect the evolution of computers since the mid-1970s. Beginning in the mid-1970s, for example, there was *Pong*, Atari's simple electronic table tennis game. *Pong* was followed by *Space Invaders* in which row-on-row of alien spacecraft descended toward the earth and were shot at by the player whose mission it was to stop the alien invaders from taking over the planet. *Space Invaders* was followed by *Missile Command,* in which the player destroyed incoming nuclear missiles before they could annihilate civilization. From *Space Invaders* and *Missile Command*, video games evolved into *PacMan,* with its obsessive "munching" and consumption of every object in sight. More recently we have seen the introduction of home machines by companies such as Nintendo and Sega, with games like *Super Mario Brothers*, *Double Dragon II,* and *Mega Man*.

Each successive generation of video games has become more technologically sophisticated, more realistic, and more interactive. The newest wave of video games, based on CD-ROM technology (the same technology people use for music recordings and computer databases), is in fact becoming more like film and television than what we traditionally expect of a video game. This is a major evolutionary step beyond the simple graphics of the

Space Invader arcade game or the tiny animated cartoon figures of the Nintendo system that have dominated the video game market in recent years.

In addition, virtual reality technologies have been on the market for several years now that make it possible to participate physically in what takes place on a television or computer screen. The game company Sega, for example, for several years has marketed a device called the *Activator!* It has a plastic sensor ring that is laid in a circle around your feet; when you jump, your character jumps, when you punch, your character punches, when you kick, your character kicks.

The *Activator!* is a crude device and provides only a glimpse of the type of interactivity that will almost certainly be possible in years to come. The real significance of this type of technology is that, as computers and televisions become increasingly merged with one another, these devices suggest some of the broad outlines for a new type of television—an interactive medium as different from traditional television as television is from radio. The remaining years of this decade will see the emergence and definition of this new media form in much the same way that the late 1940s and early 1950s saw television emerge as a powerful social and cultural force. Its potential is enormous, as are its limitations.

What happens when we have a type of television we no longer passively view, but can physically interact with? If, as the psychological research seems to suggest, viewing violent television encourages aggressive behavior, then what happens when we can actually physically participate in what goes on in front of us on the television screen? Will our interaction with television characters affect our interaction with real human beings in our real lives?

📖 SOURCES

Bradbury, R. (1989). *Fahrenheit 451.* New York: Ballantine.

Computer Dictionary. (1994). (2nd ed.). Redmond, WA: Microsoft Press.

Huxley, A. (1969). *Brave new world.* New York: Harper & Row. (Original work published 1932)

Provenzo, E. F., Jr. (1997). Video games and the emergence of interactive media for children. In S. R. Steinberg & J. L. Kincheloe (Eds.), *Kinder-culture: The corporate construction of childhood* (pp. 103–113). Boulder, CO: Westview Press.

GLOSSARY

People give lip service to learning to learn, but if you look at curriculum in schools, most of it is about dates, fractions, and science facts; very little of it is about learning. I like to think of learning as an expertise that every one of us can acquire.

--Seymour Papert

Acceptable Use Policy (AUP): an agreement signed by students, parents, teachers, and administrators concerning the agreed on rules for using the Internet in a particular school.

Adaptive Computer Interface: a computer interface that has been adapted for individuals with special needs.

Adaptive Technology: is the use of computers—both hardware and software—to help challenged individuals overcome a limiting condition in their lives.

Alphanumeric: pertaining to letters, numerals, and symbols.

Alternative Communication: communication by other than traditional means.

Alternative Keyboard: a keyboard adapted to meet the special needs of an individual.

Analog: continuous variable quantities such as voltage fluctuations. Signals of continuous nature that vary in frequency and amplitude.

Analog Computer: processes continuously variable data such as that created by voltage fluctuations (see Digital Computer).

Application Software: software written for a particular purpose, such as word processing.

ARPANET: a predecessor to the Internet funded by the Department of Defense.

ASCII: stands for American Standard Code for Information Exchange. It is a common standard used in computer programs for converting 0s and 1s into letters of the alphabet, digits, and punctuation marks.

Assistive Technology: technology that assists individuals in doing something that they could not do by themselves.

Augmentation: to supplement, enhance, or support.

Augmentative and Alternative Communication (AAC): a set of approaches, strategies, and methods used to enhance, the communication abilities of individuals who do not speak or whose speech is unintelligible.

Augmenting Intelligence: to supplement, enhance or support intelligence.

Authoring Program: software for coordinating the graphics, video, animation, text, and sound in the development of multimedia.

Backup: copy of a file, disk, or program as a safeguard against loss.

Bar Code: a linear coding system that can be read by an optical scanning device.

Baud Rate: refers to the speed at which a modem can transmit data. The faster the baud rate of a modem, the more quickly it can transfer information over a telephone line.

Behaviorism: learning theory that focuses on observable behavior and investigates relation between stimuli and responses.

Binary Number: information represented by 0s and 1s.

Bit: is the smallest amount of data or information handled by a computer. In binary code, it is represented as either a 1 or 0. Bits in groups of 8 are called bytes. Bytes can be used to represent different types of information, including numbers and the alphabet.

Buckley Amendment: the Family Education Rights and Privacy Act of 1974; legislation to safeguard students' and parents' rights to correct problems in the collection and maintenance of public records.

Bundled Software: software sold with a computer, generally at a deep discount.

Byte: see Bit.

Calculator: any device that performs arithmetic operations on numbers.

Cathode Ray Tube (CRT): the basic element used in a video terminal or television.

CD-ROM: an acronym for a "compact disc read-only memory." CD-ROMs are aluminum discs coated with plastic that are "read" by a laser. They are only designed to have information read from them and not to have information recorded on them (see CD-ROM Drive).

CD-ROM Drive: is a device that reads the data from a CD-ROM into a computer (see CD-ROM).

Central Processing Unit (CPU): the main computing and control device on a computer. It is also called a microprocessor. Single chip central processing units are used in most personal computers.

Clip Art: commercially available art and photographs that can be bought by users interested in incorporating them into their own projects.

Color Monitor: color video screen that allows the computer to output graphical information—pictures, text, and so on.

Communication Device: any device used to enhance an individual's ability to communicate.

Computer-assisted Instruction: programs that use drills and tutorials combined with question and answer models. CAI programs have their origins in programmed models of instruction.

Computer-based Training (CBT): refers to computer-based training that involves special tutorials written for the computer (see Computer-assisted Instruction).

Computer Disk: a round, flat piece of plastic or metal coated with a magnetic material on which digital material can be stored.

Computer Literacy: the knowledge of how to use computers, including how to start and stop them, and how to use basic applications and associated peripheral devices such as a printer.

Computer-managed Instruction: a type of computer-assisted instruction that emphasizes management and evaluation programs, as well as instruction.

Connect Charge: the fee that is paid to connect to a commercial communications service such as *Compu Serve* or *America Online.*

Constructivism: view of learning that emphasizes the active role of students in learning and understanding.

Copyright: the exclusive legal right to reproduce, publish, and sell the matter and form of some type of work.

Cyberspace: According to the science fiction writer William Gibson, cyberspace is "a consensual hallucination experienced by billions of legitimate operators in every nation, by children being taught mathematical concepts... A graphic representation of data abstracted from the banks of every computer in the human system. Unthinkable complexity. Lines of light ranged in the nonspace of the mind, clusters and constellations of data. Like city lights, receding." Cyberspace has come to mean the place where data is transferred back and forth in our worldwide computer systems.

Daisy Wheel: an impact-type printer that produces characters when a wheel with type characters strikes a ribbon.

Database: a file or collection of data. It could be a mailing list, a student roster, a grade sheet, or any of thousands of other similar collections of information or data.

Demo, or Demonstration, Program: either a prototype program that shows the look of a program still under development, or a disabled program that shows how a commercially available program works. A demo program only has limited functions.

Desktop Publishing: involves the use of computers to create text and graphics for the production of pamphlets, newsletters, and books.

Digital: pertaining to a single state or condition. A digital circuit controls current in a binary on or off state.

Digital Computer: electronically stores information by representing information in two states, On and Off, + and -, 0 or 1 (see Analog Computer).

Digitized Speech: speech that has been recorded and converted to digital format to be used by computers and electronic communication devices.

Disk: a round, flat piece of plastic or metal coated with a magnetic material on which digital material can be stored.

Disk Drive: an electrical and mechanical device that reads and writes data to a disk (see Computer Disk).

DOS: an acronym that stands for disk operating system. This is any operating system that is loaded from a computer's floppy or hard drives when a computer is rebooted or started up again. MS-DOS refers to the proprietary disk operating system developed by the Microsoft Corporation.

Dot Matrix Printer: a printer that creates characters by using a wire-pin print head. This is an impact device in which the wire heads strike a print ribbon like the keys on the typewriter. Dot matrix printers are inexpensive and durable, but do not usually produce printing with the quality of laser or ink-jet printers.

Download: to transfer data from one computer to another.

Drill and Practice Software: software that drills students in a specific subject area or skill such as multiplication.

Electronic Bulletin Board: is a place where people post messages and announcements that can be shared with others. Unlike e-mail, they are not addressed to a specific individual.

E-mail: stands for electronic mail. It is a messaging system that allows Interent users to send messages back and forth much like the postal system.

Emulation: the use of hardware or software that permits programs written for one computer to be run on another.

File Transfer Protocol (FTP): allows a user to be transferred across different sites on the Internet.

Firewall: a system that allows access to only some areas of computer systems to unauthorized users.

Floppy Disk: a mass storage device used mainly with microcomputers; made of flexible polyester film covered with magnetic coating such as iron oxide.

Freeware: software that is given away free of charge (See Shareware).

Gopher: a menu-based system for searching data on the Internet.

Graphical Interface (GUI): allows the computer user to run the machine by pointing to and activating a pictorial representation or icon shown on the screen. Apple pioneered the use of graphical interfaces in educational and home computing. Windows is a graphical interface for DOS-based machines.

Grammar Check: software that checks for grammar errors.

Graphics/Video Card: circuit board that generates the video signal that appears on the computer's monitor.

Gutenberg: Johannes Gutenberg (c. 1400-1468) is credited with having invented moveable type and the first modern printed book.

Hacker: a computer expert; person for whom extending the computer's capabilities is a consuming interest.

Hard Disk: Many different types of discs are used with computers. Floppy (5.25 inch) disks or microfloppy (3.5-inch) disks are designed to be removed from machines and easily copied. Hard disks are sealed inside of machines and have much greater storage capacity (typically 3.5 to 4.1 gigabytes).

Hard Drive: mass storage device for a computer.

Headset: a head-mounted device that control devices are set in.

Home Page: a WEB screen that acts as a starting point to go to multiple sites on worldwide computing networks.

Home Version of Software: refers to an edition of software intended for consumer use. It will typically include a copy of the program and one set of instructions (see School Version of Software).

Hyperlink: is a highlighted graphic such as a button or illustration, or piece of text that connects a user to another web site or source of information or file on the Internet.

Hypermedia: is any combination of text, sound, and motion pictures included in an interactive format on the computer. It is an extension of hypertext emphasizing audio and visual elements (see Hypertext).

Hypermedia Stacks: a hypermedia data set.

Hypertext: a model for presenting information in which text becomes linked in ways that allow readers to browse and discover the connections between different sets of information (see Hypermedia).

HyperText Mark-Up Language (HTML): a coding system for creating hypertext links on Web documents.

Icon: specialized graphic image that represents an object or program that can be manipulated by the user.

Information Superhighway: refers to the idea of vast sources of information being available to computer users through online sources.

Ink-jet Printer: a printer that sprays tiny drops of ink onto paper using an electrostatic charge. Ink-jet printers provide very high quality printing at a very low price.

Input Device: a device such as a keyboard or mouse that allows information to be put into a computer.

Integrated Circuit: a silicon chip on which transistors and other circuit elements are packed.

Integrated Learning System (ILS): the name given to some of the more recent versions of computer-managed instructional systems currently available from commercial vendors.

Integrated Software Package: a collection of programs that work together to provide a user with multiple tool capabilities (word processing, spreadsheet, graphics, etc.).

Interactive: refers to the user being able to react to the computer through a command and have the system respond. This may be as simple as a user striking the wrong command and having the computer correct the user, or a user telling a computer to go in a certain direction in a virtual adventure game or simulation.

Interface: the place where a connection is made between two elements User interface is where people communicate with programs. Hardware interface is the connection between devices and components of the computer.

Internet: an experimental network built by the U.S. Department of Defense in the 1960s. Today it is a loosely configured system that connects millions of computers from around the world.

Joystick: a small boxlike object with a moving stick and buttons used primarily for games, educational software, and computer-aided design systems.

Keyboard: device for imputing information into the computer. It works very much like a typewriter keyboard, but has a much wider range of capabilities.

Keyboard Emulator: hardware device that connects to the computer and allows input from sources other than a standard keyboard.

Lab Pack: typically includes five copies of a particular piece of software and the right to load it on to five computers. Lab packs often come with a single set of instructions and teaching materials.

Laptop Computer: a portable computer.

Laser Printer: uses the same technology as photocopiers to produce printed material. A focused laser beam and rotating mirror drum are used to create an image that is then converted on the drum into an electrostatic charge.

Liquid Crystal Display (LCD): uses a liquid compound positioned between two sheets of polarizing material squeezed between two glass panels.

Liquid Crystal Display Projection Panel: device that projects the contents of a computer screen via an overhead projector.

Local Area Network (LAN): interconnected computers and related peripherals, such as printers and scanners, in one location such as a building or office.

Logarithm: in mathematics, the power to which a base must be raised to equal a given number.

Logo: a programming language designed for children by the MIT professor Seymour Papert.

Mailing List: in the context of e-mail, an electronic list of addresses. Mailing lists make it possible for a single message to be addressed to many people at once. This function is particularly helpful when sharing information with a group, or in getting people to work together on committees, and so on.

Mainframe: a high level computer designed for sophisticated computational tasks.

Mathematical Processor: a type of computer system that graphs different mathematical formulas and equations.

Megahertz: a measure of frequency equivalent to one million cycles per second.

Metropolitan Area Networking: a series of computers linked on a regional basis.

Microchip: a computer chip on which are etched the components of a computer's central processing unit.

Microcomputer: a computer that uses a single chip microprocessor.

Microprocessor: the main computing and control device on a computer. It is also sometimes called a central processor. Single chip central processing units are used in most personal computers. These devices can be thought of as the "brain" of the computer.

MIDI: an acronym for Musical Instrument Digital Interface; allows for the connection of music synthesizers, musical instruments, and computers.

Minicomputer: a midlevel computer whose capabilities are between those of a mainframe and a microcomputer.

Moore's Law: was first formulated in 1964 by Gordon Moore. Moore, one of the co-founders of the computer chip manufacturer Intel Corporation, argued that the number of transistors that could be put on an integrated circuit would double every 2 years. The law has been modified and now maintains that the number doubles every 18 months and increases fourfold every 3 years. Since basic prices for computers tend to remain constant, this means that the computer you bought 18 months ago can be bought for the same price today, only with twice the computational power.

Modem: an electronic communications device that allows a computer to send and receive data over a standard telephone line. The modem itself is an electronic device and is run by means of a communications program that is resident on the computer where the modem is installed.

MOO: an acronym for Mud Object Oriented. It is essentially a technically more sophisticated MUD.

MOUSE: a pointing device that allows the user to input commands into a computer (see Trackball).

MUD: an acronym for Multiple-User Dungeon. These are imaginary adventure games resident on computer networks.
ser Dungeon. These are imaginary adventure games resident on computer networks.

Multimedia: the combination of sound, animation, graphics, video, and related elements into a single program or system.

Netiquette: the rules of proper behavior on the Internet.

Network: a collection of computers and peripheral devices that are connected by a communications system. Networks can be run in a small office or classroom or can operate on a worldwide basis. A local area network (LAN) refers to a network that is run in a limited area such as an office, school, or campus.

Network Version Software: a program specifically designed to run on a computer network where multiple computers or workstations have access to a single file server.

Notebook Computer: a very small portable computer.

Online: connected to the Internet by means of a modem and a computer.

Operating System: software that controls the computer and allows it to perform basic functions.

Optical Character Recognition (OCR): computerized scanning technology that can interpret characters on the printed page.

Optical Scanner: an input peripheral that reads an image by reflecting light from its surface.

Outliner: a type of software that assists in organizing ideas and developing outlines for projects.

Output Device: a device that displays information sent from a computer.
Password: a code word that lets you into a computer account. It protects unauthorized use of an account.

Peripherial: a device such as a printer, scanner, or CD-ROM drive that is external to the computer. Data is passed between the computer and peripheral through some kind of cable.

Personal Computer: another term for microcomputer.

Pixel: one dot on a computer's screen; the smallest element a scanner can detect on a monitor display.

Platform: the foundation technology of a computer system.

Pointing Device: a sensing device that translates executable commands in a computer.

Post-Typographic Culture: a postmodern culture.

Presentation Graphics: systems designed by the presentation of visual and textual materials. Primarily developed for business use, they have excellent classroom applications

Printing Device: any one of a wide range of devices for producing a hardcopy version of a document, usually on paper.

Processing Speed: the speed at which data is manipulated within a computer.

Program: software or the sequence of instructions that are executed by a computer.

Puff Switch: a type of computer switch input that is activated by sipping or puffing through a tube.

RAM: an acronym for random access memory. This is information that can be read or used directly by a computer's microprocessor or other devices (see ROM).

Removeable Hard Drive: a hard drive that allows its storage disk to be removed. This is very helpful when using large graphic or sound files that are very storage intensive.

Resolution: the clarity or detail of a monitor or printer.

ROM: an acronym for read-only memory. This refers to information or data that can be read by the computer, but not modified or changed (see RAM).

Scanner (Optical): a device that uses a light sensitive reader to scan text or images into a digital signal that can be used by a computer.

Scanning Array: a group of letters, numbers, or symbols highlighted on a computer screen that can be selected by the user, one at a time.

School Version of Software: contains one disk and the legal right to load the program on one hard drive. Teaching materials are generally included along with the instructions (see Home Version of Software).

Scientific Visualization Program: a computer program that visually represents scientific information and concepts.

Sensor/Probe: a computer input device that converts nonelectrical energy into electrical energy.

Server: a program or computer that is set up to provide users or clients access to files stored on a computer at a Web site.

Shareware: software distributed for a free try-out, but the user is expected to pay the developer if they decide to use the software (see Freeware).

Simulation (Computer): uses the power of the computer to emulate something in a real or imagined world.

Site License: when a software publisher agrees to make a software program available to be copied at a single site for a set fee. Such agreements are an excellent way to use multiple copies of a program at a greatly reduced rate.

Snail Mail: the name e-mail users have given to traditional, slower mail sent by the postal service.

Software: runs the computer by giving it instructions to perform certain operations. A computer program is simply a set of instructions telling the computer to complete a certain task.

Sound Card or Board: an expansion board added on to a computer, which improves the computer's capacity to process sounds.

Speakers: output devices that allow the computer to generate sound.

Speech Recognition: the process by which speech is translated into an information format that can be used by devices such as computers.

Speech Synthesizer: a device that takes information on the computer and translates it into speech.

Spell Check: software that checks for spelling errors. Typically part of word processing software.

Spreadsheet: application software that allows numerical data to be entered into cells arranged as rows and columns. Calculations can be performed on these data by entering formulas in appropriate cells.

Surge Suppressor: an inexpensive device for protecting computers from increases in the current of an electrical line.

Switch: an on-off device for activating a computer and its programs.

Synthesizer: a computer device that generates sound from digital instructions rather than through manipulation of physical equipment or recorded sound.

Tape Drive Backup: an inexpensive device for making archive copies of a hard drive's programs.

Telnet: allows access to computers and their databases, typically at government agencies and educational institutions.

Terminal: a device consisting of a video adapter, a keyboard, and a monitor where data can be input or output.

Text-to-speech Capability: converts text into speech on a computer using a speech synthesizer.

Thermal Printer: printing technology that uses specially treated paper that darkens when it passes over a heated print head.

Touch Screen: an input device for computers that is activated by touch.

Trackball: a type of pointing device similar to a mouse. Unlike a mouse, it is stationary and can be used in areas with restricted space (see Mouse).

Transistor: an electronic device made of semi –conducting materials which amplifies or controls the flow of electrons in an electrical circuit.

TTD: Telecommunications Device for the Deaf; a device that allows individuals who are deaf to talk on the telephone by typing messages.

286, 386, 486, or Pentium-based Computer: The different numbers that accompany the descriptions of most computers refer to various types of microprocessors. The higher the number, the faster the machine. Pentium is the name used by the Intel Corporation, the main manufacturer of microprocessors, to identify their 586 chip. The microprocessor is the same as a central processing unit (CPU). Modern microprocessors can contain over a million transistors in a chip that is only a square inch in size.

Typographic Culture: culture or society based around the technology of printing.

Uniform Resource Locator (URL): is like an address for a web site. It tells your computer where the web site is, and who is in charge of it.

User Friendly: a term that means easy to learn and use.

Videodisc: a read-only optical disc that is used to store still pictures, motion pictures, and sound.

Virtual Reality: refers to the idea of creating highly realistic simulations with computers. The most sophisticated of these simulations allow the user to manipulate objects and experience things (sex, walking through a museum, etc.).

Virus: a program that infects or corrupts other computer programs. An antivirus program identifies virus programs and purges them from computer systems.

Web: system providing access to Internet resources based on hypertext documents.

Web Browser: graphical used interface used to view documents on the web.

Web Page Address: the Universal Resource Locator (URL) for a particular World Wide Web page.

Web Server: a computer on which a web site resides and that can be connected to through the Internet.

Web Site: a collection of documents found on a single computer.

Wide Area Information Servers (WAIS): computer servers that allow full-text keyword searchers of information resident at sites on the internet.

Windows: a multitasking software that creates a graphical user interface that runs MS-DOS-based machines introduced by the Microsoft Corporation in 1983.

Word Processor: a type of software program that makes it possible for a writer to write or compile text, edit, and revise what has been written, save what has been written, and print it.

World Wide Web (WWW): a browsing system that makes it possible to navigate the Internet by pointing and clicking one's computer mouse. The web connects diverse sites by the use of hyperlinks.

INDEX

A

A.D.A.M · 134
Abacus · 44, 254, 255
AbleNet, Inc. · 156, 160
Acceptable use policies (AUP) · 195,
   206-208, 210, 219-220, 240
Activator · 276
Ada · 27
Ada Project, The (TAP) · 27
ADAMLAB · 156
Adaptive computer interfaces · 148
Adaptive Firmware Card · 152
Adaptive input devices · 148-152
Adaptive output devices · 152
Adaptive technology · 152
Adaptive technology on wheels · 154-
   155
Adobe Photoshop · 51, 52, 66
Advanced Research Projects Agency
   (ARPA) · 198, 199
African-American Mosaic, The · 204
Alphanumeric · 263
Alphaville · 177
Altair 8800 · 30
Alteration of digitally coded
   information · 142
Alternative communication (AAC) ·
   155
Alternative keyboards · 148, 160
*American Journal of Distance
   Education* · 87
American Memory Project (Library of
   Congress) · 200-201
American Sign Language (ASL) · 158
American Standard Code for
Information Interchange (ASCII) ·
   258
Analog · 124, 256, 258, 263, 265, 269
Analog computers · 256
Analytical Engine · 25, 27
Apollo 11 · 110, 197
Apple Computers · 31, 59, 77, 85, 151,
   152, 184, 225, 252, 259, 270
Apple IIGS · 31
ARPANET · 198, 199, 259

Art Gallery CD · 130
Arts, computers and the curriculum ·
   126-130
Arthur's Birthday · 174
Artificial intelligence · 18, 19
ASCII · 258
Assessment with computer-supported
   curriculum · 136-137
Assistive · 152, 165
Atari · 31, 259, 275
Augment (intelligence) · 37-43, 154,
   165
Augmentation Research Center · 38
Augmentative · 151, 155, 161, 162
Augusta Ada Byron · 27
Authoring programs · 184
Authorware Professional · 184
Availability of computers · 225

B

Babbage, Charles · 24, 25, 26, 27, 258
Ballard, Robert · 119
Bar code · 265
Baudrillard , Jean · 69, 79
Bell, Alexander Graham · 258
Bell Laboratories · 28, 259
Bellingham Public Schools · 207
Benedikt, Michael · 18
Berenstain Bears Get in a Fight, The ·
   174
Berenstain Bears in the Dark, The · 174
Beyond the Gutenberg Galaxy · 3, 32
Binary computer · 25, 257
Bionic Man · 167
Bionic Woman · 167
Blocks in Motion · 160
Bolter, Jay David · 173
Bootstrap Institute · 39
Bootstrapping · 39
Bowers, C. A. · 1, 3-4, 7, 20, 222, 218,
   243
Bradbury, Ray · 275
Braille · 148, 152, 159
Brainerd, Paul · 59
Brainstorm · 178
Brave New World · 274
Bruner, Jerome · 103
Bug (computer) · 6, 237, 238
Burbank, Luther · 95
Burning Chrome · 18

Burroughs Computer Corporation · 259
Bush, Vannevar · 178, 188, 193, 258
Byron, Lord · 27

C

Calculator · 2, 3, 28, 31, 52, 253, 259
Capacitors · 28
Cape Kennedy · 196
Carnegie Mellon University · 167
Cartopedia · 182
Carver, George Washington · 95
Catholic Church · 34
CD-ROM · 105, 128, 251, 252, 253
Center for Democracy and Technology · 235, 236
Central processing unit · 28, 29, 75, 251, 269-271
Cezanne, Paul · 127
Cezanne · 127
Chalkboard · 35, 102, 133
Child safety and censorship on the Net · 206
Child safety online · 206
Children with hearing impairments · 158
Children with limited cognitive abilities. · 157
Choices, Choices · 133, 134
Clip art · 54, 107
Closing The Gap, Inc. · 161
Cobol · 78
Collective intelligence · 38-39
Communications device · 2
Compton's Interactive Encyclopedia · 125, 181
Comptons' New Media · 125
Computer access, problems arising from · 228-229
Computer ethics · 221
Computer journals and publications (list of) · 87-90
Computer monitor · 266, 267
Computer support of teaching · 225
Computer timeline · 258
Computer, as curriculum tool · 77-81
Computer, as meditating force in contemporary culture · 4-6
Computer, non-neutrality of · 7
Computers and the movies · 177-178

Computers, how they are used throughout the culture · 3-4
Computers, individual responsible use of . 226-227
Computers, Power and Human Reason · 212
Computers, public nature of use in the classroom · 232-233
Computers, questions of personal responsibility and safety · 230-232
Computers, resposnible use of in the classroom . 224-226
Computers, types of . 260-262
Computers, use as instructional tools · 221-224
Computing, brief history of · 24-30
Computing, defining an educational model of · 13-15
Constructivist models of learning · 78, 80-82, 93, 131-132, 136
Consumer mathematics · 113
Copyright Act, Title 17 of the U.S. Code · 233
Copyright issues · 73, 91-92
Copyright protection · 217, 233-234
Corbis · 127, 128
Count Zero · 18, 20, 167, 170
Counting machines · 254-255
Crawford, Cindy · 242
Creative Writer 2 · 107
Creative Writer · 128
Cross-cultural writing activities · 108
Crosswords & More and Crosswords & Word Games · 119
Cuban, Larry · 99, 101, 102, 132, 137, 144, 222, 243
Cummins, Jim · 202
Curriculum, content of · 102-104
Curriculum and Evaluation Standards for School Mathematics · 108
Curriculum Associates · 109, 110, 182, 183
Cyber Sitter · 205
Cyber-Cookies · 235
CyberPatrol · 205, 231
Cyberspace · 17, 18, 19, 167, 217, 236

D

Dade County, Florida · 84

Daniel, Rene · 202

Daisy wheel · 65, 267

Databases · 8, 14, 18, 47, 52, 63, 64, 66, 68, 106, 114, 118, 120, 123, 126, 142, 143, 164, 175, 178, 179, 180, 275

Database software · 63-64

Davidson Company· 78, 79, 111, 112, 120, 124, 128, 136, 154

Decimal · 54, 113, 257, 258

Decisions, Decisions · 79, 121, 132, 133, 134, 158

Dedicated word processors · 53

Desk Set · 177

Delaney, Samuel · 167

Demon Seed, The · 177

Desktop publishing · 34, 51, 56- 60, 67, 68, 107, 114, 123, 126, 129, 165, 267

Difference Engine · 25, 26, 27

Digital · 2, 3, 21, 27, 37, 44, 46, 47, 54, 58, 68, 94, 95, 96, 131, 141, 142, 143, 152, 189, 191, 211, 242, 256, 263, 265, 269, 273

Digital calculating · 256-258

Digital camera · 2

Digital Chisel · 184

Digital organisms · 94, 95

Digital theme parks · 189

Digitized speech · 152, 269

Dildonic · 168

Director (Macromedia) · 184

Disabilities, students with · 152-162

Disk drive · 270

Disney, Walt · 178, 189

Disneyland · 189, 190, 191

DK Multimedia · 117

DNA · 96, 247

Dockterman, David · 133, 137, 138, 144

Don Johnston, Incorporated · 151, 152, 153, 158, 160

Download · 196

Dr. Peet's Talkwriter · 153

Dr. Seuss' ABC · 174

Dr. Seuss' Green Eggs and Ham · 174

Dragon Systems, Inc · 151

DragonDictate · 151

Drawing and illustration programs · 65-66

Drill and practice software · 154

E

Ecology of the classroom · 4, 11, 15

Edmark · 81, 85, 117, 124, 136, 150

Educational Native American Network (ENAN) · 205

Educational software, levels of · 75-77

Educational Technology Research and Development · 87

Eisenstein, Elizabeth · 58

Electric typewriter · 24, 267

Electronic calendars · 34

Electronic Frontier Foundation · 235

Electronic Numerical Integrator and Computer (ENIAC) · 28, 29, 259

Elements of a Web Page · 201

ELIZA · 212

Encyclopedia of Nature · 182

Encyclopedia of Science · 117, 182

Endangered Animals · 110

Engelbart, Douglas · 37, 38, 39, 40, 48

Enhancing cognition · 52

EPCOT (Experimental Prototype Community of Tomorrow) · 190

Ethical and legal issues in teaching with technology · 220-221

European Laboratory for Particle Physics · 200

Evaluating software · 81-83

Evans & Sutherland Company · 190

Expert Software · 119

Exploratorium · 196

Eyewitness Encyclopedia of Science · 117

Eyewitness Virtual Reality · 117

External storage · 271-272

F

Fahrenheit 451 · 275, 277

Family Education Rights and Privacy Act of 1974 (FERPA) · 234

Febvre, Lucien · 33

Fine Artist · 128

Firewall · 237

First Class Grade Book · 135

Floppy disk · 75, 252, 260, 271

Flores, Fernando · 40

FORTRAN · 78, 259
Freeware · 86, 91
Freinet, Célestin · 202

G

Gender discrimination · 4
General ethical and legal issues in
    teaching with technology · 217,
    220
Geometric Supposer · 113, 114
Gibson, William · 4, 18, 167, 178, 211
Global Schoolhouse Project · 196
Global SchoolNet Foundation · 203
Global Show and Tell · 204
Global Warming · 110
Grammar checkers · 99, 153
Graphical user interface (GUI) · 76
Graphics design system · 14
Graphing · 77, 108, 114, 118, 185
*Great Teaching in the One Computer
    Classroom* · 133
Greek mythology · 175
Gus Communications, Inc. · 161
Gutenberg, Johannes · 56
Gutenberg revolution compared to the
    contemporary computer revolution·
    32-35

H

Hackers 217, 236-238
Handshake · 6
Hard drive · 75, 200, 251, 252, 261,
    265, 272, 273
Hadley, Martha · 13
Harry & the Haunted House · 174
Hartley · 153
Headmaster Plus · 150
Headset · 151
Heidegger, Martin · 4
Helbrans, Rabbi Shlomo · 142
Hepburn, Katherine · 177
Hickman, Larry · 222
History of the World · 182
Home Shopping Network · 275
How do computers change the work
    of teachers? · 99, 137
How Your Body Works CD · 121

Hutchins, Pat · 158
Huxley, Aldous · 274
HyperCard · 78, 154, 184, 188
Hypermedia · 177, 178-183
HyperStudio · 78, 119, 131, 154, 184
Hypertext · 46, 177, 178-183, 188, 192,
    193, 210

I

IBM · 31, 32, 75, 85, 161, 184, 259,
    261, 269
IBM Special Needs Solutions · 161
Icons · 33
Ihde, Don · 4
*If Your Name Was Changed at Ellis
    Island* · 175
Inclusion · 126, 162, 166, 171, 222
Information highway · 19, 206
Information revolution · 33
Innocomp · 156, 161
Input devices · 147, 148, 151, 157, 158,
    163, 165, 251, 263-266
Integrated circuit · 29, 259, 269
Intellectual property rights · 91, 233,
    241
Intellikeys · 149, 156, 263
Interactive stories · 105, 153
Interactive television · 274
Interface · 6, 76, 148, 150, 167, 199,
    259
International Reading Association ·
    104, 144
Internet · 9, 10, 14, 18, 19, 21, 30, 34,
    35, 37, 38, 46, 74, 84, 86, 87, 103,
    110, 122, 124, 128, 129, 131, 137,
    140, 158, 160, 164, 165, 178, 187,
    188, 195, 196, 197, 198-200,
    202, 203, 204, 205, 206, 207, 208,
    209, 210, 211, 214, 215, 217, 218,
    219, 220, 221, 223, 230, 231, 232,
    235, 236, 237, 240, 246, 255, 259
Internet Filter · 231
IVI Publishing · 158

J

Japan · 183, 189, 246
Jason Foundation for Education · 119

Jason Project · 119
Jobs, Steven · 31
Johnny Mnemonic · 178
Journal of Computer Based Instruction · 88
Journal of Technology and Teacher Education · 89
Joystick · 149, 157, 264
Just Grandma and Me · 106, 153, 174

K

K.C. & Clyde in Fly Ball · 105, 153
Kenx · 151
Keyboard · 56, 61, 105, 148, 150, 151, 157, 160, 263, 265, 266
Keyboarding · 5, 51, 60-63, 67
Kid Keys · 61
Kid Pix · 65, 66, 80, 111, 129, 131, 163
Kid Works 2 · 132
KidCAD · 128
KidLink · 204
KinderGuard · 231
Kluge · 6

L

Lab pack · 91, 234
Landers, Ann · 99, 100, 137, 139
Language arts and literacy . 104-108
Laptop computer · 34, 156, 261, 264, 267
Laser printers · 59, 268
Laureate Learning Systems · 156, 157, 163
Lawnmower Man · 178
Learning Company, The · 61, 111, 112, 115, 118, 122, 134
Learning OnLine · 109, 110
Leviticus · 142
Levine, Ellen · 175
Levy, Steven · 59
Lexicographers · 58
Liberator · 156
Linear models of writing · 53
Liquid crystal display · 266
Little Monster at School · 174
Living Books · 106, 174, 175
Local area networks · 8, 135

Logarithms · 255
Logic chip · 28
Logo · 14, 23, 77, 115, 116
Loch Ness Adventure, The · 190, 191
Louvre Museum · 196
LS & S Group · 162

M

Machines that count · 251, 254
Macintosh · 31, 59, 71, 75, 76, 77, 117, 128, 151, 152
Macmillan Dictionary for Children · 181
Macmillan New Media · 181
Maddux, Cleborne D· · 15
Magic · 19, 55, 157
Magic lanterns · 24
Mainframe · 33, 34, 35, 38, 43, 58, 260, 261, 262, 263
Making Music · 128
Malcom X · 175
Mangrum, Charles T., II · 109
Mantis · 167
Maple V · 185
Mario Teaches Typing · 61
Markoff, John · 45
Martin, Henri-Jean · 33
Martin Luther · 34, 47
Master Type · 61
Math Blaster · 78, 111, 112, 131, 135, 136, 154
Math Rabbit Classic · 111, 112
Math Workshop Deluxe · 111, 112
Mathematica · 185
Mathematical processors · 173, 176, 185-186
Mathematics, computers and the curriculum · 108-116
MATHLAB · 185
Maxis · 5, 6, 78, 79, 122
Mayer-Johnson Co. · 162
McCaffrey, Anne · 169
McLuhan, Marshall · 1, 3, 242
MECC · 78, 79, 105, 122, 130
Media · 3, 12, 16, 20, 34, 69, 84, 101, 116, 129, 131, 185, 217, 228, 233, 238, 276, 277
Mega Man · 275
Memex · 178, 179
Metropolitan area networking (MAN) ·

135

Methodology, underlying use of computers · 130-132

Microchip · 28

Microcomputer · 29, 43, 261, 266, 273

Microcomputer revolution · 30-32

Microprocessor · 29, 75, 261, 270

Microscope · 40, 96

Microsoft Corporation · 54, 55, 56, 60, 62, 64, 65, 75, 107, 120, 125, 127, 128, 130, 153, 162, 181, 193, 200, 277

Microsoft - Accessibility and Disabilities Group · 162

Microsoft Encarta · 125

Microsoft Word · 54, 56, 60, 65

Mindscape · 121, 134

Minicomputer · 261

Missile Command · 275

MITS · 30

Mnemonic device · 19

Modern School Movement · 202

Mona Lisa Overdrive · 19, 211

Moore School of Electrical Engineering · 28

Moore's Law · 262, 263

Moravec, Hans · 167

Morse, Samuel · 258

Mouse · 6, 37, 38, 55, 76, 105, 131, 136, 148, 149, 150, 160, 263, 264, 265

Mouthstick · 151

MS-DOS · 75, 76, 77, 184

Multicultural education and the Internet · 195, 202-205

Multicultural exchanges · 203

Multimedia · 107, 117, 119, 123, 125, 127, 128, 131, 154, 176-178, 181, 182, 183, 184, 185, 187, 188, 189, 200, 232

Multimedia authoring tools · 184

MultiMedia Schools · 89

Muppet Learning Keys · 149, 156, 263

Musical Instrument Digital Interface (MIDI) · 128

Musical Instruments · 130

My First Incredible Amazing Dictionary · 181

Myst · 174

N

National Aeronautics and Space Administration · 196, 197, 198

National Center for Missing and Exploited Children · 231

National Council for the Social Studies · 103, 121, 123, 144

National Council of Teachers of English · 103, 104, 144

National Council of Teachers of Mathematics · 108

National curriculum standards · 103

National Geographic Kids Network · 120, 121

National Science Education Standards · 104, 116

Nativeweb · 205

Nelson, Ted · 46, 180

Net Shepherd · 231

NetNanny · 231

Neural implants · 18

Neuromancer · 6, 18, 19, 20, 167, 168, 170, 178, 211, 214

New Grolier Multimedia Encyclopedia · 126, 127

Negroponte, Nicholas · 45, 73

Net, The · 178

New Kid on the Block, The · 174

1984 · 6, 18, 20, 31, 59, 141, 170, 214, 222, 243, 259

1984 · 6, 18, 20, 31, 59, 141, 170, 214, 222, 243, 259

Nintendo · 21, 228, 243, 275, 276

Non-sequential writing · 180

Notebook computers · 156, 264

Nova · 167, 170

Number crunching · 6

O

Office of Technology Assessment of the U.S. Congress · 223

On Growth and Form · 96

Operating systems · 11, 75, 77, 260

Optical character recognition · 265

Oregon Trail · 79, 94, 122

Organization and arrangement of computer access · 225

Orwell, George · 141

Osborne · 31

OTA · 21, 223, 225, 243

Outliners · 153

Output devices · 147, 152, 251, 266-269, 273
Oughtred, William · 255
OutSPOKEN · 159

P

P. B. Bear's Birthday Party · 182
PacMan · 275
Pagemaker · 51, 59, 60
Papert, Seymour · 23, 51, 115
Parental guidance · 231
Pascal, Blaise · 258
Pascaline · 258
Passion for Art, A · 127, 128
Perelman, Lewis · 139
Personal computers · 32, 33, 38, 59, 209, 260, 261, 262
Phillips, Inc. · 171, 259
Phototypesetting · 58
Pierian Software · 184
Pilgrims · 126
Pixels · 242, 266
Pocket organizers · 34
Pointing devices · 151
Pong · 259, 275
Popular Mechanics Magazine · 251
Post-typographic culture · 3
Powerpoint · 35
Prentke Romich · 149, 150, 156
Pretty Good Grading Program · 135
Print Culture and Enlightenment Thought · 58
Print Shop Deluxe · 115
Privacy rights · 217, 234-236
Processing speed · 270
Project Xanadu · 46, 47
Protecting students using the Internet · 195, 205-206
Provenzo, Eugene F., Jr. · 3, 5, 21, 29, 32, 33, 49, 109, 170, 214, 229, 243, 277
Puff switch · 149
Putnam Valley, New York School District · 103

R

Racism · 4

Radio · 2, 101, 276
Railroad · 2
RAM · 83, 252, 261, 270, 271, 273, 274
Ray, Tom · 94
Read, Write & Type · 61- 63
Record player · 24
Reduce · 138
Reference Atlas · 182
Reformation · 33, 56, 58, 245
Refreshable tactual output · 152
Renaissance · 33, 35, 40, 45, 56, 58, 245
Renoir · 127
Resistors · 28
Resolution · 264, 266
Responsible use of computers in the classroom · 217, 220, 221, 224
Revere, Paul · 126
Richtin, Fred · 143
RJ Cooper and Associates · 157
Roger Wagner · 119, 120, 131, 184
Rogers, Carl · 211
Rogerian counseling · 211, 213
ROM · 8, 35, 64, 74, 75, 83, 105, 106, 127, 128, 130, 158, 173, 176, 177, 182, 186, 188, 200, 251, 252, 253, 260, 269, 271, 272, 273, 275
Rosie's Walk · 158
Royal Astronomical Society · 25
Ruff's Bone · 174, 175

S

SAM-JOY · 149
Sammy's Science House · 117
Sayers, Don · 202
Say-It-All · 156
Scanner · 2, 265
Scanning · 3, 37, 151, 159, 160, 265
Scholastic, Inc. · 90, 175
School Library Media Quarterly · 89
Schools, use of technology in · 7-8
Science, computers and the curriculum · 116-121
Scientific Memoirs · 27
Scientific visualization programs · 176, 186
Sega · 228, 275, 276
Semiconducting materials · 28
Shakespeare · 41, 247, 256

Shareware · 86
Sheila Rae, the Brave · 174
Sheingold, Karen · 13
Ship that Sang, The · 169
Silicon · 28, 29, 269
SimCity · 6, 78, 79, 94, 122
SimCity 2000 · 6
SimEarth-The Living Planet · 5
Simulations · 5, 6, 14, 18, 36, 68-69,
    70, 75, 77, 79, 80, 82, 93, 94, 117,
    118, 121, 122, 124, 132, 134, 157,
    177
Singularity, computer as a · 23, 35- 37,
    43, 49, 245, 248
Site license · 91
Slide projectors · 24
Slide rule · 255, 256
Smart Books · 175
Smart keyboard · 56
Smith, Winston · 141
Snyder, Tom · 79, 121, 125, 132, 133,
    144, 147, 158, 245
Soap bubbles · 96
Social studies, computers and the
    curriculum · 121-126
Software, sources for · 84-90
Software evaluation · 81-83
Software Evaluation Form · 83
Software Publisher's Association · 234
Sony · 259
Sources for software · 73, 84
Space Invaders · 275
SpeakEasy · 156
Speakers · 148, 152, 266, 268
SPECS for Kids · 231
Speech and language impairment · 155
Speech synthesizer · 156, 159
Spell checker · 39, 107
Spreadsheet · 14, 64-65, 68, 75, 77,
    112, 113, 114, 120, 123, 202, 253
Sputnik · 199
Standard keyboards · 148
Stanford Research Institute · 38
Steam engine · 2
Steck Vaughn's World of Dinosaurs ·
    175
Stellaluna · 174
Stirrups · 1
Stowaway · 182
Sunburst Inc. · 55, 113, 114, 129, 149,
156
Super Mario Brothers · 275

Super Solvers Gizmos and Gadgets ·
    118
Surf Watch · 205, 231
Switches · 28, 31, 105, 149, 150, 151,
    155, 157, 160, 253, 256
Synthesized speech · 152

T

Talk Time With Tucker · 156, 157
Tape recorder · 24
Taylor, Richard · 27
Taylor, Robert · 13-15, 21, 52, 71, 77-
    78, 97, 101
Teachers, how computers change their
    work · 137-139
Teachers, promise of technology for ·
    8-12
Teaching, how it changes with use of
    computers · 13
Teaching and Computers · 90
Technology · 1, 2, 3, 4, 7, 11, 12, 13,
    14, 15, 16, 17, 18, 20, 21, 24, 29, 31,
    34, 38, 40, 44, 58, 59, 60, 67, 68, 69,
    84, 85, 87, 94, 101, 102, 103, 104,
    105, 108, 109, 114, 116, 117, 119,
    122, 123, 129, 130, 133, 134, 138,
    139, 140, 141, 142, 144, 147, 148,
    150, 152, 154, 155, 158, 159, 160,
    161, 163, 164, 165, 166, 167, 170,
    171, 173, 176, 177, 178, 180, 186,
    187, 188, 189, 191, 192, 193, 195,
    199, 203, 211, 218, 219, 221, 222,
    223, 224, 226, 228, 239, 240, 241,
    243, 245, 246, 247, 248, 253, 259,
    265, 267, 274, 275, 276
Technology & Learning · 90
Technology for inclusion · 162-164
Telegraph · 2, 258
Telephone dialer · 258
Telephone switching devices · 27
Telephones · 1
Television · 1, 2, 4, 10, 16, 24, 68, 69,
    101, 139, 167, 186, 210, 274,
    275, 276
Telstar I · 259
Tempest, The · 41, 247
Terminals · 59, 260
Texas Instruments · 31, 255
Texas School for the Deaf · 158
Text-to-speech · 153, 154, 159

Thinkin' Things · 81, 117, 118

Thomas · 9, 10, 66, 147, 241

Thompson, D'Arcy Wentworth · 96

Thomson Learning Tools · 153

Three for Me Library · 174

Tierra · 94

Time Magazine · 9, 10

TimeLiner · 125

Timex · 31

Titanic · 175

Tool, computer as · 10, 14, 18, 21, 39,
    40, 52, 62, 63, 66, 71, 74, 77, 78, 79,
    93, 97, 101, 112, 116, 124, 125, 131,
    133, 136, 139, 167, 171, 180, 184,
    192, 195, 202, 223, 229, 242, 253,
    268, 270

Toolbook · 78, 184, 188

Tortoise & the Hare, The · 174

Touch screen · 105, 157, 264

TouchWindow · 150

Tracey, Spencer · 177

Trackball · 149, 264

Transcontinental Railroad · 2

Transistor · 28, 259

Tron · 178

Trudy's Time and Place House · 124

Turkle, Sherry · 195, 217

Turing, Alan · 54, 258

Tutee, computer as · 14, 21, 71, 77, 78,
    93, 97, 101

Tutor, computer as · 14, 21, 63, 71, 77,
    78, 93, 97, 101, 106

Type I uses of computers · 15

Type II uses of computers · 15

Types of computers · 251, 260

Typesetting · 54, 58, 59, 60, 202

Typographic culture · 3, 19, 21, 49,
    142, 143, 191

U

Ultimate Human Body, The · 182

Ultimate World, The · 182

Ultimate Writing Center, The · 115

Understanding Media · 3

United Nations · 204

U.S. Department of Defense · 27, 198,
    199

Use of computers as instructional
    tools · 217, 221

Utilization, of computers · 132-136

V

Vacuum tube · 28, 258

Vernacular languages · 33

Victrola · 24, 101

Video game player · 3

Video games · 3,4, 18, 177, 228, 229,
    241, 259, 274, 275

Videodisc · 83, 117, 131, 179, 186,
    188, 253, 272

Videodisc technology · 173, 186-187

Vinge, Vernor · 35

Virtual reality · 117, 178, 192, 276

Viruses · 11, 217, 236-238

VisAbility · 159

Visualization software · 142

Voice input · 151, 159, 160

Voice recognition · 150

Voyager · 128

Vredeman de Vries, Jan · 57

W

War Games · 178

WatchDog · 231

Way Things Work, The · 182

Web browser · 200, 205

Web sites · 85, 103, 110, 166, 200, 203,
    231, 235, 236

Web Track SE · 231

WebNet Journal · 90

Weizenbaum, Joseph · 212

*Where in the World Is Carmen
    Sandiego?* · 79, 124, 132, 158, 174

White House for Kids · 197

Wiener, Norbert · 95

Windows · 76

Winograd, Terry · 40

Wireheads · 166, 167

Wolf · 156

Word Art · 55

Word Munchers · 78, 79, 105

Word prediction · 56, 160, 163

Word processing · 15, 37, 39, 53, 54,
    56, 59, 60, 75, 106, 107, 114, 118,
    120, 123, 126, 129, 132, 152, 153,
    160, 165, 179, 251, 253, 265

Word processor · 2, 3, 10, 14, 38, 52-
    56, 67, 68, 73, 75, 77, 100, 115, 137,

142
WordPerfect 5.1 · 54
World Wide Web · 19, 21, 27, 35, 37,
    110, 119, 128, 187, 188, 195, 197,
    199, 200,-201, 202, 203, 205, 209,
    210, 217, 238, 259
Wozniak, Steven · 31
*Wright Brothers and the Invention of
    Powered Flight, The* · 110
Write This Way · 158

Z

Zookeeper · 124
Zoom text · 159
Zuse, Konrad · 27, 259